of the United States Soccer Federation

The official playing and coaching Manual

SOCCER

HOW TO PLAY THE GAME

SOCCER

HOW TO PLAY THE GAME

The Official Playing and Coaching Manual of the United States Soccer Federation

EDITED BY
Bobby Howe

FOREWORD BY
Hank Steinbrecher

INTRODUCTION BY
Steve Sampson

CONTRIBUTIONS BY
**the Staff of
the United States
Soccer Federation:
Tim Carter,
Clive Charles,
Tony DiCicco,
Mike Haas,
Jay Hoffman,
Al Kleinatis,
Peter Mellor,
Jay Miller,
Bob Moullin,
Hughie O'Malley,
Jeff Pill,
Sigi Schmid,
Jan Smisek,
and Tony Waiters**

WRITTEN BY
Dan Herbst

UNIVERSE

Design and Illustration: Mirko Ilić Corp.

The United States Soccer Federation would like to thank Tom King, Jim Trecker, Jim Moorhouse of U.S. Soccer; Charles Miers, Publisher; and Carla Sakamoto, Giulia Pesaro, Ellen Cohen, and Stephanie Iverson of Universe Publishing; Mirko Ilić, So Takahashi, Ringo Takahashi, Aleksandra Prokić, and Lauren DeNapoli of Mirko Ilić Corp.; and a special thanks to Hank Steinbrecher, Secretary General of U.S. Soccer for his encouragement

Principal Photography by Mark Leech Photography, Any Chance Productions, and J.B. Whitesell/International Sports Images

First published in the United States of America in 1999
by UNIVERSE PUBLISHING
A Division of Rizzoli International Publications, Inc.
300 Park Avenue South
New York, NY 10010

Library of Congress Cataloging-in-Publication Data

Soccer : how to play the game : the official playing and coaching manual of the United States Soccer Federation / U.S. Soccer.
  p. cm.
ISBN 0-7893-0338-8 (alk. paper)
 1. Soccer—United States. 2. Soccer—Coaching—United States. 1.
United States Soccer Federation.
GV944.U5 S63 1999
796.334'2—dc21

99-10249
CIP
rev

Printed in England

Cover credit: Design by
Mirko Ilić Corp.

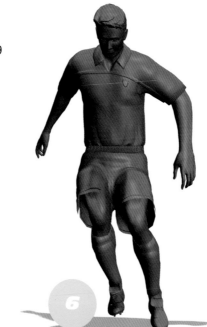

At the heart of every soccer fan is the "game." We all love to watch and follow the sport, but it's the sheer attractiveness of our beautiful game that drives the true soccer aficionado. The way the ball is played. The way players move off the ball. The motion of a team as it links passes, and the criss-crossing runs as players move down the field.

In *Soccer: How to Play the Game*, it is the players playing the game that the authors have focused upon, and that's what makes it such a special, revolutionary coaching manual. The need for this type of literature is part of an educational mandate for coaching soccer in the U.S., where we haven't seen a comprehensive publication of this nature in more than 15 years.

To me, teaching the game to others is the soul of our sport. It is important to us that this marvelous representation of our sport can therefore be applied equally to boys and to girls, to men and to women. It is complex enough to be informative and helpful to a veteran of the game, while also simple enough to assist the newcomer.

Our desire has been to create a volume that expresses our knowledge of teaching the game and our coaching philosophy to the national soccer executive as well as to the young parent learning the game by helping to coach a child's team. All have a strong hand in making soccer a preeminent sport in the United States and are vitally important to our development.

A former coach myself, I grew up in Brooklyn, New York, and played soccer on the local city fields. I was fortunate enough to receive an athletic scholarship to attend college, where I eventually moved toward coaching at the university level. In all of my years involved with the sport, which has included senior management positions for three Olympic soccer tournaments, two World Cups, and the creation of a professional league, I still look back on my time as a coach as the most rewarding.

And I think that's the way many of us "old coaches" feel. Delight in this wonderful, groundbreaking book as it enriches your enjoyment of our sport.

Hank Steinbrecher
Secretary General
U.S. Soccer

TABLE OF CONTENTS

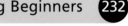

Several years ago the great Dutch coach Rinus Michels was invited to the United States to observe our programs and to make recommendations as to how we should proceed in order to elevate the game in this country. At that time he told us that unless children had played the game between the ages of six and twelve, they would almost never derive a true passion for the game nor would they become top players. If Rinus's statement is true—and I believe it is true—then it behooves all of us who are committed to the improvement of the game to ensure that the environment we create for our youngest players will not only be realistic for their development but also will give them a true love for the sport.

There have been three distinct periods in my career: the first created my passion for soccer; the other two formed the basis of my philosophy as to how the game should be taught and played.

I grew up in England in the years immediately following World War II and unlike many of my contemporaries throughout Europe at that time who used the streets as their playgrounds, my friends and I had the luxury of a grass field upon which to exhibit our skills. Our games started in the morning when the player who owned the ball came out to play and ended much later in the day when his mom called him in for tea. I loved those games. We improvised fields and improvised rules and the selection of teams was always fair. There were no distractions: we did not own a telephone or a television, computers were a figment of somebody's imagination, and there were no adults around to mess with our fun. The games belonged to us. The game was our teacher.

During the 1960s and early 1970s I played for West Ham United. I had the privilege of playing with great players: Bobby Moore, Geoff Hurst, and Martin Peters—three of England's 1966 World Cup–winning team—and against players of superb quality such as Pele, Bobby Charlton, George Best, and Franz Beckenbauer. While the game was still the great teacher, I had the good fortune to play for a manager, Ron Greenwood, who was at that time way ahead of his counterparts in training methods and philosophy. He believed implicitly in the simplicity of the game. "Simplicity is genius" was his favorite saying. While he encouraged players to improve their skills in practice, he urged players to play to their strengths in games.

In the late 1980s and early 1990s I had the honor of coaching the United States U-17 national team as an assistant to Roy Rees and then as head coach to the U-20 national team. The experience of working with Roy was invaluable. He believed in the value of carefully creating a training environment appropriate for each level of player so that it challenged the participants at their levels and instilled in his players a high demand of excellence. He did not stifle their creativity, but encouraged them to learn from the game. The game was their teacher.

If the game is the teacher then what is the role of the coach? The coach is a facilitator, an assistant to the game as a teacher, and an assistant to the players in their understanding of the game. The job of the coach is to create the environment in training for players to be challenged at their levels of ability. The demand and realism of training should replicate the game so that players on match day are not asked to make decisions nor execute the skills of the game at levels or at speeds they have not experienced.

Soccer is a player's game, therefore, players should be considered first when all coaching, administrative, and political decisions are made. The length of the season, challenge of the competition, numbers of players on the field, and the duration of games and practices must always take into consideration the age and ability of the players.

Adults must understand that young players are not mini–adults. Therefore, young players cannot comprehend adult games nor can they understand adult expectations. They should play a game on a field and with rules suited to their skills and maximizing their enjoyment. Adults must let them play, take responsibility for their behavior around children, and recognize that they hold the key to their children's love for the sport.

The game of soccer has grown dramatically in this country in the last ten years. The philosophy of U.S. Soccer has changed considerably to meet the demands of that growth, to be equal to the challenges of the modern game, and to ensure progress in the men's game and continued superiority in the women's game at the international team levels. As we have not produced a coaching manual in the last fifteen years, it is most appropriate at this time to reflect the changes. Therefore, the purpose of this book is to provide coaches with many examples of practice games that create realistic conditions for players and much supplementary information to enable them to assist their players and to understand the underlying philosophy.

There is no magic formula for success. Coaching at youth level is all about working with players to improve their performance so that they may aspire to a higher level of play. It is not about recruiting players to build teams to win championships.

Soccer mirrors life. Just like life, soccer is a game with rules where everybody must have an equal opportunity to participate but we must understand that there is no such thing as equality; some players naturally will be better than others. Soccer is a game requiring great individual skill, imagination, creativity, and decision making. Coaching is not about stifling regimens, it is about enhancing those elements.

PART 1

INTRODUCTION

So much of adult life is spent running around attending to necessary chores that we rarely engage in an activity that makes us feel as though we are really making a difference in someone's life. Coaching represents a unique opportunity to touch youngsters profoundly and to be of an incalculable benefit to them throughout their lives.

There will always be a very special place in my heart for a select handful of coaches who taught me the joys and skills of what is quite rightly referred to all over the planet as "the people's game." An enormous feeling of inner satisfaction will come to you from nurturing a young player and watching that individual grow as both an athlete and as a human being. There will be few things as rewarding as when that person matures into adulthood and fully appreciates your contributions.

The adventure that awaits you will be filled with thrills and, quite probably, some disappointments. Enjoy the former while viewing the latter as the relatively small price that one must pay for engaging in such a worthwhile activity.

Chances are that you fall into one of the two primary categories of American youth soccer coaches—some of you grew up playing the game, while many of you are neophytes who have volunteered your time out of a sense of altruism. If you belong to the latter group, please be assured that the task ahead isn't as daunting as it may now seem. Some of America's outstanding youth coaches had limited or no soccer exposure during their developmental years. By making a significant effort to educate yourself, you can become as good a coach as your determination will allow. You can learn quickly by playing the game, reading books, attending clinics, taking coaching courses, such as those offered by the United States Soccer Federation, and watching top-class matches.

As a youth coach one of your key roles is that of facilitator, a job that demands, above all else, enthusiasm and commitment. One of the greatest services you can perform for your players is to help them become fans of the game. Doing so will provide them with dreams to inspire them as well as heroes whose breathtaking skills they can emulate. Just as I'm sure that Michael Jordan has a tremendous influence on how today's NBA stars play basketball, so must today's top American soccer players reach and inspire tomorrow's headliners.

Because soccer is a fabulous game that is relatively simple to play, inexperienced coaches have a great advantage over their counterparts in other sports. You can assure your team a great time merely by letting them pick teams, throwing a ball out, and providing them with enough supervision to promote a safe environment. For good measure, toss in some verbal encouragement. Unlike some other American sports, soccer does not demand

A common scene at an uncommon club: youth training at Holland's world-famous Ajax football club.

The world's game and the simplest game: requiring but a ball (or its equivalent) to play, soccer games are daily fare from the fields of Thailand (top) to the streets of Iran.

a rigid structure in order to be played in a manner that will help develop the abilities of the participants. You would be amazed at how many world-class soccer stars owe much of their talent to childhood pick-up games (what might be referred to as "street soccer").

That approach will put you in good stead until you can acquire the knowledge you need to begin teaching the game. The U.S.S.F. coaching staff has made certain that the pages ahead will provide important information on soccer's many skills and how you can teach them. Your next step would be to take a coaches licensing course (or the next higher level course if you have a license already).

In any endeavor, there is no substitute for knowledge. You may start without knowing much about the sport that is so popular that the television audience for the World Cup dwarfs that of an Olympics, Super Bowl, or World Series. However, it is unacceptable not to work hard at educating yourself. The kids with whom you have been entrusted deserve the best experience possible. The more you learn, the greater should be their enjoyment of the sport.

But being knowledgeable about soccer is not sufficient in and of itself. Those of you whose childhoods were inspired by Franz Beckenbauer and Pelé and who grew up with a ball at your feet have an advantage. However, knowing about something and being able to teach it are two entirely different propositions. Coaching is teaching and teaching is different than knowing.

Moreover, the game continues to evolve. The sport that you and I played in our youth has changed, and has done so for the better—so have coaching techniques.

Regardless of whether you are a newcomer or a soccer aficionado, this book will prove helpful because it represents the combined thoughts of some of America's foremost developers of soccer talent. Those of us who coach professional players remain proactive in furthering our own educational process. The U.S.S.F. coaching staff has long been enthusiastic about traveling around the globe to study coaching methodology. We endeavor to translate what works in Brazil, Holland, Italy, and other top soccer-playing nations into an approach that is suited to the American player. The pages ahead therefore represent the most up-to-date ways to teach the game in our country.

This book will help you devise a long-range plan, so your athletes can play in an environment conducive to the development of the wide range of skills soccer demands. Scores of exercises and practice games will help you accomplish this task. The lessons on techniques are presented in an easy-to-understand, step-by-step format. In addition, common mistakes are discussed, so it will be easier to correct them.

You will note that the text includes a

lengthy discussion of coaching philosophy; it is very useful to examine your priorities before your first practice. This will help you best serve the needs of your team, your players, and yourself.

Becoming a good coach isn't easy, but it is enormously rewarding. As I look back to the people who coached me, I realize that I owe much of the very nature of my value system to their guidance. A coach is equal parts educator, role model, and mentor. This is a very important position, and I hope you will make every reasonable effort to do it to the best of your ability. If you make that commitment, you will be compensated with a richness that money truly cannot buy.

As someone who has known the privilege of coaching the U.S. Men's National Team, I am grateful to you and all individuals like yourself who devote time to producing the next generation of American star players, referees, administrators, and fans. In a very real way, you represent the future of American soccer.

Good luck!

—Steve Sampson

The USA joined the world in 1996, launching MLS, our own professional first division. D.C. United's Marco Etcheverry (left) was 1998 MLS player of the year.

This book has been structured as an ongoing companion manual that assists with your day-to-day coaching. While you may immediately feel apprehensive about how to organize your practices, or improve them, Part Six is dedicated to this aspect of coaching. Particular attention has been paid to helping with the planning and execution of a team's training sessions. We know from experience that this is the area where most coaches desire assistance and so we have provided you with more than one hundred outstanding training games that are fun to play and developmentally sound.

Step one will be for you to identify an aspect of the game that needs addressing for your next practice's theme. Then consult the Games section. Using the accompanying dividers you will find games that incorporate the skill and/or tactical consideration to be emphasized. Refer to the age listings for games that are appropriate for the team that you coach. The games you play should be preceded by useful and relevant warm-up exercises, for which you should consult the section on the Model Training Session and the Technical Training Session.

A vital part of youth coaching is to develop fundamentally accomplished players. Towards that end the comprehensive Technique section of the book covers every key skill and the necessary movements, giving you instructions to help players to execute techniques properly.

Also included are the most common correctable mistakes players make in performing skills.

To get the most out of any game it is important that your method of teaching is well grounded. While you are encouraged to refer to the Games, Technique, and Model Training Session sections for day-to-day use, be sure to familiarize yourself with the information contained in the rest of this book. Without the proper context and teaching techniques, much of the value of the games will be compromised.

Similarly, understanding the overall philosophy of U.S. Soccer, which is imbedded throughout this book, will be greatly helpful to your enjoyment of the game and to your ability to teach its principles to the coming generation of America's soccer stars. Your players and your team will be the beneficiaries.

A coach is more than a teacher, your moral (and legal) responsibilities also include providing the safest possible environment for all participants. Thus, you are urged to implement the steps recommended by U.S. Soccer's medical staff in the chapter on the prevention and care of injuries.

Although considerable amounts of experience and expertise went into the writing of this book, your reading and referring to this work should represent but a small percentage of your educational process. There remains no substitute for attending clinics, coaching courses, and games.

English Premier League's Ginola goes aerial with a spectacular bicycle kick. Ultimately, the best players must make their own decisions—combining intuition, technical skill, and tactical judgement—to win games.

At the start of the twentieth century, soccer's growing global popularity demanded common rules and an international governing body. In 1904, seven European nations met in Paris to found the Fédération Internationale de Football Association (FIFA). Since then, the sport's growth has been remarkable. FIFA, headquartered in Zurich, Switzerland, now oversees more member states than does the United Nations, with the number of soccer matches contested worldwide in any calendar year being measured in the millions. FIFA's crown jewel, the World Cup, which was contested first among only 13 countries in Uruguay in 1930, has grown to become by far the globe's most-watched sporting event.

For the uninitiated, it is hard to describe the unbridled passion and national pride that accompany World Cup matches. Each team is composed of a country's top players and is invested with extraordinary national expectations. Quite literally, a war was once fought over the result of a game, and the fate of more than one government has been attributed to a team's performance.

The men's World Cup finals tournament covers a four- to five-week span every four years and is now contested by thirty-two nations, but qualifying rounds involve close to 200 countries and begin nearly two years prior. Only the host nation and reigning champions are granted an automatic berth to the finals. This is the world's single most popular sporting event, witnessed by billions of viewers. The economic impact of hosting the World Cup finals is such that a serious candidate nation allocates a seven-figure budget just for the bidding process.

FIFA also administers world and continental championships for Under-20 men, Under-17 boys, as well as the Olympics (men's and women's tournaments), and an indoors (five-a-side) championship. Like the World Cup, all of these are contested by national teams, which are all-star squads composed of the very best players among a country's citizens.

FIFA has more recently added a Women's World Championship (now known as the Women's World Cup). The United States won the inaugural edition, in 1991. Our women's team also captured the gold medal in the 1996 Olympic Games.

Directly under FIFA are six continental confederations (see next page). The United States is one of about three dozen member nations under the CONCACAF umbrella.

Each confederation holds competitions to determine which teams will qualify to partake in each of the FIFA finals events as well as running championships for its own zone. The European Championships (now known simply as Euro) is itself a major international event. Its finals traditionally have been held every four years, in the even-numbered year between World Cup finals. There are equivalent tournaments in every confederation, with the Copa America

The ultimate moment in soccer: France's captain, Didier Deschamps, hoists the World Cup after defeating Brazil, 3–0, in the 1998 final.

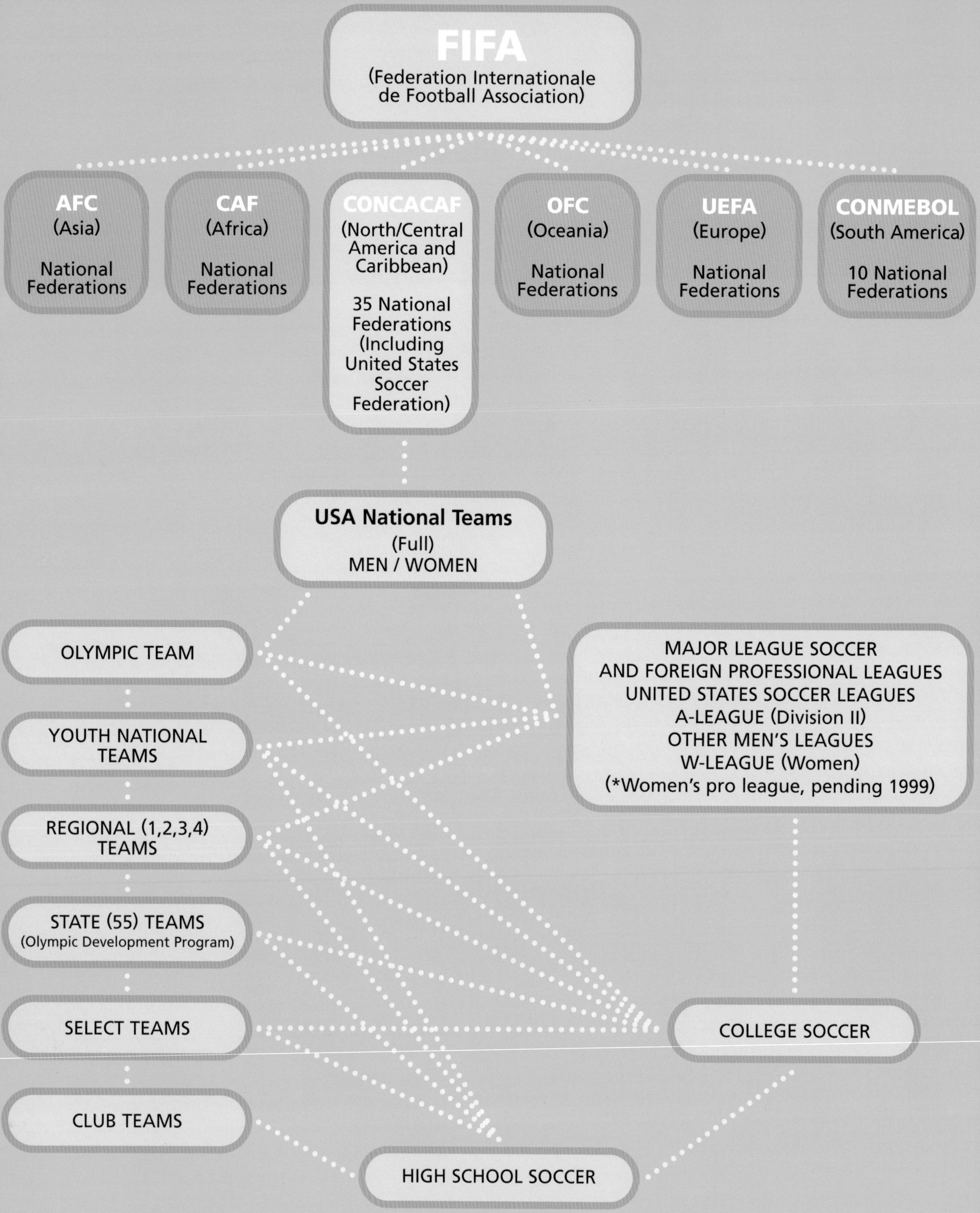

FIFA
(Federation Internationale
de Football Association)

AFC (Asia)	CAF (Africa)	CONCACAF (North/Central America and Caribbean)	OFC (Oceania)	UEFA (Europe)	CONMEBOL (South America)
National Federations	National Federations	35 National Federations (Including United States Soccer Federation)	National Federations	National Federations	10 National Federations

USA National Teams
(Full)
MEN / WOMEN

OLYMPIC TEAM

YOUTH NATIONAL TEAMS

REGIONAL (1,2,3,4) TEAMS

STATE (55) TEAMS
(Olympic Development Program)

SELECT TEAMS

CLUB TEAMS

MAJOR LEAGUE SOCCER
AND FOREIGN PROFESSIONAL LEAGUES
UNITED STATES SOCCER LEAGUES
A-LEAGUE (Division II)
OTHER MEN'S LEAGUES
W-LEAGUE (Women)
(*Women's pro league, pending 1999)

COLLEGE SOCCER

HIGH SCHOOL SOCCER

From matches that attract two billion television witnesses, such as the 1998 World Cup Final (top), to the game's grass roots, as in Jamaica (below), soccer's popularity far eclipses all other sports.

The women's game has seen an ongoing boom at the international level since the late 1980s. Across the globe, such teams as Germany, Norway (both top), Brazil, and the United States (both below) have become powerhouses.

(South America) and the African Nations Cup having the highest profiles. The CONCACAF Gold Cup is held every other year. The American men captured the first edition, in 1991.

Within almost every FIFA member nation there is a thriving national league. The most prestigious of these are Italy's Serie A, Germany's Bundesliga, England's Premiership, and Spain's Primera Liga, which are the top divisions of the pro leagues. In 1996, two years after the United States hosted an enormously successful World Cup, Major League Soccer was launched with teams in ten cities. Its subsequent growth has been steady and sure.

Most nations have an integrated league system in which the teams finishing at the bottom of the first division standings at the end of each season are relegated to the second division for the subsequent season. The top second division teams are promoted to the first division and so on with subsequent divisions. As a result, a tiny club such as England's Wimbledon can fulfill extraordinary ambitions by working its way up from the world of semi-professional soccer to the Premiership (or vice versa).

Moving up a division means a club will draw bigger crowds and sponsorship dollars and have a higher profile. While the U.S. does not have a system of promotion and relegation, its club structure is patterned after the global model—the A-League is one notch below MLS and enjoys official division two status. Its member teams play occasional exhibition and cup games against MLS clubs. It is the top rung of the United Soccer Leagues (USL), which also includes semi-pro and amateur divisions and a women's league.

Winning a first division league title is very lucrative. The league champions defend their domestic title the following year and compete against the champions of the other leagues within their confederation. The Champions League in Europe, which began in 1956 (then known as the European Cup), attracts a worldwide audience for its annual final. Its winner then faces the victors of the Copa Libertadores (the South American equivalent of the Champions League) in the Inter-Continental Cup final.

Similarly, CONCACAF's league champions meet in the Champions Cup. In 1998, D.C. United defeated Mexico's Toluca to become the first U.S. club team to reign in CONCACAF. A subsequent upset of South American champions Vasco da Gama of Brazil for the Inter-American Cup meant United was the first U.S. club team to be champions of the western hemisphere.

All the top soccer nations also hold domestic cup tournaments, which run concurrently with the league competition. Cups follow a single-elimination format. Amateur and semi-professional teams battle in the early stages. A handful of survivors thereby earn berths to the juncture at which the professional teams enter the brackets. In every year, in almost every country, there are fantastic match-ups in which a small, local team has earned the right to face one of the sport's heavyweights. On occasion, a lower division "minnow" club will eliminate a first division powerhouse, introducing great excitement to the contest.

Cup finals are glamorous events, with the most famous being England's F.A. Cup, held since 1871. Cup winners also advance to their own confederation tournament for the following year. Europe's governing body further organizes the UEFA Cup, a tournament for the previous season's best teams (based on division one league records) from each European country, excluding the one or two teams from each nation that qualified for the more prestigious Champions League.

Within each nation there is a sub-structure for amateur competition. U.S. Youth Soccer has four regions composed of fifty-five state associations (five of the largest states have two associations). The state associations hold competitions (some of which lead to regional and then national title competitions) for various age groups of boys, girls, men, and women.

American soccer features a logical structure for the identification and subsequent training of our best players. Most clubs offer developmental, in-house, and travel programs. The latter involves play against other club sides in the same age and gender grouping within a league. Usually starting at about the Under-12 level, each age division within that league gathers its top players to form a select team that engages primarily in summer tournaments. The next step is for athletes to earn a spot on their state team; better players are subsequently chosen for regional teams and, finally, selected for the National Teams Program.

Also prominent on the domestic scene are high school and intercollegiate soccer. For some time, more NCAA-member schools have fielded soccer than gridiron football teams. With the advent of Title IX, introduced in 1972, women's intercollegiate soccer experienced a boom, really starting in the late 1980s. Although the quality of the campus game has improved, the progress of our most talented players has often been retarded by limitations on the number of games that a school or college team may play and by not permitting student/athletes to participate for club teams during the academic year.

Thus, for years the lack of a soccer-intensive environment for our athletes ages 16 through 22 stood in marked contrast to that of the most competitive nations. Throughout Europe and South America it has long been common for teenagers to serve an apprenticeship with professional clubs. The cream of this crop subsequently turn pro. Attempting to replicate that system, MLS and U.S. Soccer jointly launched Project-40 in the late 1990s. High school grads and underclassman now have the option of turning pro with additional monies being set aside for tuition to continue their academic pursuits.

1999 NCAA Division One Final Four action: on campus more NCAA member institutions field varsity soccer than gridiron football squads.

For the United States to win a men's world championship in soccer we must first take the bold step of publicly stating that objective. On April 19, 1997, the United States Soccer Federation announced Project 2010, which laid the foundation to claim soccer's most coveted prize: the World Cup. To complete most projects, thirteen years would seem an eternity. But for the most popular team competition in the world, thirteen years is just around the corner.

How we prepare our players to be able to compete against the world's best soccer teams is fundamental to our success. Equally important is our ability to attract many of our best athletes to our sport. Those of us at the top of the soccer pyramid are working hard so that our best players will soon reap rewards similar to their counterparts in other major team sports. The founding and the growth of Major League Soccer coupled with the successes of our men's and women's National Teams are going a long way toward helping soccer to attract and retain gifted athletes.

Of equal importance is that youngsters have a positive soccer experience. That's where you come in. We firmly believe that the formula for success begins with your understanding that soccer is a player's game. At all stages you must remember that the game exists for the players. To teach soccer you should understand that it is inherently different from other team sports with which you may be more familiar. When Italy's 1982 World Cup-

winning coach, Enzo Bearzot, was at an American coaches' convention several years back the question was posed as to how he formulated his strategy that allowed his team to defeat Argentina by shutting down their superstar, Diego Maradona. Bearzot replied that he had spent several hours working out the tactics, but once the match began, his players did not think that the scheme would work and so they completely changed it on their own! Can you imagine an NFL quarterback throwing out a game plan in the huddle? Therein lies a very significant difference between the two sports. Our form of football belongs to those who actually kick the ball. The most skillful player on the planet will not be of much use unless that talent is married to the ability to "read the game" and to make his own good split-second decisions predicated upon understanding the ebb and flow of the match.

Players must therefore be in an environment that is fun, challenging, and competitive. Each player must perceive that he or she is integral to the success of the team, whether as a starter or a substitute. There must be a constant sense of growth that comes from improving with every training session. In general, youth soccer practices are not competitive enough while our games are overly so. Kids enjoy competing as long as it is done in a positive environment. However, the over-emphasis on winning come game day, with screaming coaches and parents

can ruin the fun. It is not a problem that we Americans strive to win. The problem lies in the manner in which many of us respond to losing. Even the most competitive professionals who make millions of dollars want the game to be enjoyable. When soccer becomes work, and practices lose their sense of fun, athletes become bored and then cease to progress.

The Case for Small-Sided Soccer

One of the greatest advancements in youth soccer has been the global acceptance of small-sided soccer. Simple logic dictates that the fewer the amount of players who must share the ball, the greater the number of times that each will touch it. More touches equal more fun and better skill.

After much thought and study of the youth developmental approach taken by the better soccer nations, U.S. Youth Soccer mandated that children under age 10 must not play more than a maximum of eight-per-side. Of equal importance is a gradual building up to that number.

There has been much discussion within soccer's coaching community as to what is the ideal number of children to involve in a game at each given age. Although specifics can vary, experts know that the game must be scaled to the needs of its participants. Having too many players for an age group will result in a human "beehive" surrounding the ball. So crowded is that swarm that it will be virtually impos-

sible for any individual to effectively utilize such basic soccer skills as dribbling or passing.

Another likely consequence of having too many players on the field is that the coach will place some players in positions and ask them to stay in that position for a period of the game. As a result, when Team A has the ball near Team B's goal there will be two or three Team A defenders standing in front of their goal just waiting for the game to come back to them. This is not fun and it does nothing to enhance their skills.

By contrast, when kids play small-sided soccer on a mini field with appropriately-sized goals, each child is involved in the game whenever the ball is in play. All get a chance to attack and all must learn to defend. Passing is possible. So is dribbling. And the scoring of goals is so common that virtually every player will know the thrill of planting a shot in the back of the other team's net.

In small-sided games, an individual's ability to combine with teammates is very important. Rendered less vital is athleticism, especially speed. The kid who is very athletic will never lose those qualities. But by not being allowed to use them as a crutch, that youngster has the opportunity to become our ideal; a great player who is also a great athlete.

A three-v-three game involves soccer's basic structure: the triangle. Look closely at any top-level team and you will observe they link through many triangles through-out the field. This allows them many passing possibilities. Four-v-four encompasses diamond shape play. While three-v-three involves but one triangle, there can be four separate triangles present merely by adding an extra player per team.

Another benefit to the progression is that four-v-four gives the attacking team width and depth. There will usually be a teammate to either side of the player in possession and there will also be a teammate either in front of or behind the player on the ball.

Even when kids graduate to six-v-six, there should remain little or no emphasis on playing a position, on winning, or on restricting decision-making. The individualist who would rather dribble than pass may not quite be the pariah that he's assumed to be. The ability to dribble past several defenders in a limited space is a quality that only a handful of the game's greatest players have acquired. Kids should not have their creativity stifled, especially at younger ages.

So great are the developmental qualities of small-sided games that professional teams play a lot more of five-v-five in training than of 11-v-11. Getting back to basics via small-sided games became a major theme of the German national coaching staff starting in the mid-1990s.

As in our country, their youth sports have become far more organized in recent years. The result is that pick-up soccer games are far less prevalent than they had once been. Among Germany's senior players, there are still plenty of technically competent athletes, but players implementing improvisational qualities have become increasingly scarce. As with us, German coaches can only encourage their players to play on their own. One step their governing body was able to take––and has taken—is to make a concerted effort to replicate the "street soccer" environment in both training sessions and games.

That approach was the result of an all-out push by former long-time German national team coach Berti Vogts. A starter on West Germany's 1974 world championship side, Vogts considered a return to small-sided play to be vital. Toward that end, he had his players hand out awards on the final day of a nationwide four-v-four competition that's held for youngsters up to age 16.

The very best way to introduce soccer to kids is through informal pick-up games, such as we used to play with our friends, on our own, during our youth.

Unfortunately, the reality for today's children is that activities are usually organized for them by adults. Lost is the spontaneity and the freedom to experiment, because the kids are constantly being told what to do. You can do a great service by allowing for loosely organized free play during which time you (and any other adults who may be present) supervise but refrain from instructing.

Player Development

It is important that players become competent with both feet and can perform technical functions with a wide variety of body surfaces. Players need the skill to attack and the tenacity to defend. Soccer's free-flowing nature demands that we produce:

1. Great mobility on and off the ball. The catch phrase for youth coaches to employ: "pass and move."

2. Lethal finishers who possess outstanding judgement, confidence, and skill.

3. Players with the three varieties of speed; tactical speed (recognizing what to do), technical speed (being able to instantly apply the selected skill), and physical (sprinting) speed.

4. Athletes who excel in transition from offense to defense and vice versa.

5. Individuals with "personality" and "flair." It wasn't that long ago that we played soccer the way that Eastern European teams played basketball in the 1970s; technically correct but lacking creativity. We must continue to develop lots of players with the ability to improvise so as to deceive opposing defenders.

6. Players who can consistently strike a ball cleanly and accurately with either foot over both short and long distances.

7. Tactically sophisticated individuals who watch and analyze ample top-level games to acquire a keen understanding of soccer. Players who are as comfortable functioning with or against a zonal defensive scheme as with or against a player-to-player marking system.

Ajax, the great Dutch club that has produced many top stars, identifies youth prospects by using what they call the TIPS system. They seek out youngsters who combine outstanding Technique, Intuition, Personality, and Speed. All-around players are the ideal. But there is also room within teams for "role" players who do one thing exceptionally well while being proficient in the other phases of the sport.

Ages Six Through Eight

For our youngest participants, it is essential that they look forward to training. In our opinion, six is a good starting age for organized soccer. We recognize that many clubs begin players at age five, or even four, but prior to age six most youngsters are better served by playing in an environment that fosters creativity and is free from too much parental control and advice. In an ideal situation, the six year old will arrive at the first organized team practice already having played soccer in informal situations.

As soon as children can walk, they can start to kick a soft, small ball. A parent kicking the ball around with a toddler will provide hours of enjoyment—with the child almost always outlasting the adult. During children's first organized practice, it is easy to tell which have played with adults or older siblings because of their comfort level with a ball. Having such a head start may account in part for why several members of the men's U.S. National Team are the sons of former top-level players.

Regardless of whether a child has spent years kicking a ball or has never done so before, practice will always be enjoyable when the child has an enthusiastic coach and actually gets to play the game. The initial part of practice should be focused on developing skills with one technical (skill) theme per session. The remainder, which should be at least half of every training session, should be spent playing games. Soccer is such a simple game that you can quickly explain the basic rules (such as not using the hands, not tripping or pushing other players, learning about how to restart play, taking throw-ins, and what a goalie does, etc.).

A six year old does not have to be competing throughout the entire practice. Yet, that child should be challenged. There should be an easily understood objective to every exercise to keep each player's attention. All of a sudden you will have kids shouting, "Hey coach, watch this!"

Prior to age eight or nine, trying to teach youngsters to pass the ball can be an exercise in frustration and futility. Most children at that stage are not yet psychologically prepared to share the ball. Therefore games and activities that involve one ball per player and lots of dribbling-type movements are recommended. When playing a game with one ball, involve very few players and allow the game to be rel- atively unstructured—players should not be coached to play in a position or told to pass.

Within the small-sided game, position- al awareness is important but not to the extent that it inhibits individual flair and creativity. There is nothing wrong with a player who attempts to dribble past three or four defenders before looking to pass or to shoot. As a coach you must develop a sense of when to emphasize the pro- gression of the individual instead of the team.

During the skill developmental phase of practice, it is very important that play- ers are given the proper visual image for the performance of a skill. You need to have a command of all of the game's primary techniques to be able to demonstrate them for the team. If you do not, recruit a play- er who can perform those skills to "paint the picture."

Once again, be cognizant of the age of the players. A six year old does not yet have the agility and balance that are required to strike a shot with the instep or pass with the inside of the foot. Instinctively, they will kick the ball with their toes. While this runs contrary to how older players should play the ball, acquiring proper technique will come in due time. Not until age eight or nine can most young- sters learn fundamentals. Heading should not be taught until about age eleven.

You can take some steps to improve physi- cal abilities, particularly when it comes to

The spirit of U.S. Soccer: symbolized by veteran MLS coach Thomas Rongen (top), who donates his time linking the pros to the next generation of players and by the Fair Play gesture that linked U.S. and Iranian players prior to the kickoff of the 1998 World Cup showdown (below).

engaging in activities that improve balance, agility, and coordination (see Young Beginners games, page 234). Fitness is not a factor early on and should not be included in your training plans. Save it for the teenage years and beyond, when it is really needed. This advice runs contrary to the first instincts of the neophyte coach. Drawing upon your own experiences as an athlete you are likely to think in terms of hard work and team strategy.

Other common inquiries from new coaches include "What formation do you recommend?" and "How do I teach kids to play their positions?" What is really being asked is how to entice that child to remain in a specific area of the field even when the action is nowhere near him. Kids will gravitate towards the ball. They should want to do so because kicking the ball represents both the fun and the essence of the game. So you will always need to keep things in perspective.

At all ages, but of particular importance early on, is to use training exercises that keep the players moving. One of our cardinal rules is that drills that involve standing in lines should be avoided. By keeping the sessions organized and succinct, you will find that players enjoy themselves more. Limit your matches to one per week and practice time to no more than two one-hour sessions per week.

Most of all, there is no need to keep score during the very first years and standings with "championships" should be saved for later.

The nine to fourteen age range represents the most influential period in forming a sound fundamental base and a love of the game. Continue to make training fun while at the same time keeping it consistently challenging and competitive. Playing to win games becomes increasingly important but should never be at the expense of playing well. Avoid the temptation to have your players boot the ball long and far in the hope that one of your fast forwards can win a footrace to create a breakaway. A ball that is aimlessly kicked forward into a sea of opponents with the idea of gaining a territorial advantage is, at best, hopeful soccer. The style of playing incessant "direct" soccer, when a team always plays the ball forward regardless of whether or not it is appropriate to do so in that situation, does not develop players. Moreover, that approach has consistently been proven ineffective at the higher levels of the game. The "direct" approach should also be discouraged because it replaces skillful and creative play with an environment in which aggression and size become disproportionately important. While we want to encourage players to be "direct" by going to goal when the opportunity presents itself, there is a huge difference between being constructively direct as opposed to whacking the ball forward all the time.

A major reason why the Brazilian men's national team is so successful is the Brazilians' lifelong commitment to playing "beautifully skilled soccer." How we play the game, especially at youth level is much more important than winning. Having said that, you will discover that the more you strive to play well, the more success your team will eventually experience.

Playing well means playing an intelligent, patient, controlled game in which skill, mobility, and precision are emphasized and applied at speed. A precise pass to a well-timed, purposeful run that culminates in a shot on goal is one of the most exciting actions in any sport.

At this age players also need to learn the importance of being able to attack and defend from all positions. Concepts of providing support, positional interchange, exchanging roles, basic tactics (changing the point of the attack, and the like), as well as learning about different systems of play may be introduced.

For players about age 10 we can start to introduce the rudimentary principles of team play. The athlete should understand when it is preferable to pass or to dribble. Basic concepts can be imparted, such as creating space behind the defense; movement off the ball by attackers; creating and quickly attacking space to full advantage; and combining passes to get through the defense.

There is more structure to the game, but the importance of encouraging creativity is not diminished. Players must still be allowed to express themselves. Most players will have developed a sense of what it means to win and lose—and therefore how to achieve victory.

When athletes are competing on a regulation-size field, positions and formations are introduced. Most teams will initially opt for a 4-3-3 (four defenders, three midfielders, and three forwards) formation, while older teams will generally play a 4-4-2 or a 3-5-2, in which flank midfielders are expected to attack the opponents' penalty area and to get back to defend in their own area. Younger players cannot be expected to have the speed or stamina of older flank midfielders, who cover the length of the field, hence 4-3-3 is usually preferred.

The main goal of formations at this stage is to keep a team organized and compact, covering the field but moving as a unit with the ball (not, for example, isolating defenders from play by keeping them too far back to prevent a breakaway).

However, formations are not why teams experience long-term success or failure. Systems of play matter to pros but never at any level of soccer are they nearly as important as the quality of the squad. Your focus and priorities should remain on player development. Learning to play a position or a role is of far less importance than honing a wide range of skills. The more that you focus on "playing your position," the less you will be focusing on what truly matters.

By the early teens, the strengths and weaknesses of individuals will render them better suited for certain roles and/or positions. However, it is a big mistake to prematurely pigeonhole individuals into specific roles and positions. As they and the team mature, the more well-rounded their skills, the better the team will become.

At all levels of the game defenders must be able to attack and attackers must be able to defend. The best way to teach your "star forward" how to defend is to have him play in the back. Resist the temptation to play to win at Under-11 by putting left-footed players only on the left side of the field. What may bear short-term gains will come at the expense of a much more important consideration: the long-term development of your players and your team.

Technically, at this level, players should make significant progress in their ability to control a ball under limitations of time and space while under pressure from the opponent. That is why increased speed of play, with and without the ball, should be demanded in training sessions and during games.

Encourage your players to become two-footed. By around age 14, the better players are increasingly comfortable at using the outsides of each foot to receive and, when necessary, strike a ball. Heading, first introduced at about age 11, will become increasingly important by age 14

for attacking and defending. By the upper reaches of this age range, players need to be able to strike an accurate 25-yard pass and hone other foot skills. This is a gradual development. By age 11, most players should be able to create a push pass. By age 12, most players have the coordination to drive a ball with the instep and drive through the ball. As players progress it is important that they can adequately perform their skills with both feet.

It is during the teenage years that more involved tactical concepts can be comprehended (but ONLY after players are sufficiently skilled as to be generally in command of the ball). A 14 year old should understand how to take advantage of space, how to catch another team on the break, how to find and exploit defensive weaknesses.

Also to be taught is the importance of offensive and defensive shape. Whatever the formation of choice, there will be some interchanging of positions. To prevent counterattacks, players must understand that if a fullback on our team advances upfield to join in on the attack, one of our midfielders or forwards must drop back to provide defensive cover for that teammate.

The physical development of individuals in this age group should be limited to the natural increases in strength, power, and speed that are obtained through the demands of practices and matches. Weight training is not yet encouraged.

Ages Fifteen Through Eighteen

The most talented athletes can be identified between the ages of fifteen and eighteen. Skill development is still a priority, but now these skills must be performed with far more comfort, speed, and precision while under considerable pressure from the opponent.

By this time, better players can learn to volley and to bend the ball with insides of either feet, play with their back to goal, and have a repertoire of effective dribbling moves.

It is essential to challenge the younger players who have demonstrated physical and technical maturity in their game to be able to compete with and against older players. But because growth spurts are quite common at these ages, coaches must evaluate the physical readiness of the athlete before having that individual "play up."

Tactics become a more important element of the game. Players should be able not only to recognize and to exploit an opponent's weaknesses through intelligent and purposeful play, they should also have a grasp of how to play when leading by a goal, when trailing by a goal, with a man advantage, or when outnumbered. By the time they reach this phase, they should have begun to make more decisions on their own, with fewer instructions from the coach during the course of a game.

By this stage players' traits are well established so that individuals will be gravitating towards roles and positions that best suit their attributes. Once primary positions within the squad have been established, functional training is introduced. This involves working with small groups of players, such as your team's strikers, on the techniques and tactical considerations that are most commonly demanded by their position. Restarts will take on greater significance, offering more scoring opportunities. "Set pieces," play from direct and indirect kicks and corner kicks, need to be practiced. Getting width into the attack to be able to effectively cross and finish is required of good teams, as is the ability to play accurate longer passes. Defensive balance and "holding shape" (covering the field) is key, too.

Soccer-appropriate forms of weight training may be introduced once an athlete has completed puberty, coupled with a well-constructed regimen designed to increase an individual's functional power, quickness, and speed.

The psychological element gains in import. This is an age of attrition with the commitment (or lack therof) of athletes becoming a major issue. Your challenge is to provide an environment that is conducive to improvement so that highly motivated players will be able to grow towards achieving long-term goals. Training sessions should be purposeful and competitive with maximum sharpness emphasized and required.

Also key during the teenage years is individual and collective discipline. You are responsible for not tolerating inappropriate physical challenges against opponents during games and setting high expectations for off-the-field decorum. Please do not abdicate your principles. Being willing to make a short-term sacrifice (not winning on the day) so as to instill proper priorities is vitally important.

Caring about your players as people can make a big difference in their lives. Your relationships with youngsters can help to guide them through the pitfalls of a very tricky stage of life in which they will be confronted with critical personal choices.

Summary

From the first training session to retirement, each soccer player's development must be nurtured. Coaching is an art form. Avoid stifling a young player's creativity, as it is vital that players develop skill and confidence with the ball. Facilitate growth by gradually adding definition and discipline to each player's game. Don't ever underestimate the need for personalities on the field nor forget that each position demands different personality types. Remember, too, that attention to detail during the primary, skill-acquisition years will pay enormous dividends.

One of the great beauties of soccer is that there are no absolutes. Every playing experience is distinct from the next. Ours is a free-flowing sport without timeouts.

Unlike baseball, basketball, and American-style football, ours is not a coach-dominated sport. In soccer, every player must constantly make a series of choices. The quality of the split-second decisions that must be made demonstrates that individual's skill, tactical sophistication, and personality. As a result, soccer allows and treasures personal creativity.

Your understanding of the mentality of the game and of the players will allow you to be a more effective facilitator in helping to create an environment in which all of your players—from the most highly skilled and creative to the most basic—thrive.

Only if young players are given the freedom to make choices during the run of play will they be able to fulfill their potential. Hard though it may be, please refrain from bellowing at your players to "shoot it" or "pass it." A "wrong" decision by a player is better than a "right" decision by a coach. After the game is the time to discuss why a player made a specific choice in a specific situation. But during the game it must be left to the players to think for themselves.

What follows are ideas about how you may best help your team to improve while thoroughly enjoying playing this great game. Please accept these as general guidelines based on consultation with some of the best coaches in the United States. Keep in mind, however, that coaches help players acquire decision-making skills in practice. It is your players who must make decisions on game days.

A vital ingredient that almost all world soccer powers share is a commonality of purpose: a united approach to development, applied to the full national team as well as to the youngest youth sides. Achieving vertical integration within U.S. Soccer requires improving two-way communication within our coaching community, from the top of the pyramid to the base, and vice versa.

We cannot sufficiently emphasize that we are all part of the same soccer family. In many ways, coaches' contributions to young players are far more important than any later training, for without producing the raw materials, there will be nothing to mold into successful teams to represent us. When you cheer for the National Team it is really "we" who are competing, not just the eleven athletes who are on the field. That "USA" on the front of those jerseys stands for the work of every member of the U.S. soccer community.

We must, therefore, all work toward the same age-specific/player-specific developmental scheme. Our athletes should be playing soccer from a young age to develop sufficient skills, and acquire a passion for the game. Vertical integration requires that we on the national coaching staff convince you of the merit of the philosophy espoused on these pages. It involves you understanding and incorporating these priorities into your program so that eight-year olds aren't playing 11-v-11 on a field 120 yards long, and therefore reaching higher plateaus without having developed their skills. A player progresses from "travel" to "select" to state to regional to youth national team. If he passes each stage without proper development, or is given contradictory approaches, we will not have succeeded. Equally, the national teams' program must harbor a common philosophical tactical approach that is consistent from our youth national teams through the senior side. This way, players can graduate proficiently from one level to the next.

The ultimate step is playing professionally followed by a national team call-up. Thus, today's six-year old may be less than fifteen years removed from challenging the greatest athletes from Brazil, Germany, Argentina, Nigeria, or Italy. There is also a simultaneous progression from youth to high school to college soccer followed by the pros (or from high school soccer directly to the pros).

Since vertical integration is a two-way street, it is imperative that our professional players take the time to get back into the community to work with you and your players. Do not be shy about approaching a professional or college player or team for help. While our national coaching staff works hard to identify and train top prospects, coaches can play a role by calling the identity of outstanding candidates to the attention of those who are above them in soccer's pyramid. If we all commit to working together we (and the game) will benefit enormously.

The future of soccer: U.S. National Team veterans Mia Hamm, Kristine Lilly, and Joy Fawcett greet the team's "12th player" (Fawcett's child) prior to a recent match.

PART 2

FUNDAMENTALS

A coach performs in several important capacities. The job description includes being a facilitator, role model, leader, long-term planner, trainer, safety and health-care provider, and salesperson, as well as teacher, organizer, and philosopher.

The Coach as Facilitator

There is no greater service you can perform than to impart a love of soccer to the children who play the game. Players who have a passion for the sport are driven to excel. When asked how he developed his love of soccer, Claudio Reyna, one of the USA's stellar National Team players replied, "Everyone in my family played soccer. My brother and I played every day. I would bang shots against the side of my house—my mom screamed at me all the time. When it rained I played in the house. I'd watch a lot of soccer games, but it helps to just play around at a young age. Up to the age of 13, 14, I think you've just got to have fun and play little games; three-against-three, two-against-two. You pick up little things, street-smart things. Of course, you've got to play on a club team to learn how to play on a team as well but on the side I was always just messing around like you see basketball players doing. That's why they get better all the time."

Select almost any U.S. National Team player and you will hear a remarkably similar tale. Many of them have also spoken of childhood peers who possessed greater potential but who couldn't match their passion and their commitment. Part of the equation is being a fan of the sport and having a hero to emulate. Having that dream will prompt young players to want to watch their heroes in action. In turn, they'll see skills that they will then be inspired to attempt to perfect in their backyard. To help make that connection, here are a few things to try:

1. Organize a team trip to watch your local pro or college team in action. Get parents involved in a pre-game tailgate party.
2. Contact a pro franchise or the coach of a local college to inquire if your team can play at halftime of one of their matches and/or serve as ball boys. These teams have a vested interest in being part of the community to build their support base. They will view your offer as mutually beneficial.
3. Use pro and college teams as coaching resources. Most have active clinic programs.
4. Hold a team party during the telecast of an important MLS or National Team game.

The Coach as Role Model and Leader

A coach's decorum during games and practices must be first-rate. There is no place in youth sports for using foul language, smoking a cigarette, drinking an alcoholic beverage, or abusing referees. Your appearance should be appropriate and neat. For practices you should have the right footwear and be prepared to participate actively.

Coaches at all levels must first be careful observers of play, whether at youth level or at international level; U.S. National Team coach Bruce Arena (previous page) owns five NCAA and two MLS title rings.

You may opt to give your captain(s) the responsibility of warming up the squad at the start of training (above) though many coaches, including U.S. National Women's Team head coach Tony DiCicco, take an active involvement in all aspects of team preparation (below).

You are responsible for the actions of your players and for making certain that they use safe techniques and methods of play. It is your obligation to the sport and to the molding of the characters of impressionable young people that you never teach "tricks" that are, in fact, forms of cheating. Instruct your players to be competitive but not at the expense of the rules and the spirit of the sport. Teach them to scheme, not cheat.

Even with young kids, another dimension of discipline should also be present on game day. A player who is substituted should always run off the field directly to his/her coach. Make sure to correct any inappropriate display of displeasure on the part of an athlete who is replaced. Have the players who aren't in the game remain within close proximity of you. Except, perhaps, for very little kids, the substitutes should be paying full attention to the match while providing encouragement to teammates.

The chapter on Laws of the Game delineates the difference between a fair challenge and one that is not permissible. Under no circumstance should cleats be exposed to an opponent, elbows be thrown, shirts tugged, or a player tripped or tackled from behind. Intentional time wasting late in a match to preserve a result is unsporting behavior; as is delaying an opponents' ability to take a free kick by encroaching or kicking a ball away in anger or to make a statement. Diving to pretend to be fouled to fool the referee into awarding a free kick also has no place in the sport.

The standard of sportsmanship that you set as the coach is among the most important things you will do, of far greater significance than winning a game. This also means you are responsible for helping to keep the sidelines free of spectators who might obstruct play and to be sure parents and fans of your team do not exhibit unsportsmanlike conduct to any official or player, including their own children.

As players mature it is important that they appreciate that they owe the game of soccer something. They owe it to try their best always, to conduct themselves as sportsmen and sportswomen at all times, to represent themselves, their families, their coaches, their team, their club, their town, and their sport well both on and off of the field. Their actions in the hotel between games of a tournament are every bit as important as is their behavior during a match.

Our players on the U.S. National Teams take very seriously their responsibility to represent soccer in the manner that it deserves. As a group, they are accessible to fans, often saluting supporters at games and thanking their fans. They are available to the media and regularly hold clinics to promote the game and assist youth teams. Overall, our pro players are great ambassadors for soccer; your players should be so too; and it all starts with your example.

Every player must also take pride in giving his or her best effort whenever stepping onto the field. For players of middle school age, demand that of them and accept no less. To do so you must set the tone by constantly working to grow as well. Your desire to improve serves two great needs; it will make you a better teacher and you will gain the respect of your players. Moreover, the game is forever evolving. We must all either grow with it or be left behind.

The Coach as a Long-Term Planner

You are an architect whose long-term planning will build your players and your team. You must, of course, appreciate who it is that you are coaching. The needs, physical capabilities, and attention spans of a first grader are quite different from those of a high school student. The length of your training sessions and how they are structured must respect those differences. Nevertheless, in the long term, excellence is needed in four key realms; the physical, technical, tactical, and psychological.

Physical refers to athleticism: an individual's speed, quickness, agility, balance, size, power, leaping ability, and fitness.

Technique, or skill, involves being able to dribble, receive, pass, head, and shoot a ball while attacking, as well as to mark, tackle, and head while on defense. Also included is the ability to dive and jump as well as to catch, punch, parry, throw, punt, and drop-kick a ball while serving as the goalkeeper.

Tactical refers to the decision-making process. Individual tactics require that each player understands the basic principle of the game and is able to decide which specific technique is best selected to solve that given situation. Group tactics demand being able to comprehend one's primary function within the overall team structure and to calculate instantly how the actions of teammates and opponents can require a player to temporarily assume a different role.

The *psychological* element addresses an athlete's maturity, determination, unselfishness, competitiveness, commitment, and dedication to the game. Too often, we are so concerned with winning games that we fail to see the big picture. In the case of youth soccer, the big picture is not measured in won-loss records but in helping to develop players who feature as many of the above-mentioned qualities as it is possible to develop. The more well rounded they become, the better the odds on them succeeding at the subsequent plateau and beyond.

Moreover, an environment must be provided in which your players can be creative. Although teaching the game's basic skills is important, during the training games the offering of pointers and corrections, if any, should be minimal. Let the game flow while allowing the players to make their own decisions. Without that freedom their analytical process will be stifled. In breaks, point out alternative solutions—players tend to remember well the situations they were in.

There is a logical progression by which a coach proceeds. The first step is to provide enthusiasm and joy. The primary objective of your initial sessions is to sell soccer to those kids as a great source of pleasure.

For the first several years the two areas that require the overwhelming percentage of your consideration are the psychological and technical. There are no tactics without technique. And there will be no appreciable level of technical competence without an enjoyment of the game.

There have been countless players who were dominant at the youth and scholastic levels owing to their superior athleticism. By the time that they realized they were not as good as they had been led to believe, it was too late to overcome their shortcomings. The players you develop must acquire skill and be able to apply it effectively because they understand the basic principles of soccer.

The farther that a player and a team progress in soccer, the more demanding the game becomes. If you allow youngsters to dominate games and practices by playing on a large field where they can constantly rely on their athleticism as a "crutch" (primarily outrunning other play-

ers) they will never develop the vital technical sharpness and tactical awareness that will subsequently be demanded.

Thus, U.S. Soccer's match recommendations coupled with your emphasizing small-sided training games is important in fostering an environment conducive towards long-term success.

The Coach as a Trainer

It is on the training ground that you can wield the greatest influence. The game is the "test." Your teaching is done prior to that. In theory, there is no coaching during a match. Your influence is minimal once the game begins, especially when compared to the football coach who substitutes on virtually every down and calls the plays or the basketball coach who can break an opponent's momentum by calling a timeout.

Whether coaching pre-schoolers or a World Cup team, practice should involve lots of contact with the ball, plenty of movement, and at least a good percentage of it should consist of playing the game. Training sessions—even at the professional level—must offer incentives. Pros are highly motivated, so providing them with an opportunity to improve will inspire them to work hard at an exercise that most youngsters might find boring. Even so, a coach gets far more out of a squad of pros when allowing them to compete, because that is what athletes love to do the most.

The art of coaching is the art of communication, whether on the pitch
with four-time NCAA champion, Jerry Yeagley of Indiana University (top),
or in the huddle with a weekend youth coach (below).

Exercises should be appropriate for the age and ability level of the participants. What happens when we, as coaches, fail in that regard?:

Problem	Response	Result
Exercise is too simple	Boredom	Bad habits created
Exercise is too demanding	Frustration	Players quit trying
Exercise length too long	Concentration lags	Counter-productive
Coach interrupts exercise to give information	Annoyance	Players don't learn

Futhermore, the last thing anyone wants to occur during training is for players to have to hang around for several minutes while the coach lays out cones to mark a field for the next exercise or, even worse, to decide what to do next. Every training session should be planned out in detail (see the section on Methodology) to minimize inefficient use of valuable practice time-—and to keep the players' full attention. Avoid also spending time organizing players into groups-—find exercises and games that will allow your practices to flow from one game to the next. And for match day, write down in advance your starting line-up and list which substitutions you are likely to make. Anticipate what you will do in various contingencies.

The Coach as "Salesperson"

Whenever possible, try to coach with a smile and genuinely enjoy that time when you are helping your players to improve. If you need a barometer by which to grade yourself, here are a few:

Do your players come sprinting onto that practice field while smiling from ear-to-ear? How few kids need for you to pump their ball up with air? How many members of your team consider soccer to be their favorite sport? Do your parents complain that their kids keep banging balls all over the house? Do you have to settle a dispute between two players who both insist on getting a certain uniform number because that is the number that their hero wears? If the answers are affirmative, then even a coach whose team is 4–16 has had a "winning season."

Your attitude is very important and will help to set the tone and temperament for your team to follow. Establishing a solid commitment from your players and the support of your parents will be far less problematic if you exhibit a genuine love and enthusiasm for the game, a true caring for all of your players as people, and hard work at furthering your soccer education.

If you look forward to practice as something that is enjoyable, the chances are your players will too. As that National Team star also noted, "A kid can't be forced to play soccer, you have got to love it."

Soccer is so universal in part because it is "the simplest game," with only seventeen rules. However, soccer's rules are forever changing—so much so that soccer as played a century ago would hardly be recognizable today. Back then, goalkeepers in possession of the ball could be charged by opponents with impunity; substitutions were not allowed; and the definition of "offside" had only begun to evolve from the footballing rules of such English schools as Eton College, which declared in 1847 that "a player is considered 'sneaking' when three or less than three of the opposite side are before him and the ball behind him and in such a case, he may not kick the ball."

One of FIFA's first mandates upon its founding by seven European nations in 1904 was to provide a common set of rules under which all nations would compete. Some local modifications are permissible. These involve field, ball, and goal sizes, the game's duration, and the number of substitutions allowed during competitions for youth (players under age 16), veterans (players over 35), and women footballers. These notwithstanding, the rules for the sport are the same in Timbuktu as they are in Tampa.

The succession of annual editions of the rule book—officially entitled "Laws of the Game"—have simplified and clarified the language, and have resulted in a game that has managed to retain its essential ingredients and spirit while still addressing the need to change for the better. Thus, soccer has remained by a wide margin the world's most popular sport.

Proposed law changes may only be submitted by the General Secretary of a national federation. An eight-member committee, officially known as the International Football Association Board, meets annually, usually in March, to consider such amendments. A minimum of six votes are required for successful passage of a proposal.

Two major improvements to the Laws were introduced during the 1990s. The so-called "back-pass rule" prohibits a goalkeeper from handling a ball that is thrown in or deliberately kicked to him by a teammate. The offside rule was modified so that an attacker is in violation only when judged to be ahead of the second to last member of the defending team—before if he was even or ahead he was offside—or when the attacking team has gained an advantage by virtue of that player having been in an offside position. In the past, any attacking player needed two members of the defending team closer than him to the goal line in order to avoid being offside, whether or not he was involved in the play.

Interpretations are also often officially altered. The concept of the "passive" offside was introduced during the 1994 World Cup. A player who previously would have been whistled for being off-

Yellow and red cards—introduced to the sport after communication problems arose in the 1970 World Cup—let the transgressor and everyone else in the stadium know that official action is being taken.

side could avoid the call if he declared his non-involvement in the play either by standing still or by running away from the area of activity.

Recent changes have also given referees added ammunition to combat time-wasting tactics. For example, a goalkeeper who holds the ball for more than 5 or 6 seconds can be whistled for a foul. And while the list of fouls in Law Twelve has not been changed for several years, referees have been empowered to deal more sternly with serious foul play, which endangers other players, as well as with deliberate fouls that deny an opponent a clear goal-scoring opportunity.

During the 1998 World Cup in France, FIFA demanded that referees particularly crack down on tackling from behind. Violators were to be immediately handed their marching orders. As with previous new applications of the Laws, that change was preceded by a massive educational effort aimed at officials, coaches, and players.

One cannot hope to understand how to enforce the Laws without having had experience in the game coupled with up-to-date information. As with all team sports, the way the game is played and officiated differs from a literal interpretation of the written rules. In this respect, soccer is no different than other sports—one thinks of the so-called "area" force plays or the interpretation of Major League Baseball's strike zone, acceptable

off-the-puck contact in front of an NHL crease, or NBA players being allowed to jockey for position in the paint.

While a thorough knowledge of the written Laws is required to become a top-class referee, this is only part of the equation. That information must be supplemented by applying rules according to the spirit of the game.

Referee awareness, for example, demands understanding both teams' tactics as well as the techniques and roles of each player. The referee should soon recognize the key attacking players for each team and endeavor to provide them with appropriate protection from any opponent who might seek to injure and/or intimidate them through unsporting actions. Another vital component for officiating soccer involves communication and cooperation among the referee, the two assistant referees, and the fourth official. An assistant referee who spots an infraction when he believes the referee was unsighted will use subtle, but predetermined signals to help the referee; this way he will not undermine the referee's authority but will still ensure the game is correctly called.

Arguably, the most important skill is management of players and coaches. Great referees have a knack for diffusing potentially volatile situations. Soccer's so-called "eighteenth law" is common sense. The ability to manage and influence others in stressful situations becomes increasingly important as a referee progresses to the higher levels of soccer. This interaction—both on and off of the field—is a big factor in helping a game to run smoothly. The sport requires good work among players, referees, coaches, and administrators if the game itself is to thrive. Surrounding all these people are the spectators. Referees (and coaches) at the youth level must prevent problems arising from inappropriate sideline comments that disrupt the wholesome environment the kids are entitled to.

It is of course the duty of all coaches to understand the Laws and the current interpretation of them and to communicate this information to their players. Their doing so benefits everyone.

The Field

Law One mandates that the field must be rectangular, with its width ranging from 50 to 100 yards and its length from 100 to 130 yards. A range of 70 to 80 yards in width and 110 to 120 yards in length is required for international matches. The field is lined with sidelines, goal lines, and other markings.

A securely anchored 8-foot–high x 8-yard–wide goal with white posts and crossbar must be in the middle of each goal line. The entire playing area is divided by a halfway line. There is a circle with a ten-yard radius drawn from the center of the field. All the field markings have significance. The halfway line, for example, is important because a player may not be in an offside position when he is in his own half of the field.

In front of each goal is a 6-x-20–yard area within an 18-x-44–yard penalty area. Within the penalty area (which does not include the arc), only the defending team's goalkeeper may intentionally use his hands or arms to play the ball. A goal kick must clear the penalty area before the ball is considered to be in play. Any direct foul that is committed by the defending team in the penalty area while the ball is in play results in the awarding of a penalty kick to the attacking team.

All goal kicks must be taken from inside the smaller goal area. All opposing players must be outside the penalty area when a goal kick is being taken. An indirect offense committed by the defending team in the goal area sees the resulting free kick moved to the goal area line that is parallel to the goal line at the point nearest to where the foul occurred.

The spot from which a penalty kick is taken is 12 yards from the center of the goal, with an arc drawn at the top of the penalty area at a radius of 10 yards from the penalty mark.

Each corner of the field has a flag post, and an arc marks a one-yard radius from the corner. The ball may be placed at any point on or inside the arc when a corner kick is taken. Prior to the taking of a corner kick no member of the defending team may be positioned inside the

*Experienced referees, whenever feasible, prefer
the human touch to maintain control of a match.*

THE FIELD OF PLAY

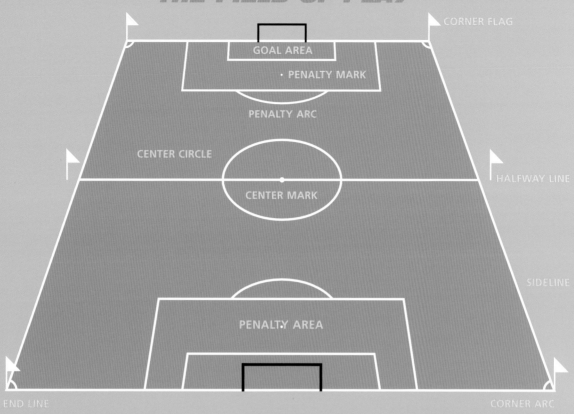

CORNER FLAG

GOAL AREA

· PENALTY MARK

PENALTY ARC

CENTER CIRCLE

HALFWAY LINE

CENTER MARK

SIDELINE

PENALTY AREA

END LINE

CORNER ARC

MEASUREMENTS

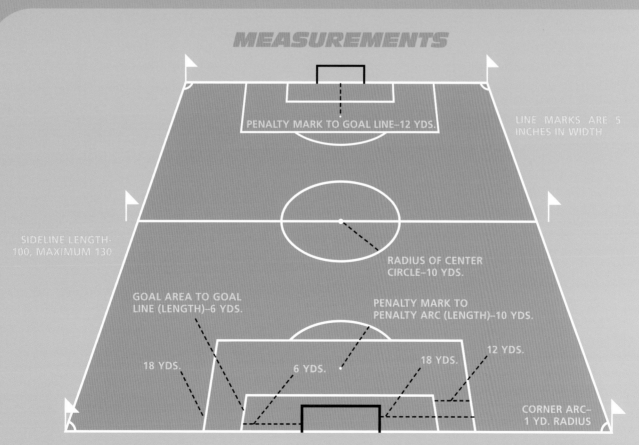

PENALTY MARK TO GOAL LINE–12 YDS.

LINE MARKS ARE 5 INCHES IN WIDTH

SIDELINE LENGTH– 100, MAXIMUM 130

RADIUS OF CENTER CIRCLE–10 YDS.

GOAL AREA TO GOAL LINE (LENGTH)–6 YDS.

PENALTY MARK TO PENALTY ARC (LENGTH)–10 YDS.

18 YDS.

6 YDS.

18 YDS.

12 YDS.

CORNER ARC– 1 YD. RADIUS

END LINE LENGTH– MAXIMUM 100, MINIMUM 50

optional restraining line that is drawn from the goal line at a distance of ten yards from the corner arc.

When a penalty kick is given, no player, except the kicker, may enter the penalty area, including the arc atop it, until a penalty kick has been struck, except for the defending goalkeeper, who may move only along his goal line.

All members of the defending team must be outside the center circle and in their own half of the field, that is behind the center line, prior to a kick-off. All members of the team kicking off must also be in their own half prior to a kick-off, but the kicker can be joined in his half of the center circle by any number of teammates.

All lines are considered part of the area they enclose. Thus, for example, a foul on the penalty area line by a defender results in a penalty; the entire ball must cross a line completely before it is out of play; a goal is only scored if the entire ball crosses the goal line.

The Basics
The Ball

Law Two mandates that the ball must be spherical, made of leather (or another suitable material), and have a circumference of 27 to 28 inches. However, smaller balls are allowed for younger players. U.S. Soccer recommends a size four ball (circumference of 24 to 25 inches) for under-12 play and a size three ball (23 inches) for youngsters up to age seven.

The Team

A team consists of not more than eleven players on the field, one of whom is the goalkeeper (Law Three). A match may not start and will be abandoned if one team has less than seven eligible players on the field. In official FIFA events (excluding exhibition games) no more than three substitutes may be used by either team; five are allowed in many other events. A player who is substituted may not reenter the game. (In U.S. collegiate, scholastic, and youth soccer such restrictions are often modified or waived.) Substitutions may occur only with the ref's permission. At many levels permission is withheld until a stoppage in play: when the ball crosses the goal line or when the team changing players has a throw-in.

All field players must have a jersey, shorts, and stockings that match those of their teammates and contrast with those of their opponents, except for the goalkeeper, whose colors must distinguish him from all of the other players and from the game officials (Law Four). Shin guards, covered by socks, must be worn. No player is permitted to use equipment or wear any item that is judged to create a danger to himself and/or others (including, for example, hard casts and jewelry).

The Referee

A referee enforces the rules (Law Five), acts as the sole timekeeper, and has the authority to discipline any player or coach by removing him from further participation in that match. The two assistant referees, once known as linesmen, provide the referee with advice (Law Six). Each assistant referee patrols a separate sideline and generally only ventures from the goal line to the midfield line, leaving the other half of the field to his fellow assistant on the opposite sideline.

Using a flag, the assistant helps alert the referee to when the ball has left the field of play, to which team a restart should be awarded, when a player may be called for being offside, when a ball is not properly placed prior to a restart, and when a significant incident has occurred that the referee was unable to see. He also notifies the referee when a substitute wishes to enter the game. In all cases the assistant referee indicates what he has seen, but only the referee has the authority to make a call. Thus, any information provided by the assistant referees is subject to the discretion of the referee.

The Length of the Game

Law Seven calls for games to last two equal periods of no more than 45 minutes each, unless the referee and both teams agree prior to the match's start to decrease the time. Should he be so inclined, the referee may make allowances: that is, add time to that half or period, for time lost due to substitutions, treatment of an injured player, time wasting, or any other cause that he feels is appropriate.

He is the game's official timekeeper and determines when 45 minutes of playing time has been completed in each half. After time expires, a penalty kick, if awarded, may still be taken. (However, the ball is dead and the half ends as soon as the ball enters the goal or the save is made.)

Starts and Restarts

Law Eight deals with the starting and restarting of play. A coin toss determines which team kicks off and which team defends which goal. A kickoff in the center of the field takes place at the start of each period (first and second halves, as well as extra time, if needed) or following a goal (then taken by the team that conceded the goal). The ball may not be kicked until it is stationary on the center mark and the referee has given a signal (whistle) to begin. The ball must be played forward, and is in play as soon as it moves forward. The kicker may not touch it again until it has been touched by another player. If the kicker does so, the defending team is awarded an indirect free kick from the spot of the infringement.

For all other violations, the kickoff is retaken. A goal is awarded should the kicker shoot into the opponent's goal directly from the kick-off, even without it having first been touched by a second player.

The ball is out of play only when the entire ball crosses an entire boundary line, whether on the ground or while air-borne (Law Nine). Unless a stoppage is called by the referee, at all other times, it is in play—including when it rebounds off a goalpost, crossbar, or corner flag or ricochets off a referee or his assistants (if the assistant has happened to enter into the playing area).

When a temporary stoppage occurs when the ball is in play in a game—such as when a medical emergency occurs—a drop ball is used for the restart. So, too, when the referee is uncertain which team last touched the ball before it left the playing area, a drop ball is used. On a drop ball, the ball may not be touched until it hits the ground.

Scoring the Game

A goal is awarded only when the entire ball crosses over the entire goal line between the posts and under the bar, providing that no infringement of the Laws has been committed by the attacking team (Law Ten). The team scoring more goals wins; the match is declared a draw if an equal number of goals are scored by each team.

Should regulation time end on level terms, competition rules can allow for various approved tie-breaking procedures to be used. These include the playing of extra time either to conclusion or to the scoring of a "golden" (sudden death) goal. If still tied, games can be decided by shootouts or penalty-kick tie-breakers.

Law Eleven states the offside rule and may be the most misunderstood of soccer's regulations. To be in an offside position in and of itself is not necessarily a violation. An offside position is defined as being nearer to the opponents' goal line than both the ball and the second to last opponent. However, an attacker is not in an offside position if he is in his own half of the field or receives the ball directly from a goal kick, throw-in, or corner kick. The attacker is only considered to be offside when in an offside position and interfering with play and/or an opponent, or gaining an advantage for his team by virtue of his positioning. The determination of offside is made only in the moment that the ball is played forward by a member of the attacking team. This usually involves a forward pass to the offside player but could include a shot that is redirected by the player in the offside position (or a shot in which a member of the defensive team is hampered from playing the ball by the attacker who is in an offside position). In no circumstance is penetration gained by an attacker's dribbling considered to constitute playing the ball forward.

When play is stopped for an offside violation, the defending team is awarded an indirect free kick from the spot where the offending player was positioned as the ball was played forward. This is subject to Law Eight, which declares that the

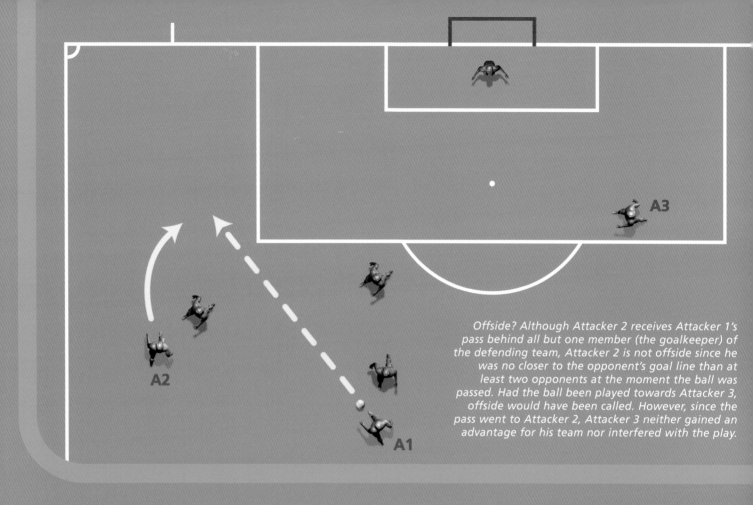

Offside? Although Attacker 2 receives Attacker 1's pass behind all but one member (the goalkeeper) of the defending team, Attacker 2 is not offside since he was no closer to the opponent's goal line than at least two opponents at the moment the ball was passed. Had the ball been played towards Attacker 3, offside would have been called. However, since the pass went to Attacker 2, Attacker 3 neither gained an advantage for his team nor interfered with the play.

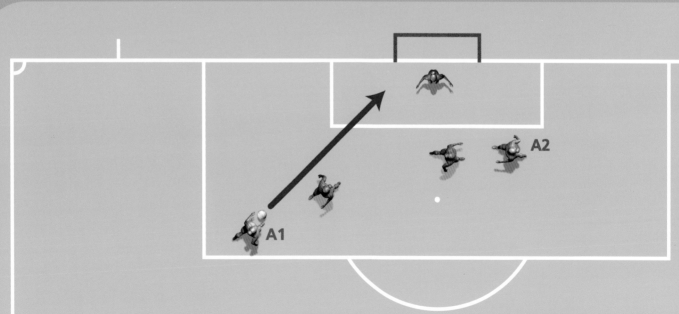

Offside? Attacker 1 aims a near-post shot while Attacker 2 is behind all but one member (the goal-keeper) of the defending team. If the shot cleanly beats the 'keeper the goal should stand. However, if the ball were to hit the post and/or be parried by the goalkeeper and subsequently ricocheted to Attacker 2 then Attacker 2 is considered offside as soon as he attempts to play the ball or his presence is judged to have gained an advantage for his team.

Fair or foul? A foul can occur without contact as Arsenal's Bould is victimized by a dangerous play even if this foe's boot misses him (top). Although two English Premier League players have collided (below), play can go on if no violation is committed or if the referee feels that number three was fouled but his team would be better served by play continuing.

ball may be moved anywhere inside the goal area for any violation that occurs in that zone.

Fouls and Misconduct

There are two varieties of fouls: those resulting in a direct free kick and those that result in an indirect free kick. A goal may be scored on a direct free kick (Law Thirteen). An indirect free kick requires that a second player (who may be a member of either team) must make contact with the ball before it enters the goal for the goal to be counted. As with all restarts, the kicker may not touch the ball after the kick until another player has touched it.

Direct free kicks are reserved for soccer's penal fouls (Law Twelve). These include either actual or attempted kicking, tripping, or striking of an opponent; jumping, charging, holding, or pushing an opponent; spitting at an opponent; deliberately handling the ball (except by the goalkeeper within his own penalty area). The latter refers to making contact with the ball by moving either hand or arm towards the ball.

A penalty kick is awarded when a direct free kick foul is committed by a member of the defensive team within the player's own penalty area while the ball is in play. All players except for the kicker and the defending team's 'keeper must leave the penalty area and may be no closer than ten yards from the penalty spot until the ball has been kicked (Law Fourteen). While the goalkeeper may move sideways, the goalkeeper's feet may not leave the goal line until the ball has been struck. After a penalty kick, should the ball ricochet off a goalpost back into play, it is live but the kicker may not play it until it is touched by another player. If a ball ricochets off the goalkeeper, it is live for any player on either team.

An indirect free kick is awarded to the team of a victim of a dangerous play, if progress has been unfairly impeded by an opponent (formerly referred to as "obstruction"); when the 'keeper has been unfairly hindered from releasing the ball; when the "back-pass rule" is violated; or when a player is called for offside. A dangerous play is when a player puts himself or an opponent in jeopardy by playing the ball in an unnatural manner. It is expected that the head or chest will be used to play a high ball. Attempting to kick such a ball is unnatural. Similarly, a ball that is near the ground is naturally played with the feet. To perform a diving header when opponents are nearby can place the individual in danger.

In youth soccer it is not uncommon to hear spectators, coaches, and players complaining, "Hey ref, that's a high kick," or, "Ref, he's playing on the ground," the latter term meaning a player is kicking the ball while lying or sitting on the ground. Both actions are perfectly permissible as long as they do not create danger.

The rules define "impediment" as a player unfairly hindering an opponent's ability to play the ball by blocking the opponent's path to the ball. However, it is perfectly permissible for a player to shield the ball if he is within playing distance of the ball (about one yard).

An indirect free kick is also awarded should a goalkeeper take more than four steps while controlling the ball with the hands while inside of his own penalty area; touch the ball again (with a hand) after having released it but before it is touched by another player; waste time (while in possession of the ball with his hands); or violate the back-pass rule. Any attempt by a field player to use trickery (juggling and then heading) to circumvent the back-pass rule constitutes an infringement, even if the goalkeeper does not subsequently use his hands to play the ball.

Time wasting cannot be considered to be an infringement while the ball is in play. Thus, a 'keeper or any other player is permitted to refrain from distributing a ball that is at his feet for as long as he wishes or is able to. Time wasting refers only to actions involved in delaying restarting play or if the goalkeeper is in possession of the ball with his hands for six or more seconds. For both time wasting and four-step infringements, most referees will use some discretion if, in their judgement, there is not a deliberate attempt by the goalkeeper to circumvent the Laws.

Law Five grants the referee the discretion to allow play to continue rather than to call a foul if awarding a free kick would in fact prove disadvantageous to the team against whom the offense was committed. A modification of the application of the so-called "advantage clause" was introduced in the 1990s. Referees may now wait up to two seconds after the foul occurs to decide which course of action better serves the team victimized by the foul. If a foul is not whistled due to the referee having employed the advantage clause, the referee, during the next stoppage, may still take further action by warning, cautioning, or sending off the offending player.

The referee's sanctions against a player are reserved for those occasions in which playing the advantage clause or the awarding of a free kick in and of itself is not deemed to be a sufficient punishment for the "crime" that was committed. The referee holds a yellow card aloft to indicate a caution. For especially egregious actions, the referee lifts a red card. The guilty party is banished for the remainder of the match. If a player is red-carded, his team is forced to play short-handed. A player who is cautioned twice in the same game with a yellow card is dismissed from the match on receiving the second card and his team must play short-handed. Cautionable actions include unsportsmanlike behavior, dissent by word or action, persistent infringement, delaying restarts, "encroachment" (the failure to respect the required distance that a defender must provide during an opponent's restart), and entering or leaving the field without the referee's permission. An immediate sending-off is required for serious foul play; violent conduct; spitting at any person; denying an opponent a goal or an obvious scoring chance by deliberately fouling (including tripping, handling by a defender, handling by a goalkeeper outside the area, etc); and using offensive, insulting, or abusive language.

Free Kicks

For all free kicks the ball must be stationary before being put back into play, and the kicker may not contact the ball a second time until it has been touched by another player (Law Thirteen). Should a team inadvertently shoot a free kick into its own goal without the ball being touched by a second player, no score is recorded, but a corner kick is awarded to the opposition. To signal an indirect free kick, the referee raises one arm and holds it aloft until a second player touches the ball or it goes out of play.

All members of the defending team are required to retreat a minimum of ten yards from the ball, until it has been put in play. Exceptions are made for kicks that originate inside the penalty area.

Opponents of a team taking a free kick in its own penalty area must be at least ten yards from the ball and outside the penalty area until the ball is in play (which occurs when the ball has left the penalty area). When the attacking team has an indirect free kick in the opponents' penalty area, members of the defending team may be within ten yards only if they are on their own goal line and between the goalposts.

Law Thirteen also provides sanctions for free kick infringements. Should a retaking of the kick be potentially advantageous to the attacking team, the referee may order the kick to be retaken after a defender has "encroached," or if the goalkeeper has saved a penalty by leaving his line prematurely. A goal kick is also retaken if the ball does not leave a team's own penalty area after it has been kicked.

If the taker of the free kick touches the ball a second time before another player has touched it once, the opposing team is awarded a free kick from that spot. The resulting restart is indirect, unless the original kicker's second touch was with his hands and that player is not the goalkeeper in his penalty area.

Law Fourteen defines penalty kick procedures. These include clearly identifying the shooter prior to the kick and the goalkeeper being on his goal line, between the posts, and facing the kicker. Other players are allowed on the field but must be outside the penalty area, behind the penalty mark, and at least ten yards from the penalty spot. The kick may be taken only after the referee has signaled (whistled) to do so.

When the entire ball crosses the entire touchline (sideline) a throw-in is awarded from that spot to the team that did not last touch the ball (Law Fifteen). The thrower must face the field, have at least a part of both feet on the ground on or behind the touchline, and deliver the ball from behind and over his head with both hands.

The thrower may not touch the ball again until it has been contacted by at least one other player. A violation of this stipulation calls for an indirect free kick to be awarded to the other team, with all other infringements calling for a throw-in to be awarded to the other team from that spot. Any defender who unfairly distracts or impedes the thrower shall be cautioned.

When the entire ball crosses over the end line (without having entered the goal) a goal kick (Law Sixteen) or a corner kick (Law Seventeen) follows. The former occurs when a member of the attacking team last touched the ball. A corner results when the ball was last contacted by a member of the defending team. A goal is to be awarded when the taker of a corner kick strikes the ball directly into the goal.

For a goal kick, the ball is placed with-in the goal area (the 6-x-20–yard box in front of the goal) and kicked out of the penalty area in one kick by any member of the defending team. The ball is not in play and may not be played by another player of either team until it has left the penalty area. Violations result in retaking the kick.

For a corner kick, the ball is placed inside the corner arc (any part of the ball may touch any part of the line) with the flag post not to be moved. Members of the defending team are required to retreat ten yards, but the attacker need not wait for this to occur before taking the kick.

Although not covered by any Laws, there are official provisions for restricting individuals to what FIFA terms "the technical" (bench) area and reporting on breaches of the law he has seen, when requested by the referee. An individual, or fourth official as he is known, assists with administrative duties, including making substitutions during the match and checking the equipment of any substitute prior to that player entering the field. The official's assistance to the referee can include helping keep order in the technical areas.

In knockout stages of competitions, in which a game cannot end in a draw, matches are often decided by a round of penalty kicks. Each team nominates five of its players from a pool of those playing in the game when the final whistle sounded. All penalty rules apply, except rebounds are not live. Each side has five kicks. The teams alternate taking the kicks against the opposition's goalkeeper until such time as one team has an insurmountable lead.

Should the score be tied after five rounds, a sudden-death situation occurs in which the outcome is decided when one team scores and the other fails to do so. No eligible player may take a second kick until all of the eligible team members have had one turn.

Using the same alternating shooter format, some competitions break deadlocks via a "shootout." The ball is placed 35 yards from the goal line with the goalkeeper starting on his line. Upon a signal from the official, the attacker has five seconds to attempt a shot, with no restrictions placed on either participants' movements (the goalkeeper still being prohibited from handling the ball outside the penalty area). The shooter may not play the ball after it has been touched by the goalie.

Summary

Soccer's Laws are based on common sense and generations of trial and error. While the Laws are universal, their application is not. There is ample room for interpretation—the same challenge that would bring a whistle in one nation might be deemed acceptable behavior in another. What matters most is that referees are consistent, so that the players understand the limits being placed on their actions. Players, in turn, have a responsibility to play fairly, and coaches are charged with not tolerating unsportsmanlike behavior from anyone connected with their team.

In recent years FIFA has reacted boldly to confront what had been a rising wave of violent play. A clear dictum to referees to protect skillful players and not to tolerate thuggery has resulted in a game that is safer, more enjoyable to play, and far more attractive for spectators.

To build on these constructive steps requires that all who love the game—a list that surely includes players, referees, coaches, and administrators—work together for the good of soccer. Workshops that bring together these factions help build mutual trust and understanding. U.S. Soccer strongly encourages attendance at such important events.

Final Words

Soccer's Laws have been slightly modified for youth, high school, and college soccer. Those involved at these levels of the sport are encouraged to consult the appropriate rulebook to uncover any discrepancies from the Laws as have they are described in this chapter. Because the Laws are forever being improved, by the time you read this chapter, some of the material may be dated. To receive a current copy of the Laws, contact your state association or the Refereeing Department in U.S. Soccer's offices.

Coaches are responsible for providing players with the safest available equipment and environment, trying to prevent injuries from occurring, and being well-versed in knowing how to treat them.

Preventing Injuries

Youth soccer is one of the safest team sports there is. Still it can be safer if these common sense steps are implemented:

1. Have all players undergo a comprehensive pre-season medical screening. Communicate, as needed, with parents or doctors to uncover any areas of concern.

2. Create an information sheet for each athlete that is accessible to you at all times. In addition to relevant medical information (such as listing any allergies or preexisting conditions of concern) should be the names, addresses, and phone numbers (both home and work) of parents/guardians as well as an emergency contact. Also to be included is the phone number of the player's physician.

3. As children approach their teenage years, preventing injuries becomes a greater concern. A large percentage of injuries occur during the last 30 minutes of games, when players are tired. The greater a player's fitness level, the less vulnerable that individual. Among the objectives for your pre-season preparation is to have several vigorous practices prior to the first full-field scrimmage or game so as to be able to compete safely and successfully; but don't make your ini-

tial pre-season sessions too testing for the players' fitness; it will be counter-productive or even injurious. The desired fitness level should be achieved and maintained throughout the pre-season and season with economical training (see Methodology). Always remember that one gets in shape to play soccer matches, one does not play soccer matches to get in shape.

4. Initiate a program to improve the flexibility of your players. A comprehensive stretching regimen becomes increasingly important as players mature, and their muscles become more prone to injury. Although this is absolutely vital for teenagers and beyond, a child is never too young to stretch. Doing so will help to make muscles more supple. Studies have proven that improving flexibility enhances performance coupled with a significant lessening of the incidence and severity of injuries.

The U.S. Soccer training staff recommends light running to be followed by stretching as a team with the coach or captain as the leader. The warm-up segment should take 10 to 15 minutes. As an alternative to light running, employ a soccer activity that involves a lot of movement (but not explosive movement, such as shooting). While it is not uncommon to have players run to the nearest goal and start shooting on their own prior to the start of a practice, as a precaution players shouldn't be allowed to do so prior to having warmed up.

A professional trainer, wearing gloves, treats England's Graham Le Saux in a Premier League match.

All stretches should be held in position because bouncing may cause harm. The key muscle groups for soccer are the hamstrings, quadriceps, groin, lower back, and calves (see sample stretches on the following pages).

5. Make sure that all equipment is used properly. Wearing shin guards during every practice and game is a must. Uniforms should be appropriate for the weather conditions. Balls should be properly inflated but never over-inflated (bring an air pump and inflater needles with you for every game and practice). We urge the use of hand-stitched balls rather than plastic or laminated balls. Do not use a waterlogged or rock hard ball.

Shoes should fit—some players need reminding about this—and their type should match the field/gym surface. For example, on a soft (wet or muddy) field longer cleats (or screw-in cleats for older players); for normal playing surface, rubber studs; for any very firm surface, indoors or out, a rippled bottom is recommended. Not every player will own all three varieties. It is permissible for an athlete to wear rubber cleats on all outdoor services (except for artificial ones) but do not allow an individual ever to wear a shoe that will compromise his own safety or that of an opponent. Also, athletes must never wear jewelry when playing.

6. After a game or training, have players spend a few minutes cooling down by again engaging in a stretching program.

7. On all occasions—and especially on hot days—players ought to be adequately hydrated. Ample breaks need to be provided for consuming water and/or a sports drink. Avoid sodas or liquids with high sugar content. Avoid salt tablets; potassium in the form of bananas is much better replenishment.

Our typical daily intake of liquids is about two liters (eight glasses). During competition an athlete may lose three to five liters, with the depletion tending to be even greater in hot or humid weather. Whenever possible, avoid training during the hottest parts of a day and practice in light and loose clothing. Encourage your players to drink a lot of fluids the night before training or playing.

8. Eighty percent of our sun exposure occurs before age eighteen and one in five Americans will battle skin cancer during their lifetime. Aggressively promote sun safety. In summer, even on overcast days, twenty minutes before going outside players should apply a sunscreen that has a sun protection factor of 30 or greater. Whenever possible, train in the shade while striving to avoid midday hours when the sun's rays are the most powerful. If your bench is in direct sun, encourage the substitutes to wear sunglasses and hats with brims.

9. Most clubs have a commissioner responsible for knowing the club and league policies on whether a field is playable and making a determination on

game day. Always inspect fields before every practice and game. Remove any dangerous objects. Fix any divots, roles, or dips in the field. In all situations—including road matches—when in doubt, do not play until the problem(s) has been resolved to your satisfaction. Abandon or take a break in the activity during unsafe weather, especially if you see lightning (take shelter in a building or move the team to an open space).

Make sure the corner flags are the right size and materials and there are no impediments or hazards close to the field's boundary lines. Wet running tracks surrounding a field can cause players running out of bounds to skid dangerously, for example.

When transporting a portable goal have an adequate number of helpers to do the job safely. Never allow horseplay at this time. Under no circumstance should anyone ever hang from a crossbar as that can have serious consequences. Once the goal is in place, it should be secured. Portable goals have been known to tip over with serious, even fatal, injuries resulting. Expect that you will be held legally liable should a gust of wind dislodge a goal and result in an injury.

10. Never tolerate unsporting play from your team. There is no place for tackling from behind, for challenging with studs exposed, for undercutting a leaping opponent, for charging into the goalie, for throwing elbows, or even for shirt tugging.

11. By being highly observant you can help to prevent a minor ailment from becoming a major injury. The immature skeleton is susceptible to growth plate injuries, including minor fractures that often go undetected. Be wary of players whose movements seem to be labored, or who are unable to run with a natural gait.

12. Make certain that an athlete does not return to action until his injury has been fully rehabilitated. The operative rule of thumb is, "if in doubt, refer it out" (i.e. make sure the player gets to a doctor). Never attempt to tackle any medical issue that is beyond your capability. Require a doctor's note (which should then be kept on file) before allowing the player to train or compete again.

Strength and Conditioning Programs

Every member of the U.S. National Team programs works out regularly. Our training staff has designed individualized regimens for each of these athletes to improve their arms, chests, backs, upper bodies, and legs. Similarly, top college programs have long included year-round strength and conditioning activities as a part of their overall player development.

We are often asked at what age an athlete is ready to begin weight training. There is no set answer. Children develop at different rates and enter puberty at different ages. Some may even unknowingly have loose joints which will render

STRETCHING

1. Quadriceps:
Lean back-
wards for
a deeper
stretch.

2. Hamstring/Lower Back: Try to
keep the back straight while
pushing the chest forward and
reach as far forward as you can.

3. Groin: Stretch is accentuated by getting the knees as close to the ground as possible while keeping the back straight and pushing the chest forward.

4. Lower Back: Pull one knee or both knees simultaneously towards the chest while keeping your head and shoulders on the ground.

5. Calf/Achilles Tendon: Keep the back foot flat on the ground while leaning against a team-mate or a wall. A straight back leg stretches the calf while a slightly bent knee stretches the Achilles.

7. Quadriceps: Pull back the ankle and hold with the upper leg parallel to the ground.

6. Hip Flexor: Bend the rear leg/knee so it is near the ground while extending the front leg and hands forward.

them highly susceptible to damage when lifting. Thus, great caution should be given to starting a program prematurely. As a general rule, by the early teenage years most youngsters are sufficiently mature to begin a strengthening program. Be sure to consult your child's parents and physician prior to getting started. Usually weight training takes place primarily in the off-season and we recommend a player's program is defined by a fitness expert.

A program must be designed to meet the demands of the particular sport. Sometimes, a specific position imposes added demands. Soccer requires functional power and speed, not bulk. Our players must be able to withstand prolonged rigorous activity. As players mature, upper body strength becomes increasingly important. This can only really be done by strength training, and is especially helpful for central defenders, strikers, and goalkeepers, who are all involved in aerial confrontations.

For all players, the most important area is the legs. A soccer player's legs tend to develop earlier than the other parts of his body. In addition to functional training (playing of the game), strengthening exercises can be useful. Explosive running with rapid changes of direction and speed is also beneficial. The best method is to have training sessions with lots of economical soccer that mirrors the demands of the real game.

Very few youth coaches are sufficiently fortunate to have a physician or a certified athletic trainer attending games or practices. That leaves you to fill the void. Some of the steps to take are:

1. Become knowledgeable in basic first aid procedures. Take a course in first aid as well as learning CPR. Contact your local chapter of the American Red Cross to learn when classes will be held in your area.

2. Prior to every game and training session, the medical kit should be checked to be sure that all essential items are available: ice, sterile pads, gauze pads, scissors, antiseptic, towelettes, ACE wrap, first aid cream, bee sting medication, athletic tape and prewrap, band aids, and disposable gloves.

Include all emergency items that are needed to deal with any player's specific problem (an inhaler for someone with asthma). Also recommended: money for calling emergency numbers and spare sets of shoelaces.

3. Make it abundantly clear to all players that only the coaches and trainers are allowed access to the medical kit. This will both assure that you are aware of any injuries and that you have not run out of athletic tape at a vital time because someone has been using it to help keep their socks from falling down.

4. When beckoned onto a field by the ref-

eree to attend to a hurt player, attempt to determine the nature and severity of the injury through observation and by communicating with the athlete.

5. Should the player be unable to speak, make certain that the airway is clear by opening his mouth and making sure to remove any blockage, including checking the position of his tongue. Next, determine if the athlete is conscious and breathing. If not, your knowledge and application of CPR will save a life.

6. When in doubt, always err on the side of caution. Do not waste precious time deciding whether to call for help if you are unsure. Never move an injured player until you are positive that it is safe to do so. If the player has a neck injury or the player reports not being able to feel an extremity, he should not be moved.

7. If you decide that the injury is not life-threatening, ask about the whereabouts of the pain and how the injury happened; "Where were you hit?," "Did you twist?," "Did you hear a popping sound?," and so on. If needed, ask relevant questions of the other players who were nearby when the incident occurred. If you know first aid, these answers will help you assess the damage.

8. Further analyze the injury's nature. Observe for swelling and/or any deformities. Note the involved area versus a comparable part on the other side.

9. Remove any player who suffers an open wound. Use gloves while treating that individual and do not allow the player to reenter the game until the bleeding has stopped. Immediately rinse your hands after removing the gloves.

10. Use the "RICE Method" as the initial treatment strategy for such common soccer ailments as contusions, sprains, strains, dislocations, and uncomplicated fractures. RICE stands for: Rest (remove the player from the activity), Ice (the injury), Compression (use elastic wrap to hold the ice firmly over the involved area), and Elevation (to minimize swelling, the injured area is lifted above the height of the heart, because gravity will limit the amount of blood that flows there).

11. Never put a player back into a game until the athlete can demonstrate that he's able to use the injured body part to your satisfaction without unduly risking further damage. The athlete should be able to run without pain and pivot without limping. The injured part ought to be able to support weight (for example, an ankle or knee should be able to withstand a toe raise). If not, then wait until all pain, swelling, and deformities are gone. Always insist that a player returning from injury trains with the team before again playing in a game.

12. Bring a player who suffers a head injury to a physician. Following a concussion, a player must obtain clearance from a qualified medical authority before allowing further activity. Should an older

COMMON SOCCER INJURIES
AND TREATMENTS

Ailment	Symptoms	Suggested Treatment
Abrasion	Loss of skin surface.	Cleanse with antiseptic and apply antibiotic ointment.
Blister	Fluid buildup under skin:	Have it drained by a qualified person and clean the area.
Concussion	Severe blow to the head which can cause dizziness, dull to severe headache, ringing in ears, vomiting, disorientation, and a possible loss of consciousness.	Remove from contest and do not allow player to reenter the game even if (s)he provides assurance of being fine. As a precaution, always have the athlete seen by a professional.
Contusion	A bruised muscle or tendon.	RICE.
Cramps	Involuntary and painful muscle contraction.	Firm pressure on the area combined with a gentle massage. Hydrate the player.
Heat Exhaustion	Weakness, pale/clammy skin, profuse perspiration but normal body temperature. possible cramps, nausea, dizziness, vomiting, and fainting.	Lie the player down with the feet slightly raised. Loosen clothing, apply wet cloths, and fan player or remove to a cooler area. Provide water in small doses every one hour. If the player vomits, discontinue fluids and take to the hospital.
Heat Stroke	High temperature; red, dry, and hot skin; rapid pulse; weakness (possible loss of consciousness); and little or no noticeable sweating.	Remove clothing (without compromising privacy), sponge bare skin with cool water or place in a tub with cool water (but do not add ice!), and bring to a cooler or an air conditioned area. Avoid stimulants and over-cooling (at the risk of inducing shock). Quickly get professional help.
Sprain	An injured ligament(s).	RICE. If in any doubt, seek professional help.
Strain	Torn muscle or tendon.	RICE. If in any doubt, seek professional help.

Pre-game stretching should be used by all players to prevent an injury or expedite recovery.

player suffer a concussion, prohibit him from driving a vehicle.

13. Whenever a player has left a game with an injury, the coach should call later that day to see how he is feeling.

Planning for an Emergency

Although soccer is relatively safe, medical emergencies can occur. Being fully prepared with a well-rehearsed plan will save precious time when every second matters. Here are primary components of contingency planning:

1. Fields are often isolated, as are some game facilities. Be aware of the location of the nearest phone and test it prior to starting training or a game to make certain that it is in working condition. If possible, bring a cellular phone, especially when in a remote area. Do not take for granted that the cell phone is within its range. There are "dead zones." To be safe, when you arrive at the site, test the phone prior to getting the activities started.

2. Carry a list of that town's emergency numbers for EMS, the nearest emergency room, poison control center, and the police. This is a vital step that is often neglected by teams playing on the road.

3. Know the exact location/address of the field so as to be able to provide that when summoning emergency personnel.

4. Have defined roles for your support team. The person phoning EMS must be able to give precise directions to the field and to be able to describe the nature of the injury. When on an isolated field, another volunteer should be positioned at the entrance from the road so as to direct emergency workers to the scene. A third individual helps clear the area around a seriously injured player so that an emergency vehicle may get as close as possible.

5. At the start of every season, remind parents and players to maintain their composure and exercise common sense during stressful situations. Quite often the athlete cannot see his injury. In the event of serious injury, an onlooker's frightened expression or a careless comment can induce panic. For this reason, your demeanor is critical. It is essential for the sake of observers and the injured player that you exude calmness and confidence.

6. Your well-stocked medical kit should include notarized release forms authorizing you (plus an assistant coach and/or a designated parent) to approve whatever medical procedures are deemed necessary when the injured player's parents and/or legal guardians are not present and cannot be reached. Information contained on those forms ought to be the player's name, address, phone number, birth date, social security number, any medical problems (including listing any allergies or medications to be avoided), and all relevant insurance information.

7. During all activity periods have a list of

key phone numbers always available. Have every parent's home, work, paging, and cellular phone numbers as well as those of relatives or family friends who are authorized (in writing!) to act on behalf of the parents/legal guardians.

8. Before entering a tournament ask questions of the director regarding their preparedness for emergencies. Among the concerns to be addressed are whether there are qualified athletic trainers, EMS personnel, physicians, and ambulance on site.

Find out if the field marshals have walkie-talkies so as to be able to immediately secure help when needed. This is especially important if the fields are isolated from the main tournament area. It is recommended that you do not enter that event unless you have first received satisfactory responses.

Developing a Medical Support Network

Be a leader in helping your team and club to assemble a sports medical team. With so many youngsters playing soccer, almost every club's ranks are likely to include parents and relatives who are medical professionals. Encouraging them to attend games and practices so that they are available if there is an emergency can pay dividends. Among those whose expertise is particularly relevant and helpful whom you should try to approach ahead of time are orthopedic surgeons, pediatricians, podiatrists, trainers, and nutritionists.

Many injuries occur in practice. Always have at least two adults present at all team practices and scrimmages. It is essential that one adult be available to transport an injured athlete to his home or to receive any needed immediate medical treatment. Meanwhile, the remainder of the squad must be adequately supervised.

It is strongly recommended that you, as the coach, become involved in educating your players about the benefits of lifelong wellness. Counsel them about the dangers of illegal substances and of smoking. Advise them of the importance of proper nutritional intake. And remember that your words, no matter how eloquent, are only as strong as the example that your behavior establishes.

U.S. Soccer recommends reading *U.S. Soccer's Sports Medicine Book*, by William E. Garrett, Jr., Donald T. Kirkendall, and S. Robert Contiguglia. Feel free to phone U.S. Soccer's Sports Medicine Department if you have any questions or need advice. And take advantage of the knowledge of a general practitioner or orthopedic surgeon in your area.

Parents of players entrust coaches with their most valued treasure: their children. Make certain that their faith is never violated. But no matter how well prepared you become, never get complacent: as sailors say, "the ocean is safe as long as you know that it is dangerous."

Pelé, perhaps soccer's greatest player and ambassador, once stated that the three most important things his coach had taught him were to be a good person, a good athlete, and a good soccer player, in that order of priority.

Being a good person involves having a strong sense of integrity and being responsible to one's family and friends. To be an athlete a person must work hard to be fit, eat right, get ample sleep, and avoid pitfalls like smoking and drugs. To become a good soccer player demands honing skills, understanding tactics, and being strong psychologically. As Pelé's coach emphasized, just to become a good soccer player in and of itself is not enough.

The formula for becoming a good coach is similar. First, you must be a good person whose example helps to instill values in players. You must be a role model whose prudent behavior includes being sensitive to the needs of players, opponents, and referees, and setting a good example in your appearance, punctuality, and respect for the rules of your league and of the sport.

Part of being a good person is to truly care about all of your players as people. Coaches who have an "open door policy" hope that their players are always comfortable talking to them about anything in their lives. This includes, but is not limited to, soccer matters.

Second, as a good coach you are pre-pared and organized for games and practices. You are administratively and functionally sound. You set rules for your team about attendance, commitment and comportment that are realistic. You apply them consistently and fairly.

You know that sports should be a fun experience. You teach your players how to play before teaching them how to compete. By about age 11 the team concept of how "we" work together to overcome "them" is introduced, but winning is kept in perspective while each individual's role within the group is explained.

And, third in importance, as a soccer coach you understand the game's nuances. You are an enthusiast who watches pro games, attends clinics, and constantly seeks to observe higher level coaches to pick up information. You share your enthusiasm and information with your players. You understand that your primary function is the development of players, with the winning of games a by-product of that process.

Handling a Crisis

Even while heeding these priorities, your coaching experience will have bumps in the road. Expect that incidents will occur during the course of every season. It is highly likely that at some point you will experience a falling out with a parent or two (usually over playing time; so have a policy that focuses on development that applies to all players and is clearly under-

Soccer has become a family sport in the U.S. A coach's role is to create a big family feeling within every team.

stood before the season), an injury to a key player, a player quitting the sport or leaving your team for the so-called "greener pastures" offered by some perceived super-duper rival team.

Know that the concerns of team management are as significant at the professional levels of the game as they are at the grass roots. Every coach has to deal with issues that, if not resolved, can undermine a season or worse.

Even the most soccer-knowledgeable neophyte coach rarely comprehends the extent to which his team's success will be predicated on team management. Building commitment and bonding individuals into a genuine team are vitally important. But these aims are not easily achieved. Many children are overstretched with activities, and quite often parents are unwilling to weigh the needs of a group dynamic (the team) above that of their child.

Try not to take these issues personally. The reality is that the best you can hope for is to minimize, not eliminate, problems. By having your priorities and philosophy in order—and having communicated them in advance to the group—you are far more likely to make a right decision in handling a crisis. This, in turn, will have a positive influence on how the remaining team members react to situations.

The loss of a player is always a difficult issue, for example. To minimize the negative psychological impact on the team, meet with your players. Discuss what hap-

pened. Be honest in how it may impact on the team without painting a negative picture ("Losing Joey does hurt because he is a very good player but this is an opportunity for many of our other good players to assume more responsibility and to make a greater contribution to our team"). If needed, present them with a new set of challenges by revamping your season's goals. Make the new objectives as positive as possible while remaining realistic.

Dealing with Individuals

It is important that you understand each individual player's psychology. It is important to discover if a child is having a bad day what approach to take to help him.

Yet an approach that is ideal for one individual could poison your relationship with another child and/or that child's parents. Individuals react very differently. Some strongly object to any correction in front of their peers while to others it can be a source of motivation. Some players are angry or hurt by being removed (even temporarily) from a game to get a quiet word from their coach. Others would prefer for a correction to be handled in that manner.

The desires of your squad members may well range greatly. Quite likely, there will be some highly motivated players for whom soccer is a passion. Others like soccer but rank it somewhere behind another sport (or two). It could well be that you will one day find yourself dealing with how to prevent burn-out in a soccer-driven youngster while simultaneously trying to spark interest in a child with waning enthusiasm. You may advise one to take a break while seeking out a source of motivation for the other. Or, you might come to agree that soccer is just not the sport for him.

Either way, having each child's best interests at heart will go a long way towards your ability to influence decisions by individuals that can, in turn, greatly impact on the group dynamic.

To better understand each individual, it may be helpful to devise an informal questionnaire for your players. Know the names of their parents, the names and ages of any siblings, and what types of pet(s) they have. Find out what are their favorite activities, TV shows, academic subjects, and teachers. Ask them what makes them happy or angry during school, at home, and during soccer practices and games. Find out what they say that they want to be when they grow up. The collective information should give you a better picture of each child and, with that, a greater understanding of how to help your players to enjoy their soccer experience while striving to realize their potential.

Team Organization

Coaching can be very time-consuming. Developing a network of support among parents will help to alleviate an onerous burden on one or two people. Among the very important administrative tasks to be met are finding practice places and times to allow for maximum participation, scheduling scrimmages (including reserving a field and a referee), getting and distributing directions to away matches, entering tournaments/booking hotel accommodations, identifying fund-raising options and scheduling fund-raising events, bookkeeping, purchasing uniforms and equipment, field maintenance, filling out line-up cards, and organizing a phone chain for when messages must be relayed expeditiously.

Finding individuals within the team "family" to handle these matters will help to minimize the burnout that you could experience after taking too much on your shoulders. You will not be able to limit yourself strictly to coaching, but you should delegate enough of the workload so that you can properly prepare to coach and it is still fun. Know that at the intercollegiate level the administrative duties of soccer coaches are extremely involved. Such off-the-field matters as recruiting, scheduling, paperwork, and academic issues often take up more of the college coach's time, for example, than actually coaching the game itself.

Taking the time to build relationships based on respect with other coaches and with referees and administrators will also help all concerned to do a better job of meeting the common goal of serving the needs of youngsters. This is an all too often overlooked duty of the coach. Many of the regrettable and avoidable problems faced by all organized youth sports—such as poor sportsmanship or the jumping of individuals from team-to-team—can be minimized by coaches who work together for the common good.

The Yearly Cycles

Your team's season has three components; the pre-season, the season itself, and the post-season.

Your pre-season mandate is to adequately prepare your team for the upcoming season. For older youth sides, you may wish to assess their individual technical and physical fitness.

During this phase there are specific objectives that you have set which must be met. As best you can, attempt to have your pre-season's demands replicate those that will follow. Knowing the make-up of your team is vital for the setting of obtainable standards.

Prior to the first game you should have set short and longer term goals for the team and for all its members. This helps to provide a blueprint for improvement while fueling motivation. Articulate to your players and parents what it is that you hope will be accomplished and how you plan to go about reaching those goals. Along with that outline all your expectations and standards requiring attendance for practices and games, appropriate behavior, and

what parental support is needed.

During the season the coach tries to develop a cycle to meet the team's needs according to the demands of the game. The demands are based upon the number and concentration of scheduled matches and tournaments, required travel days, preparation days, and days off that may be needed for physical and/or mental recuperation. Training sessions the day before or after a game need to be very light in physical demands.

Your game duties start well before the day. When playing at home make certain that the field is mowed, lined, clear of any dangerous objects, and that the goals and corner flags are in place. When playing away, distribute directions and personally check the field prior to the warm-up.

On game day, an adequate warm-up for all players follows with you having a special word with the team regarding their primary responsibilities in the upcoming match. The components of an adequate warm-up are just like those that comprise a good training session: ample movement (to fully prepare the muscles for the demands of the forthcoming match) coupled with lots of touches of the ball and a comprehensive stretching regimen (especially important for older youth players and beyond). Please avoid static drills that involve long lines and limit activity. At least during a part of the preparation stage a coach or team member should warm up the starting goalkeeper with a progression of easy to more demanding touches of the ball.

With older youth sides, the coach may opt to give a leading player or two specifics regarding their primary responsibility(ies) within the team structure. That is followed by a team talk that briefly reviews tactics: key facts known about the opposition, how the team wants to play, and/or evaluating how the field/weather conditions may affect strategy (to keep the ball on the ground when playing into a strong wind or to shoot low at any opportunity on a slick surface). Of course, the "tactics" for the younger set could be as basic as stating, "Don't forget only the goalie can use his hands, and try to remember that we are aiming at the goal by the parking lot!"

During the game you must remain calm, composed, and objective if you are to accurately analyze the performance of your team/players and to note if the opposition is creating any problems that require some adjustments on your part. Provide ample notification to players of your intention to insert them in game so as to provide all substitutes with adequate time—depending on the players' age and the weather conditions—to properly stretch and warm-up.

During the start of half-time confer with your assistants and a key player or two about what they have observed and what changes—if any—will be required in the upcoming half. Allow your players

time to cool down, to rehydrate, and—especially important—to relax and to talk among themselves. But do ask them if they have any injuries.

Whenever possible, be positive. If it is unlikely that the game can be won, set a few realistic goals for the coming half (continue to work hard to improve; play as a team; defend better collectively; or set a tactical challenge, such as improving combination play, etc.). Conversely, challenge your team to maintain their sharpness with a big lead by urging them to play to the standards that are needed when you face your most accomplished rivals.

It is essential that your comments be succinct and hone in on a few specific points. Long-winded tirades are counterproductive, with the information not being retained. The tone of your voice and your mannerisms may carry as much weight as what you actually say. If the game is on the line, suggest what must occur for a successful resolution to the match and how the team must perform to meet those expectations. Only provide a very few key points of information as no player can be expected to retain a flood of details.

After the game have the team "cool down" with a stretching routine if they will be playing later in the day or the next day. You might say a few words about the game. However, if you are angry or disappointed in the result it is sometimes better to bite your tongue and save your words of wisdom for an upcoming practice. With older teams, the observations made on game day can be the primary source for the design of your subsequent training session. It is far preferable to begin your next training session by saying, "We're going to work on finishing today so that we can do a better job of converting our scoring opportunities" than to blast the team after a tough loss for missing three empty-net shots.

Before leaving the field on game day, make sure that all equipment is accounted for. Remind your players and parents of any upcoming scheduled activities.

Your post-season begins with some needed time off to allow everyone to regenerate. Consider encouraging your players to participate in a recreational sport like volleyball or swimming. This will address the need for taking a break from soccer while serving to maintain fitness and improve their overall athleticism.

After an appropriate break you begin your preparations for the following season. It is at this time of year that great individual gains can be made. Senior players may work on getting stronger and faster through conditioning programs.

All players, particularly those in youth soccer, can improve their technical ability by attending camps and clinics. A word of caution; with millions of youth players soccer has become a very viable business proposition. The burgeoning number of camps run the gamut from excellent to those that are not worthwhile. Do your research in advance before shelling out several hundred dollars for a week of instruction. Camps can be a wonderful experience and can be highly enjoyable, but be realistic with your expectations. A one-week session, no matter how good it might be, cannot develop a player. At best, the participant will get a few things that he can take home with him to work on to help him to achieve long-term improvement.

Further, do not assume that a camp endorsed or run by a "big name" inherently guarantees that that individual will personally provide instruction. Find out about whether facilities are adequate and appropriate for the number and the abilities of the campers. Inquire as to the camp's philosophy, while learning just how competitive is the overall level of that session's attendees. Know your child's needs; does he want a round-the-clock soccer-saturated environment or would he prefer to mix his soccer with swimming, boating, and other team sports?

Either way, a good camp should feature highly qualified coaches, an acceptable ratio of instructors to campers, good food and acceptable accomodations, sufficient off-the-field supervision, and a professional medical staff that is backed by a well-stocked infirmary. Finally, do not be shy about asking for references and inquiring if group/team discounts are available.

The tightly knit USA women conquered the globe in 1991, capturing the first FIFA Women's World Cup (top), while Bruce Arena helped mold stars from several lands into a well-oiled machine that won the first MLS Cup, in 1996.

PART 3

The goal of American youth soccer development is to unlock the game within each child, allowing every individual to realize his or her full soccer potential. For that to occur coaches can be helped by understanding the various phases of childhood. We must structure our practices and games to specifically fit the needs of our players during the varied stages of their development.

To the child the destination does not matter as much as the journey. We should be process-oriented, because kids play for the sake of playing and having fun with their friends. We suggest encouraging children to take risks during their age of discovery, to help them learn how to play without fear of failure. There will be ample moments later on to condition them to shy away from what they are not good at.

Primary Characteristics of Young Beginners: Children 6 and Under

During this phase the differences between boys and girls are minimal. Typical players' weights tend to be between 30 and 50 pounds while the typical height range is 35 to 45 inches for boys and 37 to 45 inches for girls. Despite being born in the same calendar year, physical and/or mental maturities among children can range by as much as three developmental years. You will therefore encounter a very wide range of coordination from player to player.

Individual athletic personalities may start to emerge with the beginnings of self-concept, body awareness, and self-image through movement. There is, however, very little comprehension of time, space relations, and boundaries. The enthusiasm and abilities of your team members will probably run the gamut from those who are quite skillful, often the younger siblings of players, to those who are far more fascinated by watching a bird fly overhead.

They will need their shoes tied often and any unusual expressions may be a tipoff for you to ask if they need a break to go to the bathroom. Most will cry if something hurts and some will cry even when nothing hurts. At least one player is likely to cling tightly to a parent's leg and will need to be gently coaxed into playing. As soon as the game starts all players—except, perhaps, the goalkeepers—will naturally swarm around the ball in a human beehive. Some will kick the ball; others will find the swarm intimidating and shy away from much ball contact at all unless the ball lands at their feet.

Six year olds tend to be self-centered. In fact, most want the ball to themselves all of the time. While they know that their team is named the Grasshoppers, they harbor little concept of collective play. Trying to get them even to understand passing is like asking an elephant to fly.

Expect that attention spans will be very short. They may or may not remem-

Elements such as turning with a ball can be learned early on but still expect even relatively coordinated younger players to strike the ball with their toes.

A ritual such as the post-game team handshake introduces sports-manship in a way that six year olds enjoy and understand.

ber which goal it is that their team is attacking, that using their hands to control the ball is prohibited, or that they should stop playing when the ball rolls out of bounds. They are constantly in motion, easily fatigued, but recover relatively rapidly.

Dribbling games in which each participant has his/her own ball are far more appealing and fruitful than games that emphasize sharing (passing). Therefore, it is important that every player brings a size three ball to practice.

An emphasis on enhancing fundamental movement skills is urged. These include running, leaping, jumping, hopping, bending, stretching, twisting, pulling, pushing, reaching, throwing, catching, and kicking. There is a need for the child to explore the qualities of rolling and bouncing a ball, tapping it, and how a ball may be controlled by using different parts of the feet and body.

Concentration should be on developing a comfort level on the ball with the feet. You can encourage turning with the ball and changing directions with the ball. Rarely will the ball be kicked far off the ground, therefore it is premature to work on receiving balls in the air. Typical practice play should consist of imagination and pretend activities.

Games in which "monsters" attempt to tag "victims" who are dribbling are appealing. Very simple and easily understood rules are required. Any game with an obvious objective or with direct competition they will enjoy. The more aggressive will challenge for the ball and push others off it—try to teach them what is fair play. Build up to each exercise or game with smaller tasks and discrete information they can absorb in bits before putting it all into action.

It is useful to create an environment in which all the children are playing soccer-related games with lots of opportunities to touch the ball and to move it around. This allows them to learn through trial and error. Also important is to allow for unstructured play and improvisation along with alleviating any pressure to perform up to someone else's expectations. If they are playing small-sided soccer, they will all get to touch the ball, shoot, and defend, and keeping track of the result will be thankfully impossible; if they are playing as many as 8-v-8, some will know the score but fortunately only a few will care.

Any corrections should be made in a positive manner without so much as an inference that an error may have occurred. A strong response can be expected from using a player to illustrate the performance of a skill ("Wow, did you guys see how Susie turned with the ball?"). Many times teaching kids a technical skill at a very young age has more to do with imitation ("Watch me, can you do this?") than through explanation. Thus, coaches must learn how to perform the skill themselves or, at the least, have someone available to "paint the picture." But remember the pupils' capabilities: eye to foot coordination is extremely limited. Physiologically, it is virtually impossible for a six year old to strike the ball with the inside of a foot without losing balance. Expect children to learn to kick before they learn to pass and that they will kick the ball only with the stronger foot. There is no need for refinements until later.

Practice should be limited to one hour once or twice per week. Make each specific activity brief. Keep things fun. Keep things moving. Whenever possible, enlist the assistance of parents for chasing balls so that practice is as seamless as possible.

Primary Characteristics of Under-8 Children

A perceptible improvement in speed and coordination occurs as children move into this age category. Nevertheless, their immature physical abilities remain obvious.

Children still have a limited ability to tackle more than one chore at a time. Whatever awareness exists will be compromised by attending to multiple tasks. Typically, just to control the ball requires their full concentration. There remains little capacity for anything else, including noticing a wide open teammate. Few, in fact, ever look up when they dribble. Concepts of time and spatial relationships are also only starting to be developed. Players will not pace themselves or understand what it means to spread apart during games. The swarm, even in 3-v-3 games, is still the norm.

There remains a great yearning for approval from authority figures, whether parents, teachers, or coaches. The need for social acceptance by all others is strong, as is feeling a part of the group. Such small things as wearing a scrimmage vest during training games is exciting and important.

Recognition of individual skills is needed. Feelings of children at this age are very easily "bruised." What may seem to be a casual, offhand remark that you make as the coach can decimate them. Their incentive for playing soccer is not to become a great player. Rather, it is to have fun. It is important that they perceive that everyone likes them.

Their universe has expanded from home to neighborhood and they probably have a few good playmates. They are still more inclined towards small group activities, but their team identity is developing in basic ways. Some of them may have sports heroes that they wish to emulate. Many will wear their uniforms to bed. Some will comprehend very basic soccer concepts; "Charlie, if there are two defenders on you, one of your teammates must be open. If you can use your great passing skill to get the ball to the open player the chances of our team scoring a goal will be very good." They are better at remembering basics than younger players, but in the excitement of a game some field player might still just pick the ball up or shoot at the wrong goal. Expect them to find the goalmouth puddle to be too enticing to resist and that there will be dozens of falls every practice (most of the players will pick themselves up right away most of the time). Anticipate that at least one child will seek individual attention by exaggerating injury.

Patience remains the coach's watchword. Due to rapid growth spurts it is normal that a player will be unable to execute a ball skill that was performed with relative ease even two weeks prior.

Playing small-sided games will provide more ball touches per player and makes for easier to understand situations, but passing remains a far less exciting proposition to them than dribbling and shooting. Do not criticize a player for being "selfish" by dribbling when surrounded by opponents. Instead, offer praise for those who choose to attempt to pass the ball to an open teammate even if the pass is inaccurate.

Challenge them to practice on their own. Encourage such initiative by having players demonstrate a new dribbling move or an improved ability to juggle. Provide occasional juggling pattern challenges as "homework." For example, to be able to kick the ball twice with the laces and catch it. Other good challenges are bouncing the ball from thigh to thigh to head or from ground to thigh to head, then to catch it. It's still early for them to be able to receive a ball in the air—nor are

they likely to encounter many. Some may be able to begin using their weaker foot to kick with. Most can change direction and keep control of the ball. They also can learn to shoot accurately and with some power.

Foster good habits. Ask that they take care of their equipment, such as a water bottle, and that they cooperate, listen, try their best, and work with others to solve problems. Provide gentle reminders when they fall short of your expectations, but always be aware of how you communicate because the one injury that might never fully heal is bruised feelings.

Primary Characteristics of Under-10 Children

Players at this stage have entered the so-called "golden age of learning." This is a time when youngsters are very keen to learn by playing and when they have both the physical ability to develop skills and a disposition to do so. They usually have wonderful relationships with coaches and parents at this age. It is a vital time in their lives and should be equally vital in their soccer development.

As gross and small-motor skills start to become more refined, boys and girls begin to develop separately. Thus, the grouping of players in games and practices by physical maturity/ability level becomes more of a consideration.

It is natural that youngsters will continue to develop at different rates, both

The progression from the early grammar school years to the teenage phase sees the advent of coordinated skills coupled with the elimination of the swarm.

psychologically and physically. A greater diversity exists in soccer skills. Nevertheless, the athletically superior youngsters will dominate the games. However, in the long term, it is often the youngster possessing superior skill who becomes the better player.

The ability of players to concentrate increases at this age and coordination begins to emerge. An introduction may be attempted to performing properly fundamental soccer-related skills, such as shooting with the instep, learning to pass with the inside of the foot, step-overs, faking and turning while dribbling. Rudimentary receiving of the ball in the air—with the thigh, mostly—can be taught. However, technical proficiency cannot precede the emergence of agility and balance. Expect that some players will be ready to use the inside of one foot while supporting themselves on the other foot to perform a push pass, while others still will lose their balance. For the more agile, goalkeeping skills, including catching, diving, and punting can be taught (emphasize the hands being ahead of the goalie's body to collect the ball to provide protection).

The quality and appropriate duration of your once or twice-weekly training sessions are of vital importance to players' development. Practices should last about 75 to 80 minutes. Allow them to compete by playing small-sided games with basic tactical and technical challenges as a great developmental tool. Keeping score

in competitions helps to maintain their focus but it is up to you to put a proper perspective on winning and losing. Expect to deal with an occasional temper tantrum from a frustrated player. At this stage children primarily remain intrinsically motivated, but there is an identification with the team and with winning.

Competitiveness emerges. They may say some very unfriendly things to opponents and might even cry after a defeat, but their disappointment does not last long and is usually alleviated by a slice of pizza. Your choosing the right words to diffuse the situation while nudging them towards a more appropriate future expression of disappointment is needed.

Indeed, continued positive reinforcement is needed. Peer pressure starts to become a factor. Not being embarrassed in any way in front of their friends is important.

In time, players should soon start to recognize fundamental tactical considerations, such as playing away from the concentration of defenders. Some team concepts may be grasped, the swarm can be reduced by support, and positional play can be introduced, but players should play all positions and not be typecast. Players will be playing up to 8-v-8 games, taking corners and throw-ins, defending as a group, and attacking with the ability to pass. The concept of players off the ball getting open is thus rewarded (on occasion!).

Whenever possible, allow the players to

solve challenges. Explanations by coaches can be somewhat more involved: for example, players may be introduced to the offside law. They will understand it if shown but may easily forget what it involves during a game.

Self-responsibility can be introduced. This includes having each player in charge of bringing a size four ball and a water jug to practice, tucking in the shirt, and having both socks pulled up. Some of the more enthusiastic and motivated players will become keen to practice on their own. Playing soccer against a sibling or a parent using a soft ball and small "goals" (usually two books or something similar) becomes a favorite indoor activity.

Parental involvement is always a plus but gently ask all to refrain from "helping" the referee or yelling out instructions to their child during practices and games. The nature of soccer works in your favor; you can state that it is vital for their children's development to learn to make decisions for themselves.

Primary Characteristics of Under-12 Children

The onset of puberty brings significant psychological and physical changes. Girls typically hit this stage at age 10 (with a range of 7 to 14) and boys at 12 (with a range of 9 to 16). Single-sex travel teams are offered by many clubs.

Socially, today's pre-teens may have many different interests, and their play is usually relatively unstructured. They spend more time with friends and less in the company of adults. With puberty, comes psychological implications for their social lives. Their popularity directly correlates to their sense of self-esteem. As such, peer pressure to conform becomes stronger. Importance is placed on their physical development vis-à-vis their peers'.

A team is an extension of a natural gravitation, among this age group, toward a larger group of friends. At the same time, because of this growth in socialization, they may be quick to "correct" a teammate's mistake and many will openly question a referee's or coach's decisions. The development of a conscience and values has accelerated. Do not be surprised if they point out any inconsistencies between what you say and what you do. Your attitude towards sportsmanship and fair play is never more important.

By this age most athletes may sustain complex coordinated skill sequences, although the differences of the skill levels, size, speed, strength, and motivation of squad members have become significant. Dribbling moves involving a series of choreographed touches can be introduced and mastered. Quicker play, taking fewer touches, and accuracy of passing can be emphasized. Heading can be introduced.

As a wider range of skills provides the player with significantly improved control over the ball in varied situations, the player can now apply fundamental tactics to the game. Players at this age should begin to think in more abstract terms in order to apply tactics to real and hypothetical situations. Placing players in training games that demand problem solving will pay dividends providing that the players are allowed to think for themselves. It is far better to ask them how to solve a challenge than to act as a soccer guru who provides every answer.

With the introduction of 11-a-side play it will soon become obvious which players are best suited for specific positions. Nevertheless, the avoidance of typecasting players into one specific position/role will assist in their all-around development.

Training pre-teenage players involves providing a consistently challenging environment. Sessions may last for up to 90 minutes and can be held twice or three times per week. Having a theme and an easily understood objective per each session is recommended. Exercises and games stressing technical proficiency that are designed to improve tactical awareness are required. Small-sided training games are still the basis for teaching, especially if they can provide tactical demands. Flexibility training takes on added importance, both for aiding the ability to perform and for avoiding injuries. Overuse ailments are now a concern, as is burnout.

There is also a tendency for children to make friends only with those who most resemble them in age, race, sex, and socioeconomic status. Soccer's diversity provides an opportunity to cross those lines and to learn to judge others by their personal qualities rather than by a label. Coaches who help to facilitate interaction with a variety of individuals will provide a very valuable lesson.

Parental concerns become increasingly frequent. Do your best to be open and communicate in a positive manner. But understand that doing all these things does not guarantee somebody will fail to understand why their child who has missed several practices should not play quite as much as another player who attends virtually every session. Some parent will think that only a conspiracy the size of the Brinks Robbery has prevented you from recognizing that their child should be either the play-making center midfielder or the high-scoring striker. And someone will leave after the season to join a rival team.

While you can attempt to influence such behavior, you cannot fully control it. However, you are still obliged to control the actions of everyone who is associated with your team during games. What you can do is set the tone both through your words and the example that you provide.

Summary

Making allowances for limitations and characteristics of the age of players is important. What does not change is that during every phase soccer should represent a positive experience that helps to improve a youngster's self-esteem, values, and fitness.

Such logistical concerns as field availability and the number of players, coaches, referees, and administrators available will always impact upon a club's ability to implement programs. In the best of all worlds, the endorsement of U.S. Soccer's efforts to promote progressive development will be aided by implementing a scheme that closely resembles these suggested formulas for the playing of "competitive" games.

However, the only mandate that is set in stone is that U.S. Soccer will not sanction games for players Under-10 or younger that involves more than eight-a-side play. In fact, with small-sided soccer you can fit more games and players in the same amount of field space used for an eleven-v-eleven game. The more problematic issue is the number of coaches or facilities needed.

Therefore, we recommend such solutions as playing four-v-four with eleven-player teams. Two teams (22 players total) can play simultaneous games on adjacent fields—your stronger four against the opposition's stronger four and your weaker four versus their weaker four with the remaining three players available as substitutes.

Each coach acts as a "referee" and takes charge of one of the two fields, with all quarters starting and ending at the same time. Provide a short break between periods, at which point the coaches work together to arrange the lineup for the next game period. Refrain from labeling players as "A" or "B" and allow movement of players from one squad to another.

Try to work with the other coach to keep the teams as balanced as possible on each field, so that every child will have ample opportunity to play the ball, to have some success, and with that, to fully enjoy the game.

In all cases the field's length should exceed the width. While the goal size should be smaller for younger players (see chart), care must be taken not to have goals that are so small as to distort the game and frustrate the players.

A modified offside law can be used, with players offside only from the top of the opposition's penalty area, rather than from the midfield line.

It is strongly suggested that a game's score not be kept prior to Under-9 except when done so confidentially in the interest of balancing teams. Only after having reached the eight-v-eight plateau at Under-10 should standings be posted.

The increasing popularity of indoor tournaments has helped keep kids playing year-round, but is vital that the number of participants be appropriate for the available space so that the action not be so crowded as to bear no resemblance to the real game. A premium on skillful play is the objective of indoor play. When the area is about that of a basketball court there should be no more than five-a-side play.

RECOMMENDED GAMES FORMAT CHART

Age	#s	Field Length (min./max.) / Field Width (min./max.)	Minimum Maximum Goal Size	Offside	Restart	Yielding Distance	Ball Size	Officials
U-6	3-v-3 *	25/30 yds.	9 X 4 ½ ft.	None	Kick-ins	5 &	3	Coach
U-7		15/20 yds.	12 X 6 ½ ft.					
U-8	4-v-4	30/40 yds.	9 x 4 ½ ft.	None	Kick-ins	5	3	Coach
		20/25 yds.	12 x 6 ½ ft.					
U-9	6-v-6	40/50 yds.	12 x 6 ½ ft.	Modified	Either	6	4	Referee
		30/35 yds.	18 x 6 ½ ft.					
U-10	8-v-8	60/70 yds.	18 x 6 ½ ft.	Yes	Throw-ins	8	4	Referee and assistant referees
		40/50 yds.	21 x 7 ft.					
U-11	9-v-9	70/80 yds.	18 x 6 ½ ft.	Yes	Throw-ins	6	4	Referee and assistant referees
		45/50 yds.	21 x 7 ft.					
U-12	11-v-11	100/105 yds.	21 x 7 ft.	Yes	Throw-ins	10	4	Referee and assistant referees
		50/55 yds.	24 x 8 ft.					
U-13	11-v-11	100/110 yds.	24 x 8 ft.	Yes	Throw-ins	10	5	Referee and assistant referees
		50/60 yds.	24 x 8 ft.					

\# - Suggested number of players per side

* - Either with or without goalkeepers.

& - The minimum number of yards opponents must yield on all restarts.

As important as a coach knowing his subject matter is the manner in which he instructs, organizes, and inspires his players. That is why a significant portion of U.S. Soccer's national coaching licenses curricula addresses methodology. We do so while recognizing that there is no set single way to teach soccer any more than there would be only one way to write, to sing, or to paint. There are no absolutes in coaching except, perhaps, that it is absolutely imperative to strive to improve and to consistently exercise your best judgement.

Under the heading of "methodology" Roget's Thesaurus offers such synonyms as progression, systematization, economy, and businesslike. All these qualities are present in a good coach's collective techniques.

To develop a well-rounded player involves a series of building blocks that you help to add to piece-by-piece in a sensible order. Just as your child's school system wouldn't attempt to offer calculus before the students had mastered arithmetic, there can be no effective tactics unless the players have acquired sufficient skill to physically execute what they have decided to try. The activities that you select should fit their psychological needs and their physical abilities.

Take note of what your team is doing well and what areas are in need of improvement. Start with the technical skills: How is our passing? How is our receiving? How is our finishing? Then technical and tactical: Do we keep posses-sion? Do we play into pressure or away from it? Do we have vision to see openings? Decide if it is the individual skill that is weak or the team play. A big part of being "businesslike" is to be an acute observer.

Teaching primarily involves addressing one specific need at a time. Prioritize what most needs to be attempted to be corrected. To try to work on several things at once is virtually to guarantee failure on several fronts. Concentrate on a key technical or tactical element of the game. Each practice's theme should be clear. Keep your team talks very brief and to the point.

Always Be Prepared

A thoughtful design of your practice session is one of the most important things that you will do as a coach. Be organized prior to the commencement of training. Know the approximate time at which each specific activity will begin, the number of minutes budgeted for that segment, and identify the participants (try not to waste time "picking" teams) and your equipment needs. Make sure the balls are properly inflated and that you have adequate medical kit supplies.

Arrive early. Inspect the field to determine that it is safe. Using cones, saucers, or whatever markings are needed, outline the areas that you will be using. Minimize the amount of time needed to arrange and rearrange your markers. If possible, lay out all of your grids prior to the start

of training. Make your scrimmage bibs accessible (when you are going to play seven-v-seven lay out one pile of seven blue vests and another of seven red ones).

Briefly discuss the game/practice if relevant. Introduce the first activity, reminding players of the key elements of performing that skill correctly.

Finally, we all know the saying about the best laid plans. A big part of the art of coaching is the ability to improvise. You might have planned a session for 12 players only to have 9 show up. By considering contigencies in advance you will not skip a beat.

Practice Progression

In addition to prioritizing what and how to teach, it is recommended that training sessions progress from the simple to the complex; from less demanding to more demanding all the time.

Add elements of the game to each exercise as you progress and from session to session. Introduce the ball, the field of play, rules, objectives, teammates, opponents, directional play, and decision-making. By the end of the session all of the elements should be present so that the practice most closely resembles a real game with similar demands. The only constant is to maintain the integrity of your primary theme.

The warm-up should be designed to prepare the body for the demands of the practice and should incur maximum repetitions with movement of the requisite technique that will subsequently be exercised.

When teaching players to make tactical decisions, begin with unlimited space and then restrict the area. For example, when working on maintaining possession, you can start with a passing/receiving exercise without any defenders. Next, you can play 5-v-2 with boundary lines. Follow by adding a goal, to place a greater demand on decision-making for both attackers and defenders. The final stage—when each side has a goal to attack—is the one that most closely resembles a real game and the match-like decisions that will be required. The "goal" can be getting the ball into a zone, such as the "zone" game (see Game 70). Activities should progress within a training session from individual to small group to large group (the latter being defined as four-v-four and above).

For a session with a singular technical theme, such as passing and receiving, the warm-up should be followed by "match-related" exercises that lead to "match-conditioned" activities. Introduce to the "match-related phase" simulated passes and/or active opposition. "Match-conditioned" is close to a real game with a goal at either or both ends of the area.

Whether focusing on tactics or techniques, end every practice with a game. This saves the favorite form of activity for last, which will help to keep your team motivated and provides the most realistic activity as the climax of the session.

Specificity of Training

Our coaching school instructors often talk of "specificity of training." They want to make certain that training accomplishes the objective of highlighting a skill or tactical factor in a way that is demanded by a real match. Apply the SAID principle, an acronym that stands for the Specific Adaptation of Imposed Demands. SAID says that all the activities and games used during training should be match-like and should expose players to the demands of the sport.

For example, to practice dribbling slalom style against cones will improve a player's ability to dribble in and out of cones. However, since defenders are not inanimate objects there is very limited value to such a drill. Instead, use games that involve changes of direction with a ball per player in a limited space with opponents. This demands that participants exploit vision to recognize where space exists and be able to ride tackles while maintaining control of the ball. A moving ball also makes all the players move. As the players move the picture changes. As the picture changes decisions have to be made. Not only must players be able to change direction, turn, evade challenges, throw opponents off balance, and accelerate while running with the ball, they must do so while making decisions whether to continue to dribble or to pass or to shoot. Exposing the player to opposition increases decision-making situations as well as introduces game-like stress.

Economical Training

Regardless of a session's emphasis, the importance of making the most of one's training time is vital. This theme was first sounded in our country during the 1970s by Dettmar Cramer.

Imported from West Germany to coach the U.S. National Team and to help launch our national coaching educational scheme, he promoted "economical training." He emphasized activities that made the most productive use of valuable time by addressing all of the four components that comprise a player: fitness, technique, tactics, and psychological strength. Not every moment on the training ground can be fully efficient. The initial warm-up and technical stage will not appreciably improve fitness or improve tactical sophistication, for example. So, running laps without a ball will not get a player in "game-shape." The best way to get fit for soccer is to play soccer. Our sport's fitness requires flexibility, agility, endurance, speed/explosive movement, strength, and power.

Tailoring Activities

As often as possible during exercises and with all games, it is essential that every participant have an obtainable objective. Coaches attempt to walk a tightrope that allows players to experience a reasonable proportion of success to failure without allowing the activity to become so easy as to lose its value. To accomplish this demands that you be an acute observer. As a coach there are many questions that you will ask yourself during the practice. Is the ratio of attackers to defenders appropriate? Is the playing area sufficient or too generous? Are the restrictions too onerous for the skill level? Is there sufficient time to work on this part of the game, without being excessive so as to risk loss of concentration? Are there sufficient incentives to keep the participants highly motivated? Are the teams comparably competitive? Restoring the proper balance between success and a challenging environment is the result of many slight adjustments that you are encouraged to make to achieve your objective.

Options to Manipulate the Environment

An activity's validity is predicated upon having the appropriate space and structuring the teams so that success is prevalent without rewarding poor execution of a skill.

The greater the space, the easier it is for the attackers to prevail. While their success is important, too much space means they are performing in an unrealistic environment in which they are not under sufficient pressure from defenders. This can lead to sloppy play and bad habits. Not enough space makes it impossible for them to carry out their task and will likely discourage them. Space is relative: the greater the ability of the players, the less space that is needed.

Another factor is the time frame allotted to each exercise. The ability of outnumbered defenders to go all-out is important, as it puts attackers under match-realistic pressure. Try to avoid exercises or games that the players are able to do without applying their 100 percent effort.

By changing the relationship between the field's width and length you can emphasize different tactical demands. The Dutch pioneered the use of various small-sided games to emphasize different points (Compare Games 78, 89 for specifics).

Using Neutral Players

Included in your menu of choices is the introduction of "neutral players." These are individuals who play with the team that has possession of the ball. For instance, your team is playing four-v-four with a point awarded for completing a predesignated number of consecutive passes. What should you do if the skills of most of your players are not sufficient to be able even to complete three straight passes? One possibility is to introduce to the exercise a few "neutrals," who are wearing easily distinguishable, bright-colored vests. These players work with whichever team is on offense. Thus, the attackers always enjoy a numerical advantage.

Another benefit of neutral players is to allow you to play small-sided games without having to exclude anyone. Let us say that you have 14 athletes at a practice and you would like to play a five-v-five game (four field players plus a 'keeper per squad). Adding bodies to the field would so crowd the area as to compromise what you hope to accomplish. Yet, you do not want to have four kids standing around with nothing to do. Take those "extra" players and place them just outside the sidelines. They can be used as targets to whom one of the active players may pass. The neutral player immediately attempts to play the ball to any member of the team from which it was received. Because exterior neutrals are not subjected to defensive pressure, you can re-create match-realism by restricting them to one or two touches or to holding the ball for a maximum of three seconds.

Not only does this keep the extra individuals involved, it also allows you to rotate the active players and lets them periodically rest from the strenuous activity. This should help to maintain peak performance without having anyone lose their mental edge.

Conditioned Games

A "conditioned game" is the playing of a regular soccer game but with a specific rule adaptation that emphasizes a particular technical or tactical demand. For example, a coach wishing to improve his squad's crossing and heading skills might add the "condition" that a goal may only

be scored on a header.

The key is to learn how to break down the real game into technical and tactical components and to make needed adjustments to highlight a certain aspect of soccer, but still keeping the game in its most simple and realistic form. For example, if a team takes too long to pass to an open teammate or players do not get open to provide passing opportunities, then limited touch games in training are useful. There are several popular conditioned games, including two-touch (Game 100), a restriction on passing forward (Game 68), and having to move forward as a team (Game 79).

Such stipulations are well-conceived approaches. But while tinkering with the game do not be overly creative. There are countless horror stories of coaches who put in so many restrictions and changes that what occurs on the training ground bears little resemblance to a real match. To achieve the purpose, be consistent with the SAID principle.

The Positioning of the Coach During Training

Whether coaching a team of pre-schoolers or a national team, your position on the training field is important. This often-neglected consideration is one of the so-called "little things" that makes a big difference to your ability to observe.

Rule number one is to be unobtrusive. In most cases it is better to stand outside

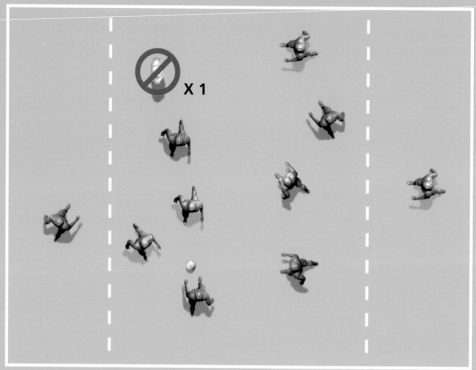

X 1

X 3   X 2

Optimum position for a coach during training.
X3 offers best field of vision with least interference with play.

of the game. Avoid a position where you interfere with play. Rule number two: be close enough to the action so as to be a viable presence yet sufficiently off to the side that you can see as much of the playing area as possible.

The diagram opposite illustrates a situation in which the coach has split his squad into two adjacent grids. In Position X1 the coach is actually in the way of the participants. Moreover, he is unaware of what is occurring in the adjacent playing area. Position X2 is slightly better. At least the coach is not in the way. But he must turn to see the opposite grid and it is impossible from this placement to see enough of the action.

The ideal is represented by X3. The coach can view what is happening in both grids and can offer whatever corrections are deemed to be important. Moreover, all the players know that they are being watched, which will encourage them to continue to train purposefully.

Experienced coaches working with large numbers (eight-v-eight and above) of senior players may have the ability to instruct from within the activity. However, doing so is not recommended for youth coaches.

When to Stop Play

When there is a common problem during the warm-up you may quickly mention it, demonstrate how to perform a skill properly, and restart the activity as soon as possible. If an individual is having a problem, work with that player one on one.

Stoppages during subsequent portions of the practice ought to be used only if your comments pertain very directly to the specific theme of the session. The key is to show the picture. When there is a significant error have the players "freeze" and re-create the situation. Make the players aware of their options and the consequences. You can do so by slowly moving the ball as you walk the players through the situation. Then step back and restart the activity by having the involved players perform the task successfully.

You are urged to keep your stoppages to a minimum, make your comments as succinct as possible, and let the game be the primary teacher. Do not make an individual feel as if he is on trial. The words you choose ought to make it obvious that you are trying to help him to improve.

Keeping Score

Allowing your players to compete exploits their inherent desire to do so. Seek to provide an obtainable objective coupled with incentives for success. Rather than asking a player to juggle a ball for five minutes, have each child keep track of how many consecutive touches he achieved. Challenge him to break his personal record. Compliment anyone who does so.

Keeping score can help to get the most out of all involved—not just attackers. As four offensive players attempt to maintain possession while stringing passes in a confined area against two defenders, keep track of the tackles, interceptions, and bad passes that those defenders force in a set time frame. Such scoring will serve as a source of motivation.

You can, for example, play in a four-v-two exercise in which the attackers win one point any time that they complete a predesignated number of consecutive passes with two points awarded for a pass that "splits" the defenders (travels between them and is received by an attacker on the opposite side). The defenders get a point whenever they touch the ball or their pressure forces a pass by an attacker that leaves the playing area. The winner is the team that first scores 10 points. Switch the defenders and repeat the game.

Or you can play "cutthroat," with any interception, tackle, or forced error resulting in the defender who won and/or touched the ball switching places with the attacker who made the mistake.

With all activities do not confuse quantity for quality. A great expenditure of time will not be productive and might even be counterproductive if participants stop focusing on the task. Remember this creed; to practice too long is to practice wrong!

Indoor Soccer

In many regions, playing soccer throughout the winter is only possible by utilizing gymnasiums and the growing number of soccer-specific facilities. For developmental opportunities to be maximized, your adherence to solid soccer principles remain essential.

Regrettably, many training sessions and tournaments are marred by a laudable but shortsighted inclination to maximize participation by placing too many athletes on the floor during games. As a result, the playing area becomes so crowded as to render virtually useless an individual's technical qualities and presents little opportunity for the team to string together passes. Similarly, the size of the goals ought to be appropriate for the age of the players, the size of the surface, and the number of participants.

U.S. Soccer's coaching staff encourages you to utilize your indoor season to continue to prioritize the upgrading of your team's technical level and tactical awareness. There are three simple steps that you can take to "force" players to attempt to play accurate passes to a teammate's feet rather than to be content to aimlessly whack the ball forward while under pressure. First, use boundary lines rather than walls with kick-ins for the restart. Second, award an indirect free kick to the defending team any time that an attacker kicks the ball that goes above head height (except when using such a large area that a well thought out long pass is appropriate). Third, on goal kicks and any distribution by the 'keeper, the ball may not cross the midfield line unless it has been first touched by an outfield player.

One word of caution; soccer burnout is a very significant issue. To go straight from outdoor to indoor soccer and vice versa without any appreciable break, risks being counterproductive. Know the psychology of your team and—especially with younger players—don't make the demands of playing soccer onerous.

Running a Tryout

In youth soccer circles annual tryouts for travel and select teams remain prevalent. While it is far preferable to select a squad based on having judged players performing in their natural environment (i.e. playing in meaningful games with their current team), that "luxury" is often not an option.

To run a tryout that provides you and your coaching staff with the best opportunity of evaluating useful and relevant information, apply the SAID principle. Simply play soccer. Start, if you wish, with small-sided games and progress to an eleven-a-side. While conditioned games can provide valuable insights into the tactical awareness of older players, they should never be used as substitutes for the real thing. But if you are running a tryout, leave the stopwatch at home. Avoid "drills" in which players must dribble in and out of saucers. Forget about shooting exercises.

Summary

Once players have established a primary position/role within the team, functional-training can be introduced at about age 15 (though goalkeepers can do functional training much earlier). This involves position-specific exercises with a player or small groups of players in the area(s) of the field in which they primarily operate. For example, strikers can work on playing with their back to the goal, on match-realistic finishing exercises, and on playing numbers down in tight spaces. Nevertheless, before high school age the overwhelming training emphasis/philosophy should remain focused upon developing well-rounded abilities.

For your methodology, it's best to follow the "I-dog-em" approach. That stands for Identify an aspect of the game which most requires attention; Devise a realistic practice session; Observe your players throughout the training session; Guide them to successful responses to their problems; Motivate them to improve their performance.

Our advice is to strive to coach the player and not the method. If the objectives of a technique are being met (i.e. passes are accurate), refrain from making minute technical corrections. In other words, "If it's not broken, don't fix it."

Coach with a positive approach and within the natural parameters of your personality. For progress to be made, a player must truly enjoy the process. Remember that the game is the best teacher. Undoubtedly, good coaching will accelerate the learning process. At the youth level, coaching means creating a realistic soccer environment to accommodate the age and ability level of the players.

On the following pages the game's primary techniques are presented in bullet form for easy reference. While performing all of the techniques, quickness of action is only made possible by quickness of thought. Therefore, every skill should be performed with vision as the player constantly looks up to assess options.

Technical proficiency is the foundation upon which all outstanding players are built. Only when a player can comfortably perform whatever skill any situation may demand while under the pressure of opposition is that athlete able to successfully compete at a high level.

The physical requirements to properly execute techniques are beyond the capability of any player until such time as that youngster has acquired the requisite agility and balance. To attempt to teach techniques to the youngest of players will be frustrating and a waste of time. It is natural and permissible that they will tend to strike the ball with their toes.

Please note that all descriptions for foot skills in this section are for the right foot. Reverse the information, as needed, when using the left foot (for example, substitute clockwise for counterclockwise).

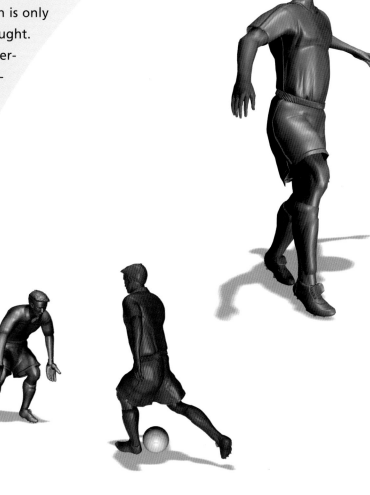

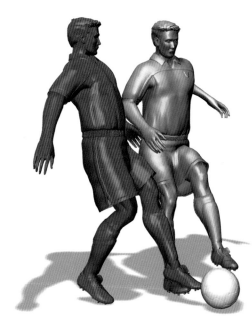

DRIBBLING

When Used:

To run with the ball at the feet, to evade challenges, to manipulate the ball, to penetrate the positions of the opposing players.

Technical Tips:

1. Maintain control of the ball while moving at speed.
2. Introduce deception moves with feints and changes of direction and speed to unbalance the opponent.
3. Advance the ball with light touches while using predominantly the insides, but also the outsides, of the feet.
4. Keep head up to observe available options.
5. Develop one or two favorite moves.

Most Common Mistake(s):

Keeping the head down and running too fast for one's skill level.

When Used:
To receive and change direction with the ball.

Technical Tips:
1. Assess the line of the ball.
2. Be aware of pressure.
3. Understand where you have enough available space and decide when to turn with the ball.
4. Turn away from pressure.
5. The use of the inside or the outside of the foot will be determined by (a) the location of the pass that is being received, (b) the location of the opponent. In the figure above, the ball is passed to the player's right foot. As the opponent is on her left side, she is able to accept the ball with the outside of the right foot and turn to her right.
6. The player's first touch of the ball is vital to success.

Most Common Mistake(s):
1. Exposing the ball to the defender.
2. Turning into the opponent.
3. Failing to accelerate after turning with the ball.

TURNING WITH THE BALL

CRUYFF MOVE

The following three dribbling examples may be used to unbalance the opponent by shifting the weight to throw the opponent in one direction and to take the ball in the other direction:

Cruyff Move

1. Fake to kick the ball with the right instep.
2. Step past the plane of the ball with the supporting foot (the left foot).
3. Rotate the right foot so the toes point downward.
4. Use the inside of the right foot to make contact with the near side of the ball so that it rolls behind the supporting foot.
5. Then play the ball with the left foot.

Scissors Move

1. Come around the ball in a clockwise direction with the right foot finishing to the right of the ball as the right shoulder dips to "wrong foot" the defender (frame 1).

2. Step over the ball with the right foot, continuing to shift the body weight and the motion so the ball is eventually under the left foot (frames 2 and 3).

3. Take the ball forward and away with the outside of the left foot (frame 4).

ZICO MOVE

Zico Move

1. Fake to strike a push pass with the right foot towards the target (frame 1).
2. Step over the ball with the right foot so it points out (as shown) and is directly in front of the supporting (left) foot (frame 2).
3. Spin the body clockwise while keeping the body between the ball and the opponent.
4. Using the instep, take the ball away with the left foot (frames 3 and 4).
5. Accelerate with the ball.

When Used:

To maintain possession by protecting the ball until an available passing option is created.

Technical Tips:

1. Stay sideways-on to the defender while keeping the body between the opponent and the ball.
2. Extend the arm that is closer to the defender to aid balance and to make yourself "wider."
3. Keep the ball on the foot away from the opponent.
4. Manipulate the ball to help create openings and to avoid the pressure.
5. Keep the head up to observe available options.

Most Common Mistake(s):

Exposing the ball to the defender.

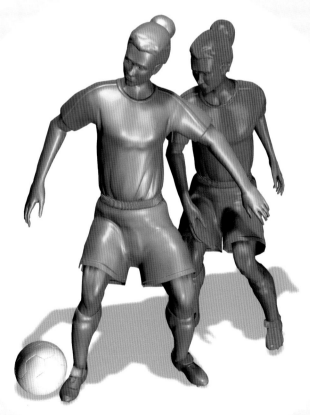

THE PUSH PASS

When Used:

Over short to medium distances (up to about 25 yards). It is used to shoot when accuracy, not power, is the key factor.

Technical Tips:

1. The inside of the kicking foot remains square to the target throughout the entire motion.

2. The toes of the kicking foot are elevated slightly higher than the heel with the ankle remaining "locked."

3. If possible, the body is square to the target.

4. The shoulders and center of gravity are forward throughout.

5. The supporting foot is pointed at the target and it is on the same plane as the ball.

6. Strike through the middle or just above the middle of the ball.

7. Follow through towards the target with the striking foot remaining open throughout.

Most Common Mistake(s):

1. Falling to "lock the ankle" at the moment of contact with the ball.
2. Planting the supporting foot behind ball's plane and/or too far away from the ball.

Notes:

These technical tips are recommended for the introduction of this technique to younger players. More proficient players will be able to execute a successful push pass without having the body aligned as described.

INSTEP PASS

When Used:

To drive a pass over a long distance or to get the ball to a distant receiver quickly on the ground. While the instep is used for both, the techniques are different.

Technical Tips:

Low Drive (this page)

1. Approach the ball from a slight angle.
2. Place the non-kicking foot alongside the ball, pointing in the direction of the target.
3. Drive diagonally across the ball, kicking the ball with the inside of instep. The knee and body are over the ball at the time of contact.
4. Follow through low with the kicking foot.

Lofted Pass (opposite frames)

1. Approach the ball from a slight angle.
2. Place the non-kicking foot alongside but towards the back of the ball.
3. Drive diagonally through underside of the ball using the lower instep above the big toe.
4. Lean back slightly at the moment of contact to impart loft on the ball.
5. Follow though towards target.

Most Common Mistake(s):

Approaching the ball from the wrong angle.
Positioning the supporting foot incorrectly.
Striking the incorrect part of the ball with the incorrect part of the foot.
Failing to follow through.

THE OUTSIDE OF THE FOOT PASS

When Used:

To pass or shoot quickly over a short (less than 10 yards) distance.

Technical Tips:

1. Point the striking foot down and in.
2. The striking foot's ankle remains "locked" throughout.
3. The knee of the kicking foot is over the ball.
4. Keep the supporting foot behind the plane of the ball to allow room for the kicking foot's movements.
5. Strike through the upper half of the ball to keep it low.

Most Common Mistake(s):

1. Loss of balance.
2. Lack of pace or accuracy of pass owing to incorrect body mechanics.

When Used:

To impart an immediate lift on the ball.

Technical Tips:

1. Imagine the ball is on a tee and strike under the ball to impart immediate loft and backspin.
2. Use the instep, with the ball contacted by the inside eyelets of the shoelaces.
3. Jab the kicking foot into the ground with no follow through.
4. Place the arms out for balance.

While the mechanics of the body are essential to the execution of a pass, the following coaching points are also vital to success.

1. Pace: The pace of the pass to feet or into space must have consideration for the receiver to enable that player to execute the next action efficiently.

2. Accuracy: The pass must be played accurately to enable team to maintain possession.

3. Timing of Pass: The pass must be played at the moment a teammate is ready to receive it. Passes played too early or too late will minimize the effect of a run or may result in loss of possession.

4. Timing of Run: As the run always initiates the pass, it is important that the intended receiver makes the run only when the passer has the ball under control and has looked up to see the potential receiver.

When Used:

To restart play whenever the ball crosses over a side-line.

Technical Tips:

1. Grip equally with both hands behind the ball.
2. To increase distance arch the back.
3. Take a long final stride with both feet remaining on the ground.
4. Complete the rhythmic motion with an extended follow through to take full advantage of the momentum of the legs, lower back, and arms.
5. After the motion is completed, the thrower immediately moves into position to be available to assist his team's attack or to help thwart any counter-attack.

Most Common Mistakes:

A successful throw-in should have all the qualities of a good pass: pace, accuracy, timing, and consideration. Young players often fail to consider these qualities and throw the ball away.

RECEIVING WITH A FOOT

When Used:

To control the ball successfully; to simplify the next action in the game; short passes, long passes, or dribbling the ball.

Technical Tips:

1. Look up to assess the situation before the ball arrives.
2. Make early selection in method of control.
3. Move into the ball's path early and come to meet the ball.
4. Play the ball across the body (top) if opponent is on the right side, or slightly withdraw foot upon contact to cushion and turn the ball if the opponent is on left side (opposite top).
5. A player can receive a ball with the outside of the foot to protect the ball from the opponent (right).
6. Balls can be controlled in the air with the inside of the foot: at the moment of contact the leg is withdrawn to cushion the ball (opposite middle and bottom).

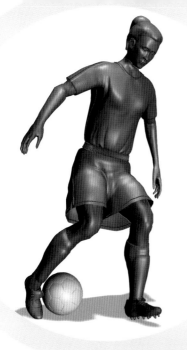

Most Common Mistake(s):

1. Being stiff when the ball arrives.
2. Failing to control the ball well enough for next action in the game to be set up.
3. Not looking up until after the ball has been contacted.
4. Failing to execute successfully after controlling the ball. Receiving the ball is not an end product. Therefore, if the action after control results in a loss of possession the control is wasted.

RECEIVING A RISING BALL WITH THE CHEST

When Used:
To control a ball that is bouncing up in front of the body.

Technical Tips:
1. Move into the ball's path early and come to meet the ball.
2. Lean forward from the waist, to be over the ball.
3. Extend arms for balance, with hands inward and thumbs down, as shown.
4. Be on the balls of both feet.

Most Common Mistake(s):
Failing to assess the line of the ball and misjudging the bounce.

Technical Tips:

1. Move into the ball's path early and come to meet the ball.
2. Help to "soften" the ball by having body weight concentrated on the balls of both feet.
3. Extend arms out, with hands open and thumbs up for balance and to expand the controlling surface.
4. Lean backward from the waist.
5. Be on the balls of both feet.
6. Withdraw the contact area slightly and relax the knees as the ball arrives. Angle and/or rotate to redirect the ball away from opposing pressure.

Most Common Mistake(s):

1. Misjudging the flight of the ball.
2. Allowing the ball to bounce up instead of controlling it down.

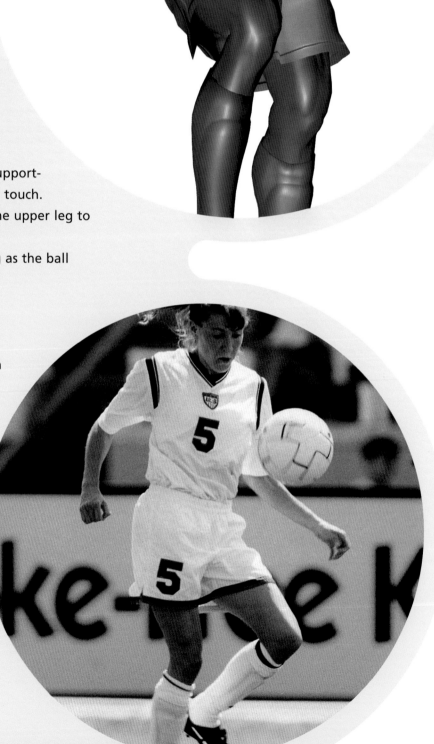

RECEIVING WITH THE THIGH

When Used:

To control a ball that is played in the air.

Technical Tips:

1. Move into the ball's path early and come to meet the ball.
2. Make early selection of this method of control.
3. Extend arms for balance.
4. Angle thigh slightly downwards.
5. Be on the balls of the supporting foot to promote a soft touch.
6. Use the fleshy part of the upper leg to receive the ball.
7. Withdraw the upper leg as the ball arrives.

Most Common Mistake(s):

1. Leaning backwards with the body weight supported by the heel.
2. Making contact with the ball with the knee.
3. Bringing leg up too late.

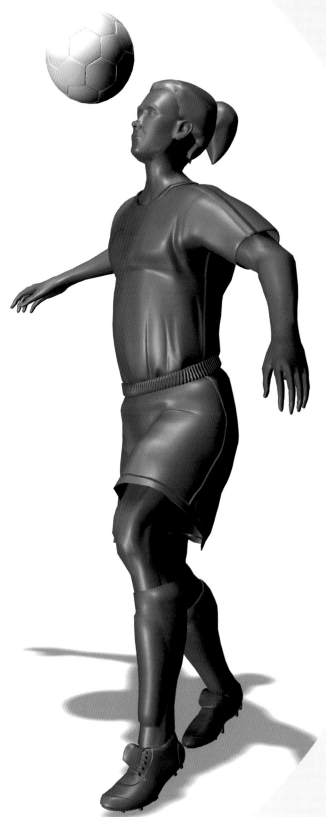

When Used:

Only rarely used and usually to pass the ball over a very short distance to a nearby teammate.

Technical Tips:

1. Move into the ball's path early and come to meet the ball.
2. Extend arms for balance.
3. Keep the eyes open and the mouth closed.
4. Be on the balls of both feet.
5. Strike the ball with the hairline of the forehead.
6. Withdraw the head and lean backward from the waist as the ball arrives.
7. If possible, keep feet on the ground and be as "light" as possible, with the body weight concentrated on the bottom of the toes.

Most Common Mistake(s):

Being rigid, which causes the ball to then travel too far.

RECEIVING WITH THE HEAD

THE INSTEP DRIVE

When Used:

Shooting for power or passing along the ground.

Technical Tips:

1. Lean forward with the shoulders and kicking knee over the ball prior to and during contact.
2. The kicking foot remains pointed downward diagonally across the ball.
3. Throughout the kicking motion the supporting foot is pointed at the target.
4. Drive through the ball.
5. To keep the ball low, follow through low and strike the upper half of the ball.

Most Common Mistake(s):

1. Incorrect positioning of supporting foot causing a loss of power and accuracy.
2. Failing to drive through the ball.
3. Failing to keep ankle locked on kicking foot.

THE INSTEP DRIVE

THE VOLLEY

When Used:

To shoot or pass an airborne ball straight ahead.

Technical Tips:

1. Be light on the feet to get behind the line of the ball.
2. Get the knee of kicking foot over the ball with toes pointed downward.
3. Use a short leg stroke (the pace of the ball will supply the power).
4. Make contact just above the center of the ball.
5. Follow through low, with toes still pointed towards the ground.
6. When time and space permit, strike the ball while it is as close to the ground as possible.

Most Common Mistake(s):

1. Misreading line of the ball.
2. Kicking underneath the ball.

THE SIDE VOLLEY

When Used:
To redirect a cross or a pass while the ball is still in the air.

Technical Tips:
1. Move into the ball's line of flight early.
2. Upper body "faces" the arriving ball but the supporting foot is pointed at the target.
3. Knee of the kicking leg "leads" the foot.
4. Dip the front shoulder towards the target and "drop away" from the ball. Prior to contact, the kicking leg is just above the ball's plane and it moves slightly downward.
5. The body rotates towards the target with the laces striking just above the center of the ball.
6. Follow through low and at the target.

Most Common Mistake(s):
1. Failing to assess the line of the ball.
2. Mistiming the contact with the ball.

When Used:

To pass around an opponent, to "widen" the goal when shooting, and to serve the ball on restarts. The inside of the right foot curves the ball from right to left.

Technical Tips:

1. Approach the ball from an angle.
2. Concentrate the weight on the outside of the supporting foot as it remains grounded next to the ball.
3. Lean backwards and away from the ball.
4. With the toes pointed slightly upwards, strike the outside of the ball with the inside of the foot.

Most Common Mistake(s):

1. Hitting too far under the ball and so sending it too high.
2. Contacting too much of the ball with too much of the foot.

HEADING

When Used:

When having to play a high ball to clear (when defending), to pass, or to shoot when attacking.

Technical Tips:

1. Assess the flight of the ball.
2. Time the jump to head the ball at the highest point of the jump.
3. Keep both eyes open and the mouth closed.
4. Strike the ball with the hairline of the forehead.
5. Lock the neck and keep the upper body rigid.
6. Thrust forward from the waist (except for diving or flicked headers).
7. Strike through the top half of the ball to send it downwards when shooting from close range or strike below the center of the ball to send it high, wide, and far when clearing on defense.

Most Common Mistake(s):

1. Closing the eyes prior to contact, thus painfully hitting the ball with the nose or the top of the head.
2. Mistiming the leap.
3. Mistiming the thrusting of the head.

THE FLICKED HEADER

When Used:

To slightly alter the ball's plane while keeping it going in the same direction. This is often done by an attacker at or beyond the near post to set up a scoring chance for a teammate behind him.

Technical Tips:

1. Extend the arms.
2. Keep the eyes open and the mouth closed.
3. The bottom of the ball needs to glance off the very top of the forehead.
4. Lift the chin slightly so as to "open" the angle of the forehead.

Most Common Mistake(s):

Poor timing of the leap: hitting too much of the ball or missing it entirely.

FUNNELING THE OPPONENT IN POSSESSION

Technical Tips:

1. Approach the opponent rapidly but in a controlled manner.
2. If possible, try to approach at an angle to limit the attacker's options.
3. While nearing the opponent shorten the strides with the knees bent and the weight on the balls of the feet.
4. Keep the body well-balanced, with the eyes on the ball.

Most Common Mistake(s):

Over-commitment from sprinting at the attacker, allowing the attacker to push the ball into space and run around the defender.

Technical Tips:

1. Keep weight evenly balanced on the front of the feet.
2. Keep the eyes on the ball.
3. Bend slightly from the knees and the waist.
4. Be slightly angled, with one foot moderately closer to the attacker to encourage the opponent to go in the least dangerous direction.
5. Be close enough to make the attacker look at the ball but be retreating at a pace that is slightly slower than the attacker is advancing.

Most Common Mistake(s):

Running out-of-control at the attacker or being too far away, so that the opponent still has many options and little pressure exists.

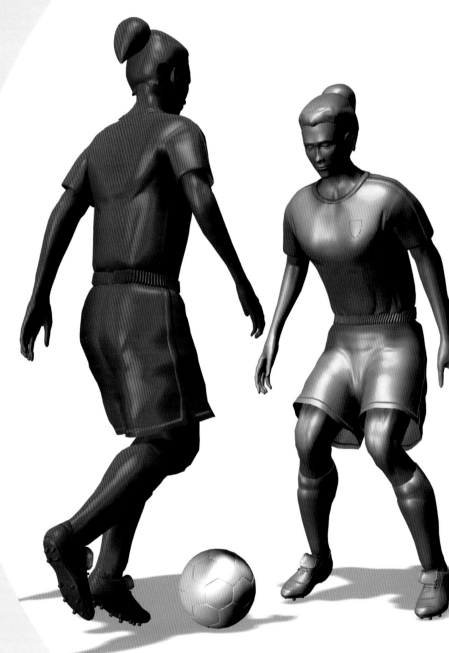

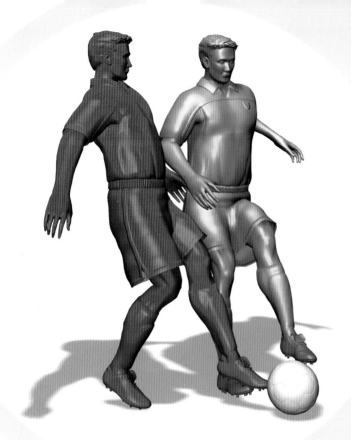

When Used:
To quickly tackle the ball when it has been exposed by the attacker.

Technical Tips:
1. Lock the ankle.
2. Use the foot that is closer to the ball.
3. Play the ball into space away from the opponent(s) and/or towards a teammate.

Most Common Mistake(s):
Deflecting the ball back to the attacker.

THE BLOCK TACKLE

When Used:

To win the ball when risk-taking is appropriate.

Technical Tips:

1. Keep supporting foot next to the ball.
2. Lean forward from the shoulders.
3. Lock the tackling foot's ankle with toes pointed slightly upwards. Drive through the ball just above its center.
4. Tackle with the full body weight.

Most Common Mistake(s):

Failure to fully commit to the tackle.

HOOK SLIDING TACKLE

When Used: To dispossess the opponent and gain possession of the ball.

Technical Tips:

1. Ideally, initiate the challenge as the ball is separated from the opponent.

2. Strike just above the middle of the ball with the instep of the upper foot.

3. Swing the challenging foot in a slightly downward trajectory, with the ankle remaining locked throughout.

4. With the body weight behind the ball, wedge the ball against the opponent and the ground so that the opponent falls over the ball.

5. To avoid fouling, challenge only with one foot and play the ball first.

6. Weigh risk vs. reward, as a failed attempt can concede a foul.

7. Recover quickly to an upright position to initiate a counter-attack.

When Used:

To dispossess an opponent of the ball, usually near a touchline or in front of goal.

Technical Tips:

1. Challenge from the side and not from behind.

2. Always weigh the consequences of failure; only challenge when absolutely necessary, and/or when fully confident of success, and when the ball is not likely to ricochet into an opponent.

3. Initiate movements when the ball is separated from the opponent.

4. The challenging leg swings into the plane of the opponent and strikes against the near side of the ball to clear it out of opponent's path.

5. Usually use the right foot when coming from the left (although the outside of the near-sided/bottom foot can also be used when near the touchline, as shown here). 6. To avoid fouling, challenge with only one foot and make contact with the ball first.

7. Immediately recover to a standing position.

CONVENTIONAL SLIDING TACKLE

Athletes tend to be judged on what they do best. But a soccer goalkeeper is primarily assessed by the ability to avoid mistakes. All 'keepers—from youth up to international stars—will concede some "soft" goals. The best 'keepers make the least mistakes and are able to recover their composure quickly while retaining their confidence after having suffered a blunder.

It is not a coincidence that goalkeepers typically reach their prime at a later age than do field players. While athletic parameters like agility, coordination, and leaping ability are important, they are not nearly as significant as judgement, leadership, and positioning.

Former professional goalie and World Cup coach Tony Waiters has identified the position's 13 key principles:

1. Providing a "second barrier" to back up one's hands
2. Having "soft" hands
3. A good stance
4. Proper positioning/angle play
5. Diving forward to make saves
6. Maintaining preferred (concave) body posture
7. Producing an instant recovery when required
8. Having outstanding diving technique
9. Maintaining concentration
10. Having a good situational sense without having to guess or anticipate
11. Staying on one's feet for as long as possible in one-v-one confrontations
12. Handling crosses well
13. Giving positive distribution

The Techniques of Goalkeeping

Even the hands of great 'keepers fail them on occasion. This is especially so when confronted with shooters who impart spin and power on their strikes and/or when a 'keeper must catch a shot on the short hop off bumpy ground. A goalie must present as big a "second barrier" as possible by getting the maximum amount of body behind the ball and the hands. This second barrier should be perpendicular to the trajectory of the incoming shot.

While the body presents a hard barrier to the ball, the hands act as shock absorbers. There are two hand positions for catching. The so-called "welcome" or "scoop" position is used for shots at the keeper's body but below the chest (see page 173). For all other shots in which a catch is attempted the hands are in the "W" (also referred to as the "diamond") position (page 171).

When catching, the palms are turned outwards and are extended in front of the body. Under no circumstance should an opposing attacker be shown the back of the goalkeeper's hands. By extending the hands the initial ball contact is in front of the body, which makes it possible to withdraw them upon impact to absorb the ball. 'Keepers who do this well are said to have "soft" hands. Their valuable ability to hold difficult shots minimizes dangerous rebounds. Having soft hands requires a relaxed body. The stance is never rigid and the palms face the shooter. Also important is a steady head, which allows the eyes to watch the ball into the hands.

Another part of that equation is angle play. To make the goal appear smaller to the shooter, the 'keeper dissects an imaginary line from the ball to the middle of the goal.

Goalkeeping at all levels demands instinctive bravery as well as requiring excellent judgement.

The distance from the goal line during the starting position is a matter of personal preference, confidence, and experience. The 'keeper wishes to be far enough off the line when the shot is taken to lessen the available target space to the attacker but not to come so far so as to become vulnerable to having the ball chipped over his head. Tall 'keepers with great leaping ability can afford to be more aggressive at advancing off the line since they are less vulnerable to a chipped shot. Conversely, a goalie who is diminutive or less athletic should be more conservative.

With experience a goalkeeper learns to recognize clues that allow him to extend his range. An attacker who is under pressure and/or has the ball rolling away from him will find it very difficult to dip a shot. But a shooter with ample time and space or one who has the ball rolling across his path or towards him has conditions that are far more favorable to lofting the ball over the goalkeeper and having it dip under the crossbar.

Other factors to take into account are the skill level and angle of the shooter, the positioning of open attackers (if any), and the conditions, such as a wet or bumpy field or a strong wind that can be unpredictable and suggest the goalie be more conservative.

The ability to "read" situations is not to be confused with guessing or anticipating. Goalies should only react to shots and crosses after they have been struck. Many a 'keeper has been embarrassed when failing to heed this fundamental principle.

The goalkeeper's starting position is such that he can move forward and then become set just as the shot is struck. There are several important reasons for this; it is easier to take steps forward than steps backward: it is almost impossible to get any impetus for a dive while retreating; narrowing the shooter's angle makes the goal appear "smaller" and improves the odds that the attacker will hit the ball at the 'keeper or miss the goal altogether; and, to attack the ball, the 'keeper wishes to dive sideways and slightly forward. Only under the rarest of circumstances should he be retreating as a shot is being taken.

No 'keeper will hold every attempt. When rebounds occur it is important that the goalie recovers as quickly as possible. The ability to reassume rapidly the ready position is important.

Diving technique takes years to perfect. The movement is sideways, with the 'keeper landing on his side. The body forms a barrier that is perpendicular to the trajectory of the incoming ball. The hands move in such a manner that the arms create a "window" that allows the goalie to focus intently on the ball throughout the dive.

Remaining ready and alert at all times is important. While lapses in concentration are common among younger players, the ambitious goalie must learn to "stay focused" for the entire match.

The farther that a 'keeper progresses in the sport, the more important it is to be able to command the spaces in front of the goal. The 'keeper is responsible for covering the gaps between the defenders and himself. He must stay connected with the defense throughout the entire game. A ball played "over the top" by the opposition calls for leaving the line to arrive before any attackers. This often means exiting the box. Coupled with the rule banning the use of the 'keeper's hands on an intentional back pass from a teammate's foot, the modern goalie must be every bit as skillful with both feet as his teammates.

To win through balls, the starting position can be at or beyond the top of the penalty area. Only as the attackers advance forward with the ball under their control must the 'keeper begin to retreat so that he can be at his preferred distance from the goal line as soon as the opponents move to within shooting range. The 'keeper should be within a personal comfort zone whenever the possibility of a shot being taken exists.

Dealing with crosses requires judgement, confidence, technique, and timing. Once the decision to collect or fist away a ball has been made, the goalie shouts "'keeper!" to alert his teammates that he is coming for the ball. Any player could state "mine" but it is a foul for an opponent to trick the defense by saying "'keeper." When deciding to remain on the line he yells "away" to advise teammates to clear the ball upfield.

When in doubt about his ability to catch a cross, the 'keeper must opt for safety by fisting the ball out of danger. Whether using one hand or both simultaneously, the priorities (in order) are to hit the ball high, wide, and far. This is known as "boxing" the ball.

At the game's higher levels 'keepers must decide in a split-second whether to come for a cross. Making the wrong choice or even a slight hesitation can result in conceding a goal.

While winning the ball is ideal, it is but one part of the equation. Once in possession the 'keeper becomes the team's first attacker. Distribution by passing hands via throwing, punting, or drop-kicking can either launch a counterattack, help to maintain possession, or put the team in trouble. Throwing the ball to a teammate who is in traffic or is running away from the keeper, for example, is risky.

Psychological Considerations

Coaches must comprehend the fragile nature of the psyches of 'keepers, especially with younger players. The 'keeper knows if he is having a tough game. He needs his coach to give positive reinforcement rather than to compound his problems.

Whenever possible, give your goalkeeper the benefit of the doubt. Rather than tell the 'keeper what he did well or poorly, ask him to evaluate his performance. You will often be pleased at how he understands situations. His vantage point is far superior to that of the sideline-bound coach for deciphering what occurred.

At the highest levels of soccer the qualities that are most commonly found in successful 'keepers include:

1. controlled confidence in their ability without ever being arrogant.

2. a "level" personality based upon maintaining an appropriate perspective that allows them to avoid becoming cocky or lazy after a great performance yet not to fall apart after a difficult outing (a consistent personality leads to consistency of performance, which is one of the most treasured attributes that any goalkeeper can possess).

3. high degree of self-motivation with a keen desire to improve.

4. strong leadership qualities coupled with a high degree of intelligence to be able to

Position-specific training is necessary even for young goalkeepers; it should be fun, not exhausting and never at the expense of ignoring their overall soccer development (top). Goalkeepers have to find their own "comfort zones," learning from experience and training where to position themselves to minimize danger (bottom).

perform as a de facto coach on the field to keep the defense well organized.

5. the awareness to make instantaneous decisions and the mental toughness to deal with the demands of the game, teammates, fans, and the public both on and off of the field.

6. sufficient courage to be willing to put his body/health "on the line" when required to keep the ball out of the net.

The right attitude is essential in a position in which mistakes are immediately posted on the scoreboard. The goalie lives with the understanding that a series of great saves will be forgotten if he should subsequently make a major mistake. It takes a special type of individual to handle that responsibility.

Getting Started

U.S. Soccer recommends that for ages 6 through 12 the goalkeeping chores are rotated among the squad so that all youth players experience at least a limited amount of time playing in the goal. While a youngster may express a desire to become a 'keeper at an early age, that player must also develop the wide range of soccer skills. Thus, a coach may decide to have one or two individuals who share the majority of time in goal while making certain that those kids also get to play in the field.

Putting the Pieces in Place

By the time that a 'keeper enters high school he should have a good level of technical ability and a rudimentary understanding of the tactical role of the goalkeeping and of team defending.

Fitness will be taking on increasing importance, with an emphasis on abdomi-

nal and upper body strength coupled with leg strength, vertical leaping, and explosive quickness.

He should be taking his own goal kicks. Abdicating that responsibility to a teammate leaves one less player in the field to help win the ball. Also, the most advanced opponent will be onside while far into your team's territory if a defender is taking a kick, as there are now two players (the one taking the kick and the 'keeper) in a deep position.

Athleticism is the icing on the cake. Goalkeepers who rely on their athletic ability to get out of trouble caused by poor positioning and inadequate judgement are less valuable than an inferior athlete whose positioning and judgement are outstanding. The best 'keepers are not forced to make nearly as many spectacular saves as their lesser colleagues.

Having said that, they are fully capable of making the big play when it is most required. Great 'keepers are able to occasionally keep their team in a game in which they are being outplayed. They may even single-handedly win the game for their side. But for every spectacular performance there are several others that are only noteworthy for being solid and workmanlike.

Thus, the coaching emphasis and positive reinforcement should be more geared toward when a 'keeper gets the "little" things right than when making spectacular saves that inspires fans to shout "ooh" and "aah."

Remember too there will be times when aesthetics take a back seat to pragmatism. If a 'keeper must run cross-legged across his goal to keep the ball out of the net, so be it.

The unique needs of goalkeepers are often neglected. Not until the 1990s did it become common for professional teams to employ a specialty coach to work exclusively with a club's goalies. Having such an individual has proven to be of great benefit. Qualified 'keeper coaches have insight into the specific demands on goalies and their needs that most general coaches lack. If your team does not have the luxury of having a goalkeeper coach, arrive early and put your 'keepers through a technical session prior to the arrival of the rest of the team. Know that you must balance providing advice with keeping the 'keepers active. Both the 'keepers and the remainder of the squad must feel that the goalies are a part of the team and not apart from the team.

Charting the progress of your 'keepers over time with a written journal will prove helpful. Note the coaching points stressed and document the performance of each goalie. Using a video recorder can help the goalies to review their technique to better understand their strengths and weaknesses. Make it a point to show far more positive examples than negative.

Goalies from Under-12 through U-14 should train once or twice per week with sessions ranging from 45 minutes to one hour.

U-15s and U-16s should train for a little over an hour twice weekly, while U-17s through U-19s should have two or three sessions of 75 to 80 minutes apiece.

These workouts are always used to augment their training with the remainder of the squad and not as a substitute for working with the team.

As the coach you are responsible for inspecting the area to be used. Ground that is bumpy or hard may not be safe and is unlikely to be productive for getting positive results.

Whenever possible use a real goal with the proper field markings. As goalies mature they come to rely upon the field lines of the six-yard box and the penalty area to get their bearings. When using a different area for training, place saucers to represent those field lines.

After warming up, the training session features a 15- to 20-minute period dedicated to technical practice. Repetition of the fundamentals with an emphasis on proper execution is vital, especially with younger players.

We recommend keeping practice gimmick-free. Stick to fundamentals while reinforcing the 13 key principles. Doing so will render the goalie ready to perform when training with the remainder of the squad starts.

The 'keeper's fitness needs differ from those of teammates. Unlike a midfielder, he won't be running for five-plus miles during the course of a typical match. Instead, he must be able to accelerate quickly, to be agile and supple, and to have outstanding leg spring. Jumping rope is helpful.

Short sprints that incorporate rapid changes of direction are useful. So are plyometrics, which are a series of exercises that utilize explosive leaping movements to build power. A goalie can practice continually leaping over the ball for 30-second intervals with two-footed takeoffs from side-to-side or from front-to-back and back-to-front.

Jumping up and down from the crouch position (the one used by a baseball catcher) works, as does running interspersed with one- and two-footed takeoffs over a series of hurdles.

Footwork exercises are important and may be performed by 2, 22, or 102 'keepers simultaneously. In an activity known as "Let's Dance," the goalies face a leader/coach. They must mimic the footwork movements of the leader/coach, which, for example, include moving side-to-side, backpedaling, advancing, leaping, and taking a power step followed by a side dive that is slightly forward. In "Shadow Goalkeeping" the coach dictates the types of movements and saves to be imagined by the participants.

Serving a wide variety of shots to the 'keeper is useful. The goalie should be encouraged to move his feet to place his body into the line of the ball's trajectory as soon as possible and to catch the ball cleanly while using the appropriate technique.

Diving technique is quite challenging for the neophyte goalie. The player can learn in increments by starting on his knees as shots are kicked at a moderate pace along the ground to either side. His starting position should be upright and not with his body weight concentrated over the heels.

Progressions are to have the 'keeper start in a stance similar to that of a baseball catcher. Next, allow diving saves from an upright position but with him holding the ball from the start. Finally, the coach/server can strike shots so that he learns to deal with making saves on the line.

Among the coaching points: body square to the ball while diving slightly forwards; leading with the palm to attack the ball; looking through the "window"; getting as much of the body behind the ball as possible; propelling, bending, and lifting the knee during the dive; and trapping the ball, with the ground acting as the "third hand."

To improve dealing with through balls outside the penalty area the coach (or a server) is stationed about 10 yards beyond the "D." He touches a ball to the side and pushes it into the path of an onrushing attacker, who tries to score. The 'keepers change places after every attempt.

The server controls the pace of the passes. As such, balls can be played to favor the 'keeper, the attacker, or into a 50/50 confrontation. Since this exercise is primarily designed to benefit goalies, give consideration to placing some balls to favor the 'keeper whenever that individual appears to be struggling. This will lift confidence, and with it, performance.

As with all exercises, keep the goalie's starting position realistic (the coach/server has the option to chip a shot over any 'keeper who is "cheating"). Training is only fully useful if it is match-like. For example, when working on handling crosses to the back post, a 'keeper may be tempted to deepen the starting position. Your job is to make sure that he's learning to play the game and not the drill.

When working on breakaways, your coaching points include reminding 'keepers to advance rapidly on any long touch by the attacker, but to move under control with hands low and palms exposed to the shooter whenever the attacker maintains close control of the ball.

An alternative exercise is to have attackers, who are at least 40 yards from the goal, in groups of two with a ball between them. They pass back and forth while moving. The coach calls out one of the player's name and that individual races to goal on a breakaway. After a second or two the other player's name is called by the coach, whereupon that athlete attempts to catch his partner and to act as a second attacker. The 'keeper then must assess his options and rush out to meet the danger or close the potential shooters' angles. This produces a fairly realistic environment for both the attacking players and the goalkeepers.

Finishing exercises are also helpful for working on technique. However, coaches should take care that a goalie isn't allowed to work out for too long. Coaches who seek to make their goalies "tougher" by working them past the point of exhaustion greatly increase the likelihood of an injury.

Moreover, as the 'keeper becomes overly fatigued, the quality of his technique and his overall performance will drop. This is counterproductive to his needs and also to those of the attackers, who are now being allowed to perform in a false environment.

As goalkeepers mature, the nature of training progresses. Many goalie coaches like to use a series of exercises designed to upgrade footwork and mobility. For example, the coach/server is at the penalty spot. He flips a high ball that the goalie must advance to collect cleanly and return. As soon as that occurs a second ball is shot to either side of the goalkeeper.

Here are some other variables the goalkeeper may have to consider:

1. The ball is first dropped. The 'keeper charges out and dives on it. He must then retreat to tip a chipped serve over the crossbar.

2. A cross is hit from a wide position towards the near post. The 'keeper races forward to collect it cleanly. From the opposite side a server is wide of the other post and is positioned about 10–15 yards off of the goal line. That person hits a shot along the ground that the 'keeper must come across his goal to save.

3. The 'keeper must sprint forward to the penalty spot. He jumps up to touch a ball with both hands that is being held above the coach's head. The goalie then retreats to deal with a ball that is lofted over him.

4. The 'keeper makes a save on the line. He must recover and face an attacker on a breakaway.

As with field players, the most effective training tools are games that closely resemble match conditions. Small-sided contests (five-v-five up to eight-v-eight) in an appropriately-sized area give 'keepers ample work in an environment in which principles like positioning and the organizing of the defense are demanded.

Conclusion

The coaching of 'keepers can be an extremely intimidating prospect even for the most experienced of coaches who weren't themselves goalkeepers. Taking the time to educate yourself via books, videos, and clinics will help you overcome your reticence and to better serve players whose performances can either help your team to excel or hold it back.

U.S. Soccer offers coaching courses dedicated exclusively to helping you to work with your goalies. The curricula were put together by some of soccer's best 'keeper coaches.

The one-v-one confrontation (top and bottom) requires the goalkeeper's full confidence and supreme technique.

When Used:

To be prepared to make a save when a shot is anticipated.

Technical Tips:

1. The feet do not exceed shoulder width during the stance.
2. The hands are at the side with the palms facing the ball.
3. If the shooter is nearby the 'keeper's center of gravity and hand position are low.
4. The weight is on the balls of the feet as the shot is struck, with the body weight being forward. Alternatively, take a two-footed hop slightly upwards and forward so as to land on the balls of the feet as the shot is being kicked with the 'keeper's feet shoulder width apart.

When Used:

To catch any ball that is wide of or above the upper body.

Technical Tips:

1. Form a diamond behind the ball with the thumbs and index fingers.
2. Get as much of the body behind the ball as is possible.
3. The shoulders remain square to the incoming ball.
4. The first part of the body to touch the ball should be the hands.
5. Extend the hands forward and then withdraw them slightly to make them "softer" as the ball arrives.
6. With a locked neck to help keep the eyes steady, watch the ball intently until it is fully under control.
7. As soon as possible, the ball is curled into the chest.

Most Common Mistake(s):

Failure to extend fingers/thumbs so as to provide a barrier behind the ball.

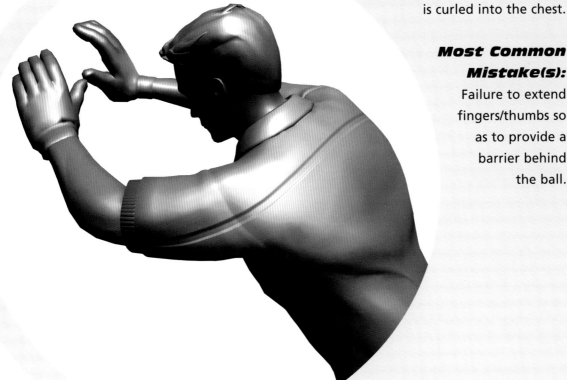

GOALKEEPING

THE CHEST CATCH

When Used:

To catch a ball that is struck at the upper body.

Technical Tips:

1. Move the feet to get the body into the ball's line of flight.

2. Get as much of the body behind the ball as is possible.

3. The shoulders remain square to the incoming ball.

4. Lean forward from the waist with the shoulders over the ball.

5. Extend both arms with palms facing upwards.

6. With a locked neck to help keep the eyes steady, watch the ball intently until it is fully under control.

7. As the ball arrives, surround the arms behind it to trap it against the chest with the elbows close together.

8. A slight jump may be used to bring an awkward shot into the chest.

9. For low shots that are at the 'keeper the body lunges forward as the ball is curled into the chest.

When Used:
To gather a ball that is rolling on the ground.

Technical Tips:
1. Move the feet so the ball arrives within the plane of the body.
2. Place the hands on the ground with the palms facing upwards.
3. The shoulders remain square to the incoming ball.
4. The first part of the body to touch the ball are the hands.
5. With the shoulders forward and the upper body over the ball, the legs form a back-up barrier behind the ball.
6. With a locked neck to help keep the eyes steady, watch the ball intently until it is fully under control.
7. The ball is scooped into the body. If the goalie has run forward to meet the ball the upper body lunges forward as the ball is caught.

Most Common Mistake(s):
Failure to watch the ball into the hands.

When Used:

When total extension is required to get to the ball.

Technical Tips:

1. The near-sided foot steps forward and sideways.

2. The initial stride is as long as possible and adjusts to the shot.

3. The far foot smoothly follows the lead foot.

4. The near-sided hand leads the body into the dive.

5. The near-sided hand comes behind the ball with the far-sided (top) hand coming over the plane of the ball to form a "window" for the keeper's eyes so that the ball may be seen throughout.

6. Dive forward to meet the ball. Proper footwork keeps the body perpendicular to the shot's trajectory. Following the catch the feet keep the body in line with the field.

7. The body remains parallel to the ground throughout.

8. After catching the ball the hands rotate slightly towards the field

so as to be above the ball. The ball contacts the ground just before the goalkeeper lands on his side.

9. The final position has the torso slightly concave as the shoulders remain square to the ball. The moderate bending of the upper body assists in attacking the ball and helps the 'keeper to fall slightly forward while smothering the ball. The body is comfortably wrapped around the ball.

10. Not all shots can be held. When opting for safety by parrying a shot over the cross-bar, the fingers extend upwards and the palm redirects the back of the ball. For shots to the upper net, the far-sided hand may come under the ball to push it over the bar. When parrying a ball past a goalpost the maximum hand surface is used.

Most Common Mistake(s):

1. Turning the body in midair to produce a belly flop (landing on the stomach).
2. Diving back-wards.

GOALKEEPING
THE COLLAPSE DIVE

When Used:

For low shots that are a foot or two to either side of the goalkeeper.

Technical Tips:

1. The feet do not exceed shoulder width during the stance.
2. The ball-side foot kicks in the opposite direction of the shot.
3. The body collapses to the ground with the hands down first.
4. The ball is caught, if possible, in front of the chest or against the chest.
5. Immediately cradle the ball to safety.
6. The knee of the top leg extends forward for protection.

Most Common Mistake(s):

Getting the body and the hands down late with the ball rolling under the 'keeper.

When Used:

To prevent an attacker from scoring on a breakaway.

Technical Tips:

1. The 'keeper stays on his feet for as long as possible, since remaining upright puts pressure on the attacker and may delay the opponent sufficiently to allow a defender to recover to provide assistance.

2. As the attacker approaches, the 'keeper advances forward with hands low and the palms exposed to the ball.

3. Separation of the attacker from the ball is a signal for the keeper to advance rapidly.

4. The goalie strides forward only at intervals in which the attacker is unable to make contact with the ball.

5. The 'keeper must remain well-balanced with feet at shoulder width. The goalie is prepared to change direction while the opponent is in contact with the ball.

6. When diving into the attacker's feet to smoother a shot, hands are close together and as near to the ball possible. The arms are extended across the face for added protection. An imaginary line drawn from the ball to the goal's center would dissect the goalie's chest.

When Used:

To safely deflect a high shot that can't be safely caught over the bar.

Technical Tips:

1. For a shot to either side, turn the body slightly sideways and use the hand that is nearer to the ball (i.e. when the ball is to the 'keeper's left the body is rotated counterclockwise with the right hand used to palm the ball over the bar).

2. For a shot directly above the 'keeper, the body remains square. A one-legged jump is used with the opposite-side knee lifted and the opposite-side hand contacting the ball.

3. When retreating for a dipping shot, the initial movement is a drop step (when turning counterclockwise the left foot is withdrawn) followed by a long crossover step by the other foot. If possible, short shuffling steps follow to try to get the body square to the flight of the ball.

4. In all cases, the fingers are elevated above the palm to expose the maximum surface area to the ball.

5. The palm is pushed upwards against the underside of the ball.

6. The goalie attempts to watch the ball for as long as possible.

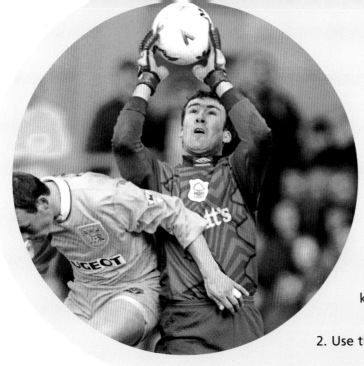

When Used:

To intercept a cross at the highest possible point so that the opposing attackers can't score with a header.

Technical Tips:

1. For maximum elevation, jump off one leg and lift the knee that is facing the play to add impetus to the leap.

2. Use the "diamond" ("W") to catch the ball.

3. If possible, slightly bend the elbows to help absorb the pace of the incoming cross.

4. Move into the ball's trajectory and make the catch with the shoulders square to the flight of the cross.

5. Immediately cradle the ball safely into the chest.

GOALKEEPING BOXING

When Used:

To fist the ball to safety when a crowded or uncertain situation creates the danger of dropping an attempted catch.

Technical Tips:

1. When retreating for a cross the 'keeper's path is parallel to that of the ball. The foot that is closer to the goal line plants while the opposite knee twists slightly to put the palms in line with the ball.

2. Time the leap while on the run to reach the ball at the highest possible point.

3. Jump off one foot with the knee that faces the field being lifted for protection and to provide added thrust.

4. To box the ball back from where it came use two fists with the thumb portions of the hands facing inwards.

5. Bend the elbows before moving arms in unison to punch the ball.

6. To box the ball in the same direction but with added height and distance the near-sided hand hits the far underside of the ball.

7. Clearance priorities are, in order; height, width, and distance.

Most Common Mistake(s):

Attempting to catch the ball when it isn't fully safe to do so. The 'keeper's mantra must be: "If in doubt, fist it out."

GOALKEEPING DISTRIBUTION

When Used:

To play the ball to a teammate to launch an attack.

Technical Tips:

1. Bowl the ball to a nearby teammate to make it easy to receive.
2. Drop-kick when faced with a brisk wind (but not on a treacherous playing surface).
3. Overhand/javelin-style throw when trying to quickly and accurately find an open teammate who is far away.
4. Punt the ball when avoiding a turnover or reducing pressure in one's half of the field is a major concern.

Most Common Mistake(s):

Throwing a ball to a teammate who is running away from and not looking at the goalkeeper. Throwing the ball to a teammate who is under pressure.

PART 5

Often, among the first courses of action for neophyte coaches to take is to seek advice on the "correct" formations to employ. That line of reasoning is easily understood given the context of a familiarity with sports like American football in which virtually every moment is dictated by coaches and scripted in a playbook.

But soccer is not about formations; it's about players. And youth soccer is all about developing good players. So while having a formation as your starting point may be a necessary evil, it must never be your focus. No formation will work with inferior players and every formation will bear fruit with superior players.

While the issues of 4-3-3 versus 4-4-2 are of some relevance, it is important that coaches and players understand the basic principles of play, which are applicable to every formation. These principles, however, only become relevant at such time as your players have acquired a requisite level of skill.

There is a soccer aphorism that there are no tactics without technique. And there are no effective tactics unless players can make quick and accurate decisions. Doing so requires information. One source is visual, as players constantly seek to calculate their options while anticipating situations that might arise. Another source is verbal, as players provide instruction to teammates whose positioning is such that their vision is temporarily limited.

The ability to make good decisions rapidly is known as tactical speed. It is a key component of successful plays and successful teams. Because effective play requires the fulfillment of both individual and collective principles, all players must understand the roles that they are expected to assume while defending and attacking.

In team sports, consider "transition" to be the actions that occur immediately following a turnover. In transition, the team that wins the ball quickly spreads out; the team that is now defending attempts to get a high number of players behind the ball and to be compact. The most important consideration is for the defender nearest to the ball to delay the opposition's ability to play forward for as long as possible.

Team transition sees one side adjusting from offense to defense while their opponents switch from defense to offense. Once the ball has been won by a defender, the player in possession of the ball becomes the attacker. The quick and decisive movements of his teammates are vital so that he can decide whether to dribble, lay the ball off to a teammate, or quickly play a penetrating pass that puts several opponents "out of the game."

While some teammates move in relation to the ball to aid the attack, several others position themselves to deal with any subsequent opposition counterattack should the ball be turned over.

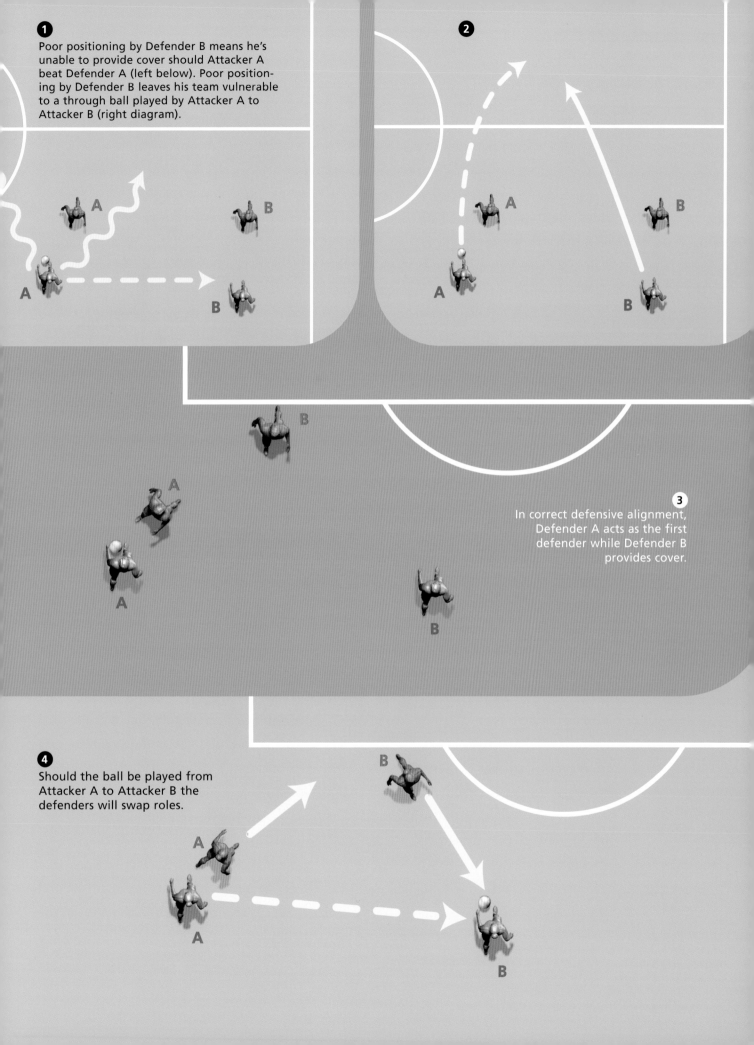

1

Poor positioning by Defender B means he's unable to provide cover should Attacker A beat Defender A (left below). Poor positioning by Defender B leaves his team vulnerable to a through ball played by Attacker A to Attacker B (right diagram).

2

3

In correct defensive alignment, Defender A acts as the first defender while Defender B provides cover.

4

Should the ball be played from Attacker A to Attacker B the defenders will swap roles.

A key issue during transition is the nature of how the ball was lost. Passes that were played forward only rarely result in quick counterattacks (unless the attacking team has so lost its defensive shape that it is vulnerable). Turnovers from square and backward passes usually allow the team that won the ball to play directly forward.

Another vital aspect of transition is that of individual transition: how players' roles alter with the movement of the ball and of other players, whether or not possession changes teams. Soccer is a free-flowing game. Thus, the role (and, with it, the primary demands) on each player usually changes as players move without the ball as well as when the ball is dribbled, passed, or shot.

The first defensive principle is that of immediate chase, as many members of the defending team sprint to get between the ball and their own goal. If possible, they quickly win the ball back. Should an attempt to regain possession not be deemed feasible or worth the perceived risk (for example, if a missed tackle might lead to a scoring opportunity), the secondary aim is to employ restraint and control so as to prevent offensive penetration while delaying the opposition. The best defenders are well positioned, patient, and stay on their feet between the attacker and goal whenever possible. This forces the offensive team to slow down, which allows more defenders to get behind the ball and become organized.

Depth is the organization of players behind the defender who is marking the opponent with the ball. It can be provided by one or several defenders. Creating defensive depth is especially important when the opponent in possession is unguarded.

Notice how in Diagram 1 Attacker A is in possession of the ball as Defender A has correctly moved forward to jockey and delay his opponent. Although Defender B is preventing a pass to Attacker B, he is not in a position to help Defender A should he be beaten by Attacker A. Nor, as shown in Diagram 2, is he able to prevent a through pass. His position in Diagram 3 discourages Attacker A from trying to penetrate by dribbling. And Defender B is now also able to prevent a through ball. Should Attacker A opt to pass the ball square to Attacker B, the defenders can exchange roles. Defender B will step up to pressure Attacker B while Defender A retreats to provide what is known as depth or cover.

Team compactness refers to the distance between the defending team's front players and its rear defenders. The greater the pressure on the opponent with the ball, the more compact that the defense can safely become. In other words, the closer the nearest defender is to the attacker in possession or the more defenders there are around the attacker, the less chance there is of a long ball being played over the top of the defense, the more compact the defense can afford to be, and the more pressure they can put on the ball and on opponents around the ball. Conversely, a lack of defensive pressure means the rear defenders need to be withdrawn so a long pass will not land behind them.

Concentration occurs as the defending team retreats towards its own goal. The outside players pinch inwards, particularly on the weak side (Diagram 5), the vertical side of the field farther from the ball. While Defender A seeks to prevent Attacker A from shooting or penetrating, Defenders B and C are providing cover. Both of them are well-positioned to deny a penetrating pass and to be able to close down their respective opponent should a pass in front of them be completed. This concentration of defenders reduces the time and space that attackers are granted in which to manipulate the ball to create a shot.

Concentration is also important in the other parts of the field to prevent penetration. It is therefore essential that the gaps that exist between the defenders remain smaller than the spaces between the attackers. This central "squeezing" of defenders behind the ball seeks to prevent passes from being played through the collective defending action. The defense's ambition must be to make the opponents play in front of them, never to let them get behind them.

Balance is the positioning of defenders relative to possible penetrating attackers who are not in immediate support of the ball (Diagram 7). To be properly balanced requires appropriate width and depth. To simply have one without the other, as shown by Diagram 6, is not sufficient.

Balancing defenders should be both goalside and ballside (on the side of the opponent closer to the ball) of the opposing attacker for whom they have primary responsibility. The positioning of balancing defenders is determined by the distance of the nearest opponent(s) to the ball. The greater that distance, the farther away the defender may be. As Diagram 7 shows, Defenders B, C, and D have taken up positions relative to Attackers B, C, and D, respectively. While Defender B provides cover, Defenders C and D offer balance.

Defenders C and D wish to be far enough off their opponent to be able to get to the ball first should a long diagonal pass land behind them and therefore deny immediate penetration. At the same time they must be close enough to be able either to intercept a pass that is played in front of them or, at least, be able to put the receiver under immediate pressure. Ideally, the receiver will be forced to accept the ball facing away from the direction in which he wishes to play. If that is not feasible, the receiver must be put under sufficient pressure so as to be denied the chance to penetrate.

These principles are applied when the opponent has possession. Players should be aware that effective defending begins with not giving the ball away unnecessarily while on offense.

5

In the diagram, with the ball in a cental attacking position, the defenders have "pinched in" to make a shot on goal very difficult. This action is known as concentration.

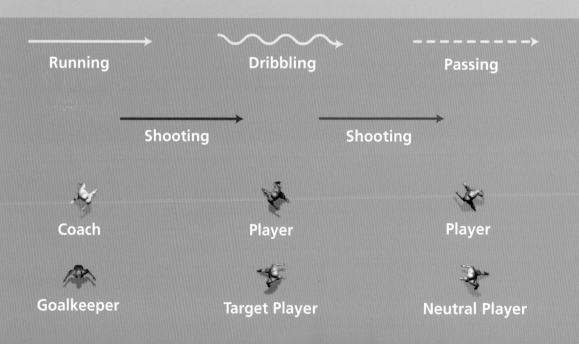

Running   Dribbling   Passing

Shooting   Shooting

Coach   Player   Player

Goalkeeper   Target Player   Neutral Player

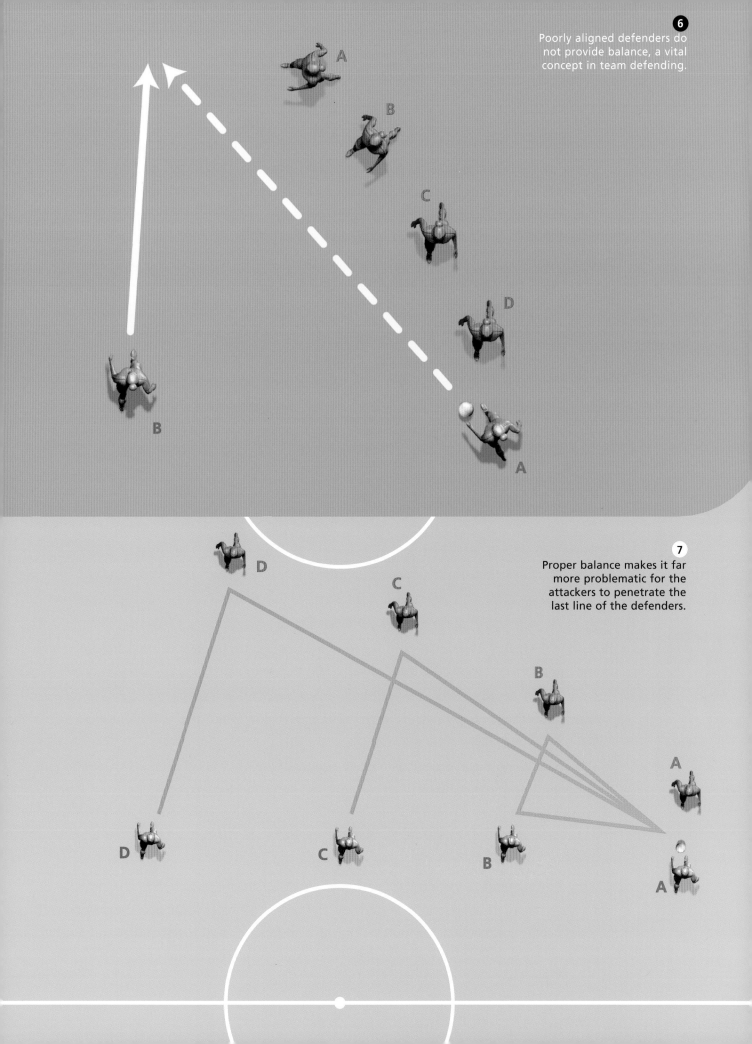

Poorly aligned defenders do not provide balance, a vital concept in team defending.

Proper balance makes it far more problematic for the attackers to penetrate the last line of the defenders.

In soccer we speak of "first," "second," and "third defenders." The first defender is the member of the defending team who is the closest to the opponent who has the ball (known as the "first attacker"). Second defenders are positioned to close down the first attacker should the first defender be beaten. This is known as providing "cover." They are also responsible for guarding ("tracking") the opponents who are in support of the first attacker (known as the "second attackers").The "third defenders" are all the other defenders, who are primarily concerned with the spaces and opponents in advance of the ball.

There are several tactical considerations that individual defenders must weigh. The most important is that the starting (marking) position before the ball is played to his opponent allows him to be first to any passes played behind him and also allows him to intercept a pass or pressurize his opponent should that player receive a pass. As the ball is traveling to the opponent, the defender may make up the distance between his starting position and the opponent at maximum speed. However, as the opponent is about to make his first touch on the ball, the first defender must slow down and pressure the attacker in a controlled manner. His priorities are: (1) to win the ball back; (2) to deny penetration; (3) to limit his opponent's vision and options.

When selecting his speed and angle of approach, the first defender measures his rival's speed and ability versus that of his own, the presence and positioning (or lack thereof) of second attackers and of covering defenders, and the area of the field in which the confrontation occurs (see Diagram 14).

If the attacker is appreciably faster than the first defender, then the defender may feint, as if to get close to the opponent (by an exaggerated forward movement of the shoulders) but quickly retreat just as the attacker is about to contact the ball. Just after the attacker pushes the ball forward, the defender can poke the ball away.

As always, decisions involving how much risk-taking is prudent should be conservative when the confrontation is in the defensive third, when the opponent is an especially dangerous player, and/or when there are no covering defenders.

By angling his approach and body position (see Technique section: "Marking the Opponent"), the first defender further hopes to limit the first attacker's options. He may attempt to funnel the first attacker into dribbling away from the center of the field, towards a tight space near one of the touchlines, into a covering defender, and/or to make the attacker play the ball with the weaker foot.

While doing so he retreats at approximately the same speed as the attacker is advancing. He hopes to get sufficiently close to the first attacker so that the attacker's eyes are forced to look down at the ball, so that the opponent's options go unnoticed, and he becomes more vulnerable. At this point defenders apply more pressure—with the covering defender attempting to win the ball while the other defenders rotate accordingly. By denying penetration and making the first attacker predictable, the first defender allows his teammates to "read" the situation. They may then assume more effective positions.

The temptation to gamble to win the ball back by the first defender must be resisted if the situation dictates prudence. The best defenders do not "sell themselves" by diving into tackles when the failure to win the ball could gift the opposition with a great opportunity. They must take special care not to recklessly challenge for the ball. This is an especially important consideration after the opponents have just achieved penetration. By being prudent, they buy time for teammmates to be able to recover from the previous penetrating action.

The nearest second defender(s) provides cover for the first defender. This is accomplished by being at the proper angle and distance from the first defender. The second defender should be able to put pressure immediately on the first attacker if that opponent gets past the first defender. He is positioned so that one move by the attacker cannot beat both the first defender and himself.

There will be situations in which the first attacker is isolated and thus lacks immediate passing options. When that occurs the first defender may force the first attacker towards the second defender so that either of them—but usually the covering defender—can tackle to win the ball. Second defenders need to be cognizant of clogging passing lanes to prevent and/or intercept attempted penetrating passes.

Their positioning is such that should the ball be played to the attacker they are tracking, they should have a chance at an interception. Barring that, they wish to be able to challenge for the ball as the attacker attempts to receive it. At the very least, the second defender must be able to quickly close down the receiver in a timely manner so as to eliminate his ability to further penetrate the defense.

The third defenders remain compact and concentrated relative to their teammates so as to limit the space that is available for the attacking team to exploit. By squeezing space towards the center of the field they aim to preserve their team's balance and defensive shape so as to prevent penetration. Those on the weak side of the field understand that the primary immediate danger for offensive penetration is the space behind them, into which a ball may be played for a third attacker. Third defenders act collectively in concert as if there was an invisible string that was linking them together. Thus, the movement of one necessitates movements by the rest. They are aided by verbal instruction from their goalkeeper since the 'keeper has the greatest field of vision of any player in the defensive team.

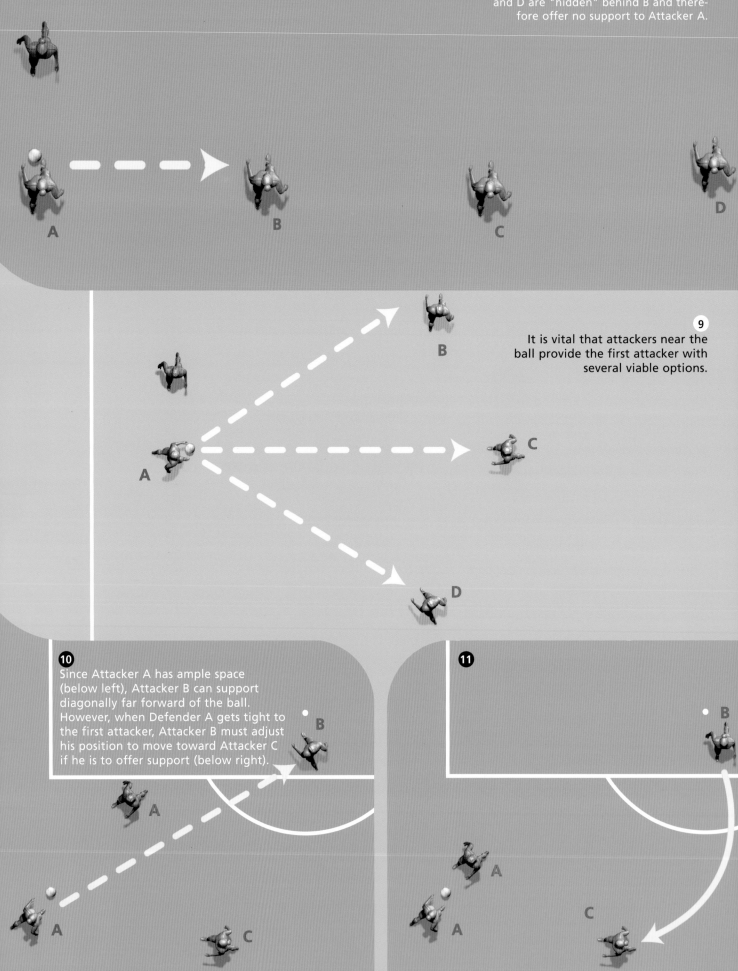

In this poorly aligned attack, Attackers C and D are "hidden" behind B and therefore offer no support to Attacker A.

It is vital that attackers near the ball provide the first attacker with several viable options.

10
Since Attacker A has ample space (below left), Attacker B can support diagonally far forward of the ball. However, when Defender A gets tight to the first attacker, Attacker B must adjust his position to move toward Attacker C if he is to offer support (below right).

11

Attacking Principles

In an effort to score goals the offense utilizes support, width, mobility, improvisation, and penetration.

Support involves the organization of attackers behind, in advance of, and in lateral positions to the first attacker. This provides immediate passing options to the first attacker and allows the offense to maintain possession despite defensive pressure, thereby creating chances to penetrate. Support, as shown correctly in Diagram 9, incorporates having adequate depth, which is the disposition of attackers in advance of and behind the ball.

The supporting player can have greater depth and distance if the first attacker is not under pressure (Diagram 10). However, the angle and distance of support changes as defensive pressure placed upon the first attacker increases (Diagram 11).

Width is the disposition of attackers and the utilization of space across the field. It is used to help pull apart the opposition so that the defending team is unable to remain sufficiently concentrated. The difference between having proper (Diagram 13) versus inadequate width (Diagram 12) is the difference between allowing the defense to keep its concentration versus pulling it apart and creating space and channels.

The movements (mobility) of attackers without the ball so as to unbalance the collective defending efforts of the opponent are also vital to helping to achieve penetration. These runs allow attackers to enter spaces into which a pass may be played to them. Additionally, movement in and of itself is valuable as it forces defenders to make decisions: to hold and let their man run free or to go with their opponent and leave space for another attacker to move into.

Penetration is a very straightforward concept: the ability to get the ball behind defenders by dribbling, passing, or shooting.

Any and all of the above attacking principles are used for one primary purpose; to create an opportunity to score. They lead to the most important aspect of soccer; a team's ability to finish.

The Roles of Attackers

In order to consistently maintain possession and to be able to penetrate the defense when appropriate, attacking players need to be comfortable performing in all three roles: penetration, support, and running off the ball.

The first attacker (the player who has the ball) attempts to penetrate, whenever feasible. He selects the technique best suited to solve the tactical dilemma with which he is confronted. That process involves weighing the game situation, his location on the

field, the positioning and relative abilities of teammates versus opponents, and his own technical strengths and weaknesses.

The preferred option of the first attacker is to attempt to score a goal or get the ball to a teammate who is better positioned to do so. If neither is possible, the next best choice is to achieve penetration by passing or dribbling.

The second attacker(s) is in immediate support of the first attacker. The distance and angle is predicated upon the defensive pressure (or lack thereof) to which the first attacker is being subjected. It is essential that the supporting angle is such that one defender cannot restrict both attackers.

The second attacker must be an appropriate distance from the ball, meaning that he is not so far away that a pass to him can be intercepted, yet he must not be supporting so closely that the first defender can slide in to place immediate pressure on him after he has received the ball.

The third attacker(s) works to unbalance the defensive team by making constructive runs that help to increase the attacking team's options. Most of these runs are intended to penetrate the defense. But, runs across the face of the defense and diagonal runs can be utilized to create space and unbalance the defense, providing openings for teammates to use.

Thirds of the Field

For tactical purposes a soccer field is defined by horizontal thirds. The ratio of risk-taking to safety should increase the closer that a team gets to the opposition's goal and vice versa.

In the rear third (see Diagram 14), the offense's primary consideration is to avoid turnovers. By contrast, in the front third, risk-taking is not only encouraged but is an essential element to creating scoring chances. The mentality of effective attackers is a key ingredient: they must be willing to endure several failed attempts without getting discouraged. Because the front third tends to be crowded with defenders, there is a premium placed on the ability of the attackers to beat opponents one-v-one (dribbling) and through combination play. The inclination to "make things happen" wins games and is a major factor separating great players and teams from the rest.

Defensive tactics also take into account the zone in which the confrontation occurs. The first defender is usually encouraged to take risks to win back the ball in the front third but must be aware of the importance of safety in his own third. The defense is most concerned with preventing penetration, especially shots. Prudence is demanded, with players having to understand the potential consequences of giving the ball away on offense or gambling on a risky tackle while defending.

Depth also changes. When the ball is in the front third the area that is being

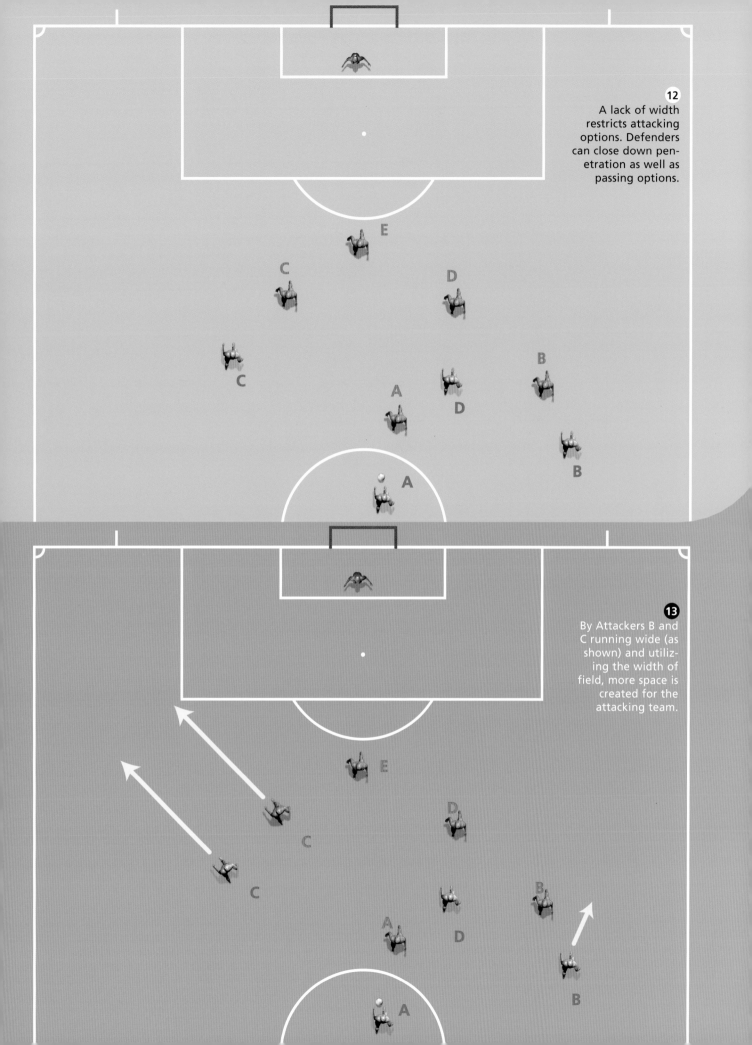

12
A lack of width restricts attacking options. Defenders can close down penetration as well as passing options.

13
By Attackers B and C running wide (as shown) and utilizing the width of field, more space is created for the attacking team.

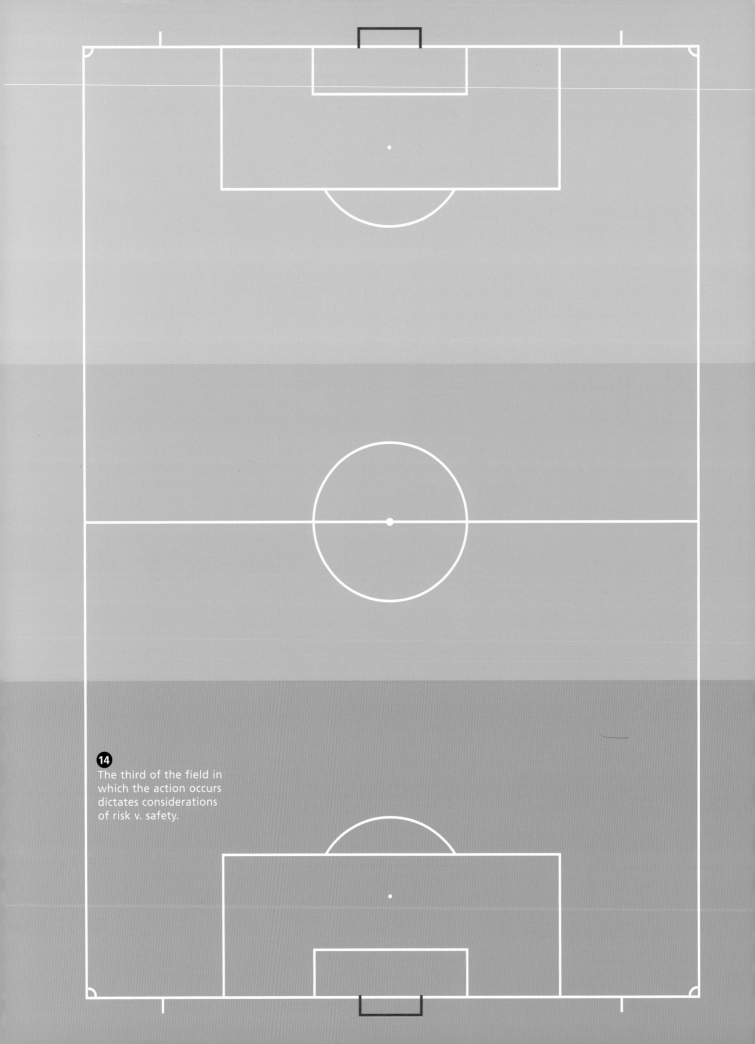

14
The third of the field in which the action occurs dictates considerations of risk v. safety.

defended is far longer than when play is in the rear third. When the ball is in the opponent's half at least some defenders must be sufficiently withdrawn so that a long pass cannot beat the entire defense.

When the action is in the rear third and within shooting range, the second defender nearest to the first defender provides cover with less depth than would be appropriate in the other two-thirds of the field. The reason is that any movement to get open by the first attacker must be immediately addressed by the second defender. The second defender must apply pressure so as to deny that opponent any chance to finish. Thus, the danger to be addressed involves not only the possibility of penetration but also any sideways movement that creates a shooting opportunity.

Considerations in the rear third include maintaining numerical superiority, defending one-v-one confrontations successfully, controlled aggression with discipline, and an added premium on adhering to the principles of pressure, cover, and balance.

Midfield Tactics

There is a balance of safety-v.-risk in the midfield third. As soon as possible, midfielders attempt to connect and combine with the forwards. Until then, possession is valued. In most situations in which an offensive player opts to dribble in the midfield third he does so by attacking a space to create passing angles and penetrating options rather than to take on a defender.

Offensive midfield decision-making includes selecting whether to go directly to the opposition's goal or to build up deliberately. The number of defenders who are goalside, available space, and the ability of attackers to penetrate must be considered.

After gaining the ball back the attacking team seeks to penetrate as soon as possible. Forward and through passes are encouraged, with attackers off the ball rushing into advanced open spaces and providing immediate options. Ideally, a quick scoring opportunity will result. Conversely, the first defender hopes either to win the ball back or, more likely, to attempt to delay the counterattack to buy time for his teammates to recover.

When the chance for a quick counter is not present, the offensive team builds up the attack. Maintaining possession until the opportunity to penetrate is presented is critical as it allows the back players time to provide additional attacking options. It also allows forwards to make positive runs to be available to receive the ball.

At the higher levels of soccer the midfield can dictate a game's tempo. There can be considerable value to maintaining possession while forcing the opposition to expend energy chasing on defense. Quite often, this will pay dividends as the opponents lose concentration and have their fitness tested.

To utilize the principles of attack (support, width, mobility, penetration, and improvisation) involves players understanding basic offensive tactics coupled with possessing a sufficient level of technical ability to execute effectively.

Penetration may be gained through improvisation, particularly dribbling, but also by team play. The latter becomes far easier to achieve when the attacking team combines support, mobility, and width/depth to pull apart the defense while providing the first attacker with viable alternatives to dribbling.

Individual Penetration

Penetration can derive from improvisation, which is the flair and creativity of individuals that is most often evident through dribbling and well-disguised passes. The ability of a first attacker to deceive defenders with cleverness is especially valued at the higher levels of the game, where time and space are at a premium.

Combination Play

Combination play occurs when two or more attackers interact via passing and moving to maintain possession and/or to penetrate the defense. Two-player combinations include the wall pass, the double pass, takeovers, and overlaps. Ideally these will lead to a pass that creates a goal-scoring opportunity, such as a through ball or a cross.

The wall pass is soccer's give-and-go. It is used to gain penetration (Diagram 15). The double pass is, basically, a wall pass plus one (Diagram 16). Attacker A plays the ball forward and moves laterally to receive a return pass. After laying the ball off, the original receiver (Attacker B) makes a diagonal penetrating run. He then gets the penetrating pass in the space behind the defenders.

A takeover occurs when the first attacker dribbles the ball towards a teammate. The receiver accepts the ball as he moves into the space that was created behind the original first attacker's run. Takeovers are most commonly used in two-v-two confrontations. They usually serve to unbalance the defense while allowing for the player taking over to immediately penetrate with a run, pass, or shot. An alternative is for the original player to keep the ball so as to penetrate while a teammate serves as a decoy.

When executing a takeover, the first attacker shields the ball from the first defender. Thus, the foot that is farther from the goal/center of the field is typically used. The second attacker receives the ball with the foot that is closer to the goal/center of the field. The "same foot" technique (right foot to right foot or left

15

Attacker A and Attacker B set up the opportunity to pull off a wall pass. Attacker A dribbles, passes to Attacker B, then runs into an open space to receive a return pass.

16

The double pass is used to spring the original receiver behind the final line of defenders (Attacker A passes to Attacker B, moves square, B passes back to A, and A passes through to B).

17

Takeovers are most often utilized in two-v-two situations in which space is at a premium.

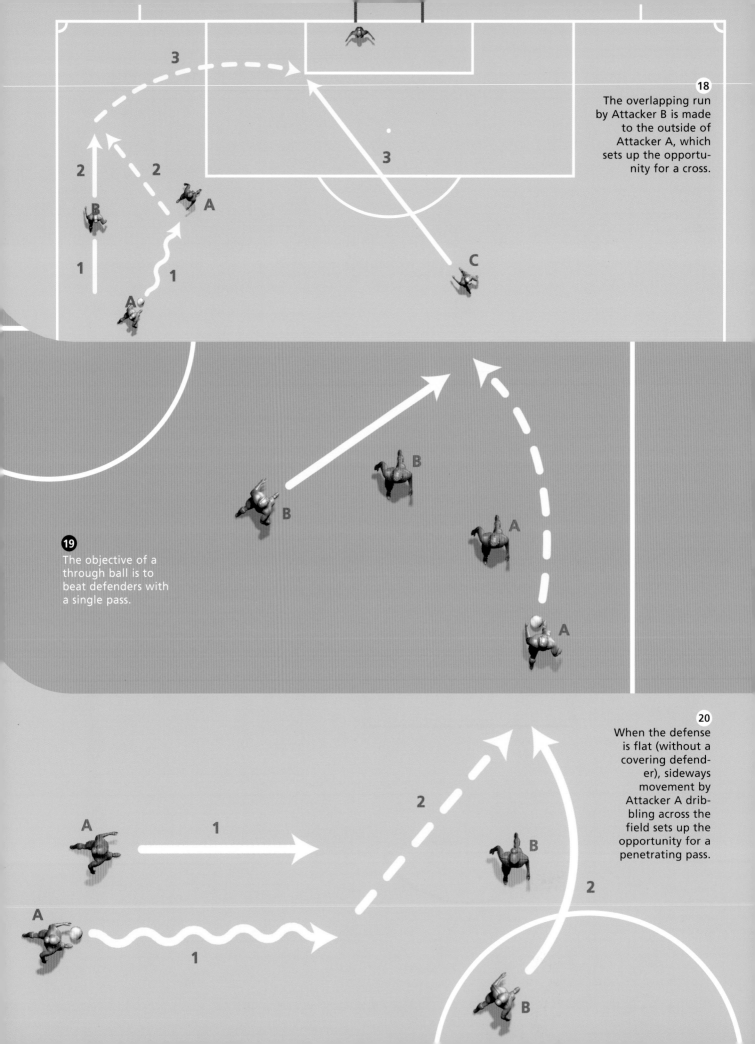

18
The overlapping run by Attacker B is made to the outside of Attacker A, which sets up the opportunity for a cross.

19
The objective of a through ball is to beat defenders with a single pass.

20
When the defense is flat (without a covering defender), sideways movement by Attacker A dribbling across the field sets up the opportunity for a penetrating pass.

foot to left foot) always applies.

An overlap sees a second attacker running in a wide position in advance of the first attacker. It is generally used in the front third of the field so as to spring an attacker around the defense's flank. (The mobility of the second attacker can also serve to make him a decoy so that the first attacker can gain penetration by dribbling). In Diagram 18, Attacker A dribbles at the first defender and towards the goal. By doing so, he creates the opportunity to play the ball ahead for his overlapping teammate. As Attacker B receives and prepares the ball, Attacker C can begin a diagonal run into the box to receive a cross.

A through ball is a pass that is played into a space behind the defense for an attacker to run onto. It is effective if there is no covering defender or the covering defender has left too large of a gap between himself and the first defender. In Diagram 19 the ball is played outside of the first defender after the second attacker has initiated the movement with an angled penetrating run.

In Diagram 20, the covering defender is poorly positioned. The first attacker prepares the ball by moving it toward a teammate before passing the ball into the space that is behind the second defender. Through balls have the best chance of working when the receiver's run and/or the path of the ball is on a diagonal plane. Attackers should try to avoid straight-line passes to straight-line runs, whenever possible.

Crosses are passes that are aimed centrally from a wide and/or deep position in the opponent's third of the field. An accurate and timely delivery creates real danger to the defense. Balls played into the near post area (as shown in Diagram 21) should be driven forcefully so that the defense has little time to react, while the receiver needs only to redirect a first-touch shot. Balls played to and beyond the far post are lofted over defenders.

Crosses are almost always aimed in the space that is beyond the goalkeeper's range of interception while still being behind the last line of defenders. The velocity and trajectory of near-post serves (hard and low) allows them to be delivered far closer to the goal line than with most balls that are lofted deep. For either a cross or a through ball, the timing of the receiver's run is important. It is initiated after the first attacker has prepared the ball so that it may be passed and eye contact has been made between the two attackers.

When an attacker penetrates to get to the defending team's byline (goal line) the ball is usually passed diagonally backwards in the penalty area. The cutback, as illustrated in Diagram 22, is an especially effective form of a cross because the first attacker has typically drawn the attention of defenders and forced the 'keeper to

come to the front post, thus leaving a large portion of the goal exposed. Attacker A moves goalward. As he is confronted, the ball is played to a supporting teammate (Attacker B). At advanced levels, three-player combinations are an option. A third player penetrates by having participated in a combination play that involved two other attackers. In Diagram 23, the first attacker plays the ball to an advanced player (Attacker B), while the supporting player (Attacker C) moves forward to be available for a layoff. Next, Attacker B passes back to Attacker C and then makes a clearing run. Meanwhile, the initial attacker completes the move by making a run to be available for Attacker C's penetrating pass.

Possession with a Purpose

Not every situation calls for trying to get behind the defense. When the opposition is well organized and has numerical superiority, it is prudent for the attacking team to play the ball across the field—and, if necessary, backwards—until the opportunity to go forward to penetrate has been created. Good teams rarely give the ball away unnecessarily. They understand that there are three major benefits from maintaining possession. The primary purpose is to keep the ball while looking for opportunities to penetrate the defense to score a goal. Second, the best defense is a good offense since—barring a huge blunder—the opponents cannot score without the ball. Finally, keeping possession forces opponents to do a lot of running, which is both tiring and frustrating. Quite often, the team that has been forced to chase a lot will struggle in the late stages of a game. Playing accurate passes to the feet of teammates or to space for a player to run onto is a key to maintaining possession. So is passing-and-moving using a minimum of touches. Also important are to dribble to open space and to have support available with which to combine. A lateral or backward pass is usually indicative that great defensive pressure exists in that portion of the field. Because of the concentration of defenders, it is rare when the receiver of a lateral or backwards pass should play the ball back in the direction from which it came.

Therefore, second attackers who are behind the ball normally provide support at an inside angle. That player has an "open" body position to view other parts of the field to allow him to assess his options prior to receiving the ball. If there are a lot of defenders between the first attacker and the goal, the offensive team may opt to switch the point of attack (see Diagram 24). As shown, this is done by playing across the field, which is often initiated by passing towards the middle of the field with the ball usually being passed diagonally backwards. In this case, Attacker A has

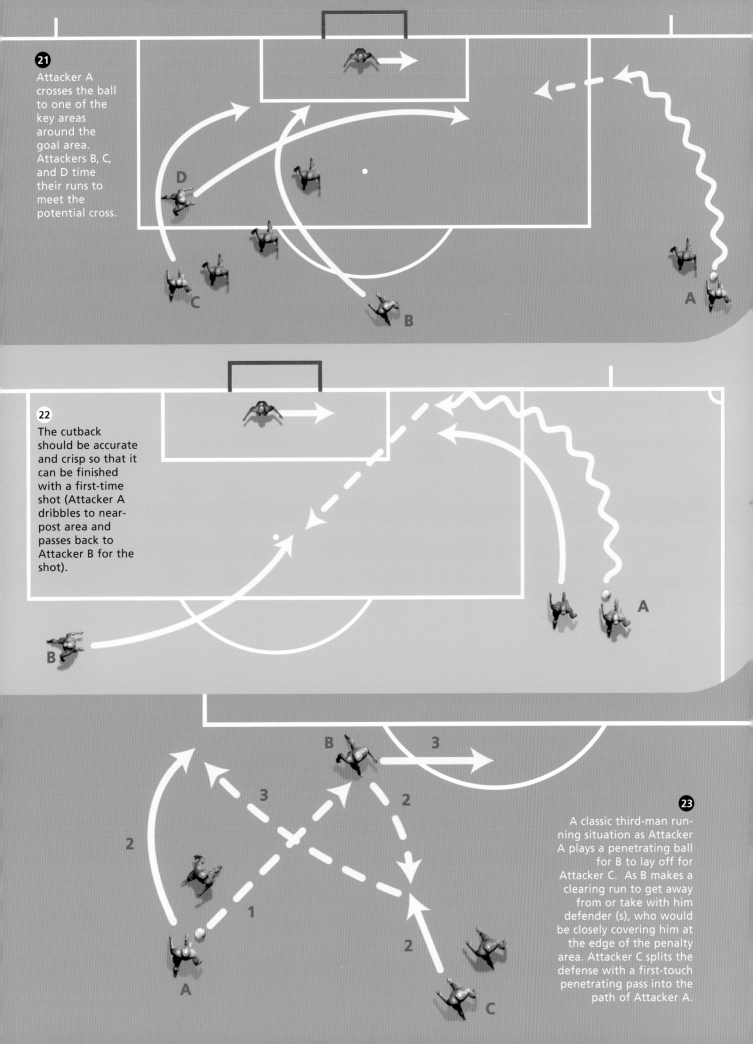

21

Attacker A crosses the ball to one of the key areas around the goal area. Attackers B, C, and D time their runs to meet the potential cross.

22

The cutback should be accurate and crisp so that it can be finished with a first-time shot (Attacker A dribbles to near-post area and passes back to Attacker B for the shot).

23

A classic third-man running situation as Attacker A plays a penetrating ball for B to lay off for Attacker C. As B makes a clearing run to get away from or take with him defender (s), who would be closely covering him at the edge of the penalty area. Attacker C splits the defense with a first-touch penetrating pass into the path of Attacker A.

24

If the attacking team is unable to play the ball forward on one side of the field, Attacker B changes direction of play to attack on the opposite side.

little opportunity for penetration. He plays the ball to Attacker B who, in turn, quickly passes the ball into the path of Attacker C's run.

When working on possession/changing the point of attack, the coach emphasizes tactical and technical speed. Achieving these will make the ball "run faster" than any defender, thus not allowing opponents to recover into effective defensive positions before the ball can be played again. This is achieved by aiming crisp cross-field passes to the foot of the receiver that is farther from the attacker. The receiver, in turn, plays the ball forward or across the field using the minimum number of passes. The receiver's first touch is away from defensive pressure. And the ball is received and subsequently passed using the minimum number of possible touches.

Of the five principles of attack, offensive mobility remains a very important quality to emphasize to our youth players, U.S. Soccer's national coaching staff has prioritized improving the movements of our players off the ball. Not only is mobility vital for players off-the-ball, so as to create space while providing viable passing options for the first attacker, but it is also useful after an attacker has passed or shot. Even experienced defenders often suffer a lapse in concentration. As that occurs, there is a brief opportunity for that attacker to move decisively and intelligently so as to be available to receive a return pass behind several (or all) of the defenders, or to be first to a loose ball after a shot has been struck.

Maintaining Team Shape

Another important coaching point is to attempt to keep a good "shape." There are several instances in which withdrawn attackers make penetrating runs without the ball. These movements usually come as a team has changed the point of attack and serve to give the attackers a numerical advantage. An overlap, for example, often unbalances the defense by forcing a central defender to move into a wide position. In doing so, valuable central space is exposed for other attackers to exploit. While such runs can be a very effective attacking weapon, they do leave the offensive team vulnerable to a counterattack should a turnover occur. Thus, the maintaining of team "shape" is very important. As that withdrawn player surges forward, a teammate should slide over to occupy the vacated space behind the ball. Meanwhile, other teammates make appropriate adjustments so as to make certain that there aren't gaps that could be exploited.

A significant percentage of goals are scored on restarts. A team's ability to take advantage of direct and indirect free kicks, penalty kicks, corner kicks, and throw-in opportunities while effectively defending against opponents' restarts takes on added importance as the teenage years beckon. The keys to success for all forms of restarts are the quality of the service, timing of the runs, and, when appropriate, the precision of the finishing.

Quite often, the sounding of the whistle alone causes players temporarily to lose concentration. The team that organizes itself and acts more quickly gains the advantage. For the defense it is imperative that opponents in potentially dangerous positions are marked. In the case of a free kick within shooting range a wall must be quickly constructed and properly positioned. If the defense is slow to organize itself the attacking team should capitalize by quickly and effectively restarting play. Even if the defense is prepared the attackers still retain several advantages. Among these are the chance to move players into prime predesignated attacking positions, the kicker/thrower being able to serve a dead ball without defensive pressure, and the chance to execute a series of choreographed (but simple!) movements.

Offensive Tactics: Corner Kicks

Most corner kicks are flighted directly into the opponent's goalmouth. These are known as long corners. Balls that curve towards the goal are called inswingers. When the ball's trajectory swerves away from the goal it is referred to as an outswinger. Balls played deep (beyond the center of the goal) are flighted to clear the initial line of defenders. Any cross aimed towards the near post area is driven at or slightly above head height. In general, the most effective corner kick option is the inswinger driven to the near post area. With all corners the decision as to how far from the goal to aim involves the kicker taking into account the range, ability, and aggressiveness of the opposing goalkeeper. Another option is the short corner kick, which helps to pull defenders out of the central area and provides a better angle from which to deliver the cross (see diagrams on following pages).

Offensive Tactics: Throw-ins

Long throw-ins are a prevalent and effective weapon in an attacking arsenal. In the offensive third of the field the priority is to create a scoring chance, with the ball usually aimed towards a centrally positioned target player, who flicks it on toward goal or across the goalmouth. Throw-ins from deeper positions are taken with the objective being to maintain possession and redeploy the team so the attacker has maximum support.

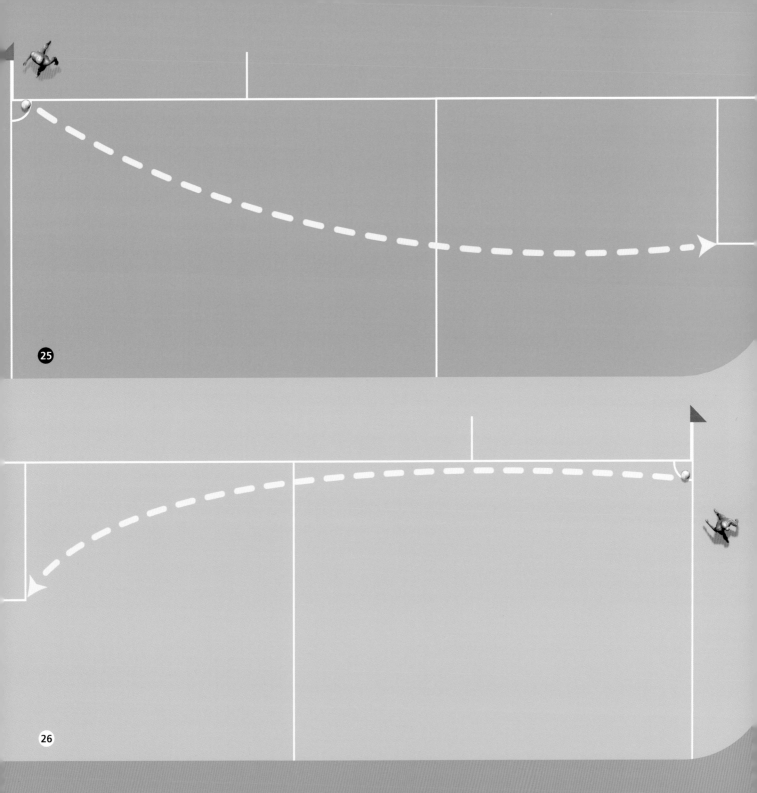

25

26

Inswinger and Outswinger

To produce an inswinger from the left corner (top diagram) the ball is placed in the corner arc as shown and the kicker stands behind the goal line. The ball is approached from an angle and kicked with the right foot. For an outswinger (above diagram) the kicker stands beyond the touchline and upfield from the flag. The ball is placed in the corner arc as shown and it is kicked with the right foot.

Long Corners

Attacker A is effective at heading. His job is to flick a cross directly into the net or to redirect the ball across the face of the goal for a teammate to shoot. Attackers B and C must also be good headers, aggressive, and find space. For balls played beyond the far post they may retreat to gain space before moving forward again. Attackers D and E read the trajectory of the cross and meet the ball in midair. Attackers F and G move horizontally to win any weak clearances and be available for a back pass. If possible, they will shoot quickly, because a shot blocked would launch a counterattack.

Short Corner Kick Option

Two common varieties of the short corner. The ball is played to a teammate on the goal line who lays back a first-touch angled pass that is immediately crossed into the box (top). Alternatively, a second attacker stands inside of the corner-kick taker (above). The ball is passed to the second attacker, who dribbles goalward as the original kicker makes a run around his teammate. When confronted with a defender the dribbler lays the ball back to the teammate, who can then shoot or cross or feint a pass and attack the near post on the dribble.

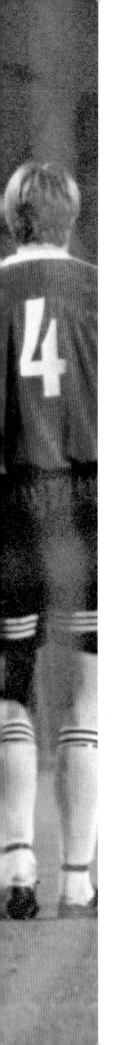

In either situation, it is advantageous if the throw can be taken quickly, before the defense has time to get itself organized. The attackers must move to get open. When throwing the ball to a teammate the principles of good passing apply—with accuracy and appropriate pace being important. Usually, the throw is aimed at the feet so that it may be controlled more easily and quickly.

Because aerial confrontations are common on long throw-ins into the penalty area it is advisable to position the players who are the most effective at heading as receivers. This often necessitates placing one or more defenders in the opposition's penalty area. When doing so be sure that other players are positioned to protect against any subsequent counterattack. The thrower's job does not end with the ball's delivery. After a long throw he immediately runs on to the field. When throwing a ball to a facing teammate's feet he may move into a supporting position to be able to receive a return pass.

Long throw-ins tend to be delivered with far greater accuracy than corners. For both types of deliveries, other attackers may make well-timed diagonal goalward runs behind the target player to get into prime scoring positions as the ball, flicked on by the target player, arrives. A player arriving too late will miss the chance. A player arriving too soon will probably have to stop himself and be still just long enough to be marked.

Defending Against Corner Kicks and Long Throw-ins

When faced with an opposition corner kick, one defender is placed on the goal line 10 yards from the ball. This forces the long corner to be struck with increased loft, thus giving the goalkeeper more time and a space to intercept the cross. Moreover, even the moderate pressure of a defender positioned in the ball's anticipated line of flight could induce a poor kick.

For an inswinger the goalkeeper stands on the line with the body in an "open" position (Diagrams 30, 31). Most 'keepers prefer to start in the rear half of their goal, as it is far easier to move forwards than backwards. However this position may have to be modified, particularly if the field is narrow or a dominating opposing target player is in the near post area. For an outswinger most 'keepers will stand a yard or two off the goal line.

Another defender is placed on the near post. It is his job to clear any balls that are played in his direction. He should "hold" the post until he is sure that the ball will arrive upfield of him. This will guard against the danger of an inswinger traveling between himself and the post while also protecting against rendering the 'keeper temporarily unsighted by his movement.

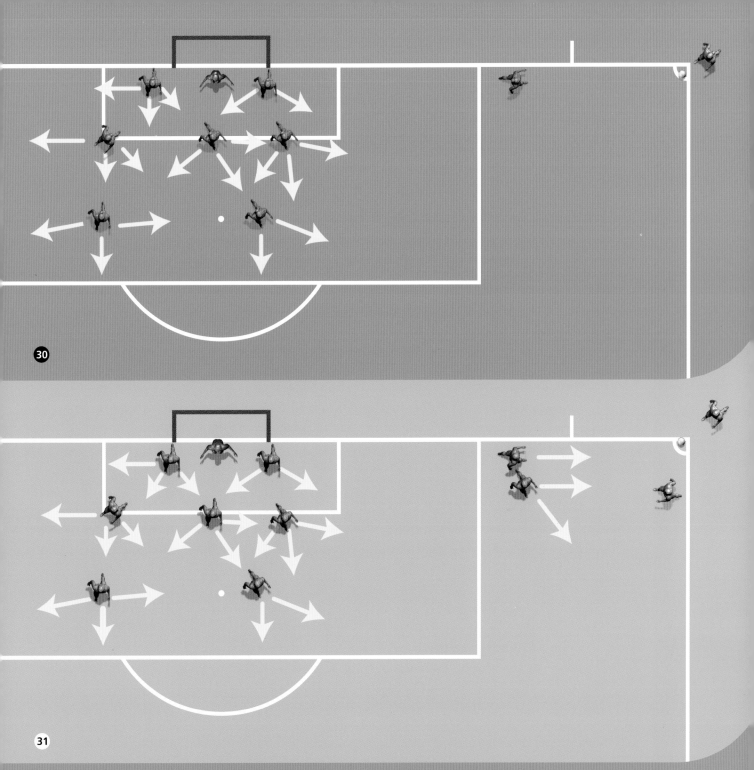

30

31

Defending Against Corners

Each defender is responsible for the danger zones to his side and front, with the defenders on the posts also required to cover the goal should the 'keeper fail to collect a cross. If the attacking team places two players near the ball, another member of the defending team should immediately move to be 10 yards from the ball (it is preferable that this individual is the midfielder on that side of the field rather than to pull a defender out of the prime central zone). The defenders around the near post and the one in the middle of the six-yard box must be very aggressive and good in the air while the defenders on the posts should be skillful enough to not miss or mis-kick shots that arrive awkwardly.

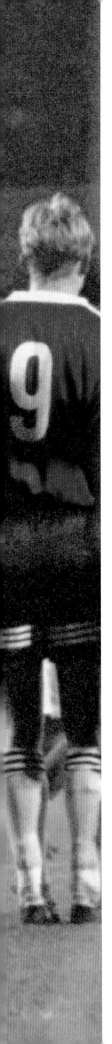

Many teams use another defender to guard the back post. Should the 'keeper leave the line to collect the ball, the player(s) on the post(s) move inward to cover the goal.

A team's most effective player in the air can be used to mark his counterpart on the opposition or be placed centrally on the six-yard box. The defending team should be sufficiently well-organized so that the key danger areas (near post, far post, and central goalmouth) are accounted for at all times. At older levels, it is the goalkeeper's job to position teammates prior to the kick or throw-in being taken.

Some teams opt to run elaborate restarts in which a number of players stand outside or near the top of the penalty box before making choreographed runs. It is a mistake for the defending team to mark such players tightly while they are far away from the goal. Doing so opens up gaps in key areas. Moreover, should the defender get to the ball first the subsequent clearance would have to be performed while running towards his own goal.

Instead, place defenders in intelligent positions at the key spots inside the penalty area. This zonal concept is predicated on the ability and inclination of every defender to attack the ball should it arrive within playing distance. It is imperative that the ball is not allowed to land inside the penalty area and that no attacker is given an uncontested touch. All clearances should be struck high, wide, and far (in that order of priority).

The tactics for defending against long throw-ins are similar. However, when tracking opponents a two- to three-yard buffer zone is advisable. That will allow time to challenge for the ball while guarding against a penetrating run. Two defenders are assigned to mark the likely target player with one defender behind him and the other between him and the ball.

In all these situations the ability of the 'keeper to organize the defense and to command the area in front of the goal are vital assets; the defenders in turn must attack the ball.

Penalty Kicks

Surprisingly often a team's most accomplished penalty-kick taker is not the superstar striker but a player whose psychological strength allows him to thrive under pressure. There is far more pressure on the shooter than on the goalie.

The 'keeper has very little chance of making a save if the shot is struck with accuracy and/or power. Thus, many goalies attempt to unnerve the shooter by moving their arms, rocking back and forth, and feinting in one direction. All of this is done in the hope of planting indecision in the shooter's mind.

The taker should concentrate on striking the ball cleanly and on hitting a predetermined target, low or high just inside a goalpost. He should pay as little attention to the goalkeeper as is possible. Also key is taking care to place the ball on the ground so that it is stationary and so that it is not inside a rut.

Before the kick, members of both teams are positioned on the nearest restraining lines. They should be determined to arrive first to any rebounds. When the ball ricochets off of a goalpost or a crossbar it is live but must initially be played by someone other than the kicker. If the penalty-kick taker plays it before another player does, the defending team is awarded an indirect free kick from the spot of the second touch. Should the ball come off of the 'keeper it is live for all players. Any defender who gets to a rebound should immediately clear the ball in the direction that he is facing, even at the expense of conceding a corner kick.

Free Kicks

If a direct or indirect free kick is awarded in the middle third of the field, a long free kick can be played. Long free kicks are typically flighted diagonally toward a target player who is in an area that extends beyond the far post. That player attempts to win the ball and redirect it into a dangerous position to create a scoring opportunity for a teammate.

One strategy for the defending team is to sprint forward in unison just before the ball is kicked so as to pull attackers into offside positions. To counter that, the offensive team may position two attackers near the ball (see Diagram 32). The first player can take the kick or step over the ball to leave it for his partner. Because the defending team cannot know who will take the kick, the timing of an offside trap becomes problematic. The second player looks up to see whether or not the opponents have collectively pushed forward. If his target player is not offside, the ball is flighted behind the line of defenders. However, if the target player is already in an offside position the second player waits until his teammates quickly recover to take the kick. The accurate delivery of the kick coupled with a good first touch by the receiver should result in a great scoring opportunity.

For free kicks in wide or deep positions in the offensive portion of the field, two potential kickers are on opposite sides of the ball. As shown in Diagram 33, Attacker B would be a right-footed kicker while Attacker A would have the ability to strike the ball with the left foot.

Thus, the defense does not know in advance if it will have to deal with an inswinging or an outswinging free kick. Another plus is that the second player could help to get free on the flank and cross the ball from a better position should the opposition neglect to bring a second defender near the ball.

When within scoring range, simplicity is the watchword for free kicks. The most effective teams usually have two or three players around the ball and have rehearsed two

or three variations from the same set-up.

Teams with older players usually have specialists who have developed the ability to bend shots over and around defensive walls. If a direct shot is intended, at least one attacker stands behind the left side of the ball with another attacker behind the right side of the ball (a left-footed player is to the right of the ball and vice versa). Having two attackers so positioned disguises the kicker's identity to the goalkeeper. It also allows for a player to run over the ball, which may cause the anxious 'keeper to move either in anticipation of a shot's direction or so as to be able to still see the ball. Either way, the 'keeper's movement may expose a greater area of the goal into which the subsequent shot may be aimed.

For an indirect kick, or to create a better shooting angle, the ball may be played by the kicker a yard or two towards the middle of the field. The ball is then immediately shot or the receiver stops it for a shooter to strike it quickly. Time will always be of the essence as a member of the defending team is typically assigned to charge the ball as soon as it moves. To counter that, instruct your player who is standing over the ball to fake playing it square. If the defender charges prior to the ball being kicked he can receive a yellow card. What will most likely happen is the defender will stop short as soon as he sees that the ball has not been kicked. To avoid being cautioned, he should retreat quickly—the ball is then played, which buys the shooter a few extra yards of space.

Another option is to have a third attacker standing a few yards to the infield side of the ball and parallel to it. The ball is played to him and he stops it with the bottom of his boot. As that occurs, a teammate runs forward to strike the ball. A clever ploy to confuse the defense's ball charger would see the receiver step on the ball. As the opponent charges, he then rolls it behind himself for another player to strike the ball.

Very often the attacking team will place a player (or two) just in front of and to the inside of the wall. This is to make it harder for the 'keeper to see the ball until after it has been struck. The subsequent free kick is aimed through that attacker's position (the player ducks or moves as the ball arrives) while bending away from the 'keeper and into the area behind the near side of the wall.

Defending Against Free Kicks

To defend against free kicks within scoring range, the defensive wall is placed 10 yards from the ball. There should be enough players in the wall that an imaginary line from the ball through the outside player will intersect the near-sided post while a line from the ball through the inside defender will intersect the middle of the goal. It is the wall's responsibility to protect against shots that are aimed at the near half of the goal. It is vital that players have sufficient courage not to duck or turn away from the ball. They may

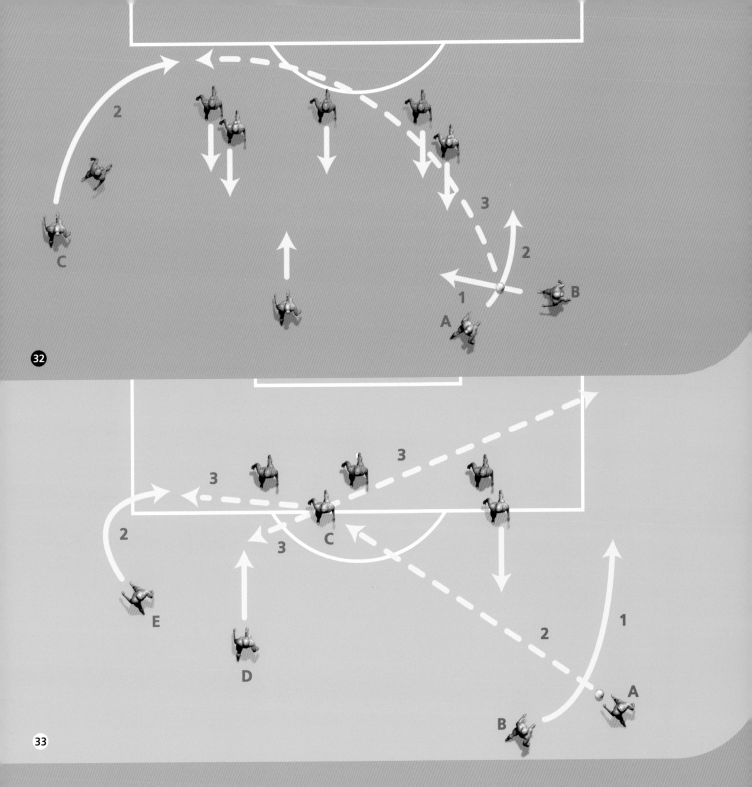

32

33

The Long Free Kick

Top: To beat the offside trap, left-footed Attacker B runs over the ball as the central attackers retreat with the advancing defenders. Attacker A approaches the ball to aim a right-footed kick behind the defenders, beyond the goalkeeper's range, and into the path of Attacker C. The other attackers then sprint forward to get into scoring positions for an anticipated cross or a rebound of a shot taken by Attacker C. Above: Should the defense be holding, the ball is aimed towards Attacker C. He, in turn, attempts to play the ball behind the line of defenders for an onrushing attacker inside the penalty box. Alternatively, the trap can be countered by A playing a short pass ahead to B (or vice versa) or the kicker hesitating during the approach to the ball.

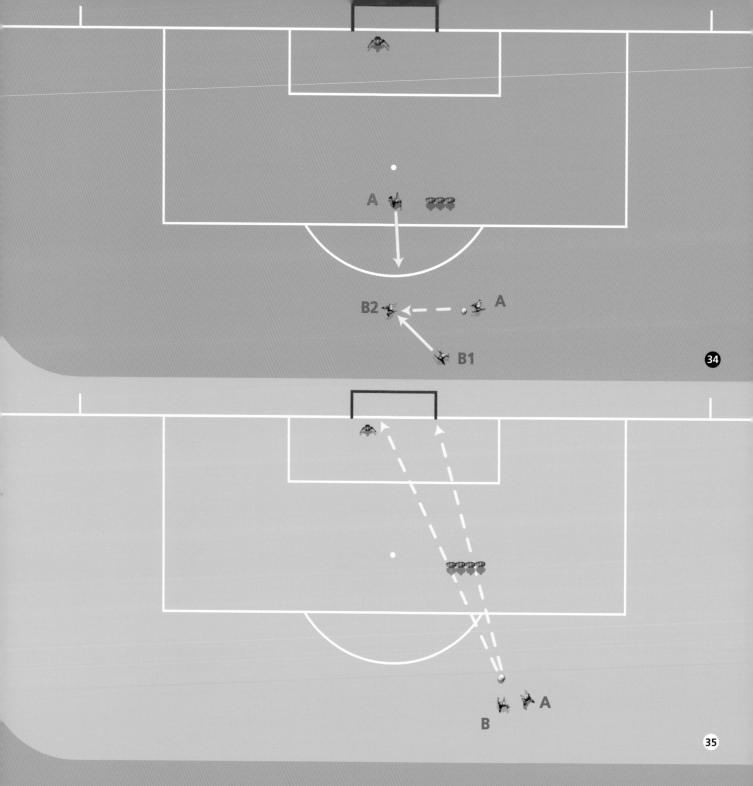

Positioning the Wall

Whenever a free kick is awarded within shooting range, a wall is set up to cover the near half of the goal (above). The defense may assign a player, positioned in or near the wall, to charge the potential shooter, if the first kicker should pass the ball to a teammate (top).

wish to use their hands and arms to cover sensitive body parts prior to the ball being put into play. As long as a defender's hands and arms do not move, a direct free kick to the offense will not be given should the ball strike him on the arms or hands directly from the kick.

The goalkeeper is charged with covering the far half of the goal but must also be ready to save a ball that dips over the wall. He stands roughly midway between the goal's center and the far post. As many teammates as are needed retreat to cover attackers and the key spaces inside of the penalty area.

Up to six defenders may be used in a wall to defend against a free kick in a central location that is just outside the penalty area. As few as two defenders may be required for a shot from an acute angle. The temptation to put too many players in the wall should be resisted, as it leaves too few defenders to mark opponents and restricts the 'keeper's vision.

As soon as a referee awards a free kick the 'keeper calls out a number to inform teammates of how many defenders are to be situated in the wall. It is preferable that midfielders and/or forwards are used in the wall so that players who are accustomed to defending may take up important central positions.

The outside-most defender serves as a predesignated "wall captain," receiving instruction to make sure the 'keeper's lines of vision are clear, and therefore making certain that the wall is correctly positioned.

A player upfield of the wall (usually a predesignated forward) can help to line up the wall so that the wall captain intersects the imaginary line that runs from the ball to the near post. All wall members line up tightly next to each other. They do not break apart until after the ball is shot. Should the ball be played sideways, the wall may move forward in unison in the direction of the ball.

Some experienced 'keepers, when time permits, prefer to line up the wall themselves. In that case, the goalie runs to the near post as the wall captain turns to face his own goal. He then follows his keeper's instructions as to where to stand. In youth soccer it is preferable to have a forward position the wall. This allows the 'keeper to concentrate on the ball at all times. Should it appear that the free kick may be taken quickly, the task of positioning the wall must be performed quickly by player who is in front of the ball.

One or two yards to the infield side of the wall is the "block player." If the restart involves a pass he charges at the ball to pressure the shooter and to try to block a shot. Another defender is stationed just to the outside of the wall to track any attacker who makes a wide penetrating run.

An indirect free kick within 10 yards of the goal—unusual at higher levels, but occasional in youth soccer especially after a goalie violates the back-pass rule—calls for bringing back every player to form a wall along the goal line, starting at the near post.

Should the ball be in a central position the defending team may opt to use two walls that come in from each of the posts with the 'keeper covering the middle of the goal. As soon as the ball is played the goalie charges out to intercept it or, at least, to block or hurry a subsequent shot.

Indirect free kicks from wider positions inside of the box are defended like other wide free kicks.

Summary

Just how important restarts can be has been illustrated countless times in high-level matches but never more so than in the 1998 World Cup Final. All three French goals during their startling upset of Brazil came from corner kicks. In the 27th minute the hosts were awarded a corner by the right touchline. Zinedine Zidane drove a header from the edge of the six-yard box into the Brazilian goal. A virtual carbon copy from the opposite flank doubled the margin during injury time. The clinching goal came deep into injury time in the second half on a French counter off of a Brazilian corner.

While France's first half goals came via a conventional approach, many big goals on restarts are due to cleverness. Argentina scored on a free kick 24 yards from England's goal. Argentina's Javier Zanetti hid in the middle of the opponents' wall. Just before an apparent shot was to be struck, he slipped behind the wall and ran to its near side. Zanetti then received the kicker's pass with his right foot, spun, and planted a 14-yard left-footed shot past a surprised goalkeeper.

Such dramatic goals win headlines but most restarts are far more mundane. Except when in the attacking third, the objective is to maintain possession. It is fine to fire a long throw-in just inside of the sideline to gain territory if your team retains the ball. But to keep doing so at the expense of possession is neither tactically nor developmentally sound. Attacking and defending against restarts that involve scoring chances are important and your team should be prepared to exploit these situations. However, at the youth level, long-term development is the first concern and practice time is always at a premium. It is not necessary to budget so much of your training sessions to dealing with restarts that you neglect more important concerns, such as improving technique and the teaching of the principles of the game.

It is recommended that the practicing of restarts be done within the context of a realistic training game. At all levels, simplicity and immediate organization are keys.

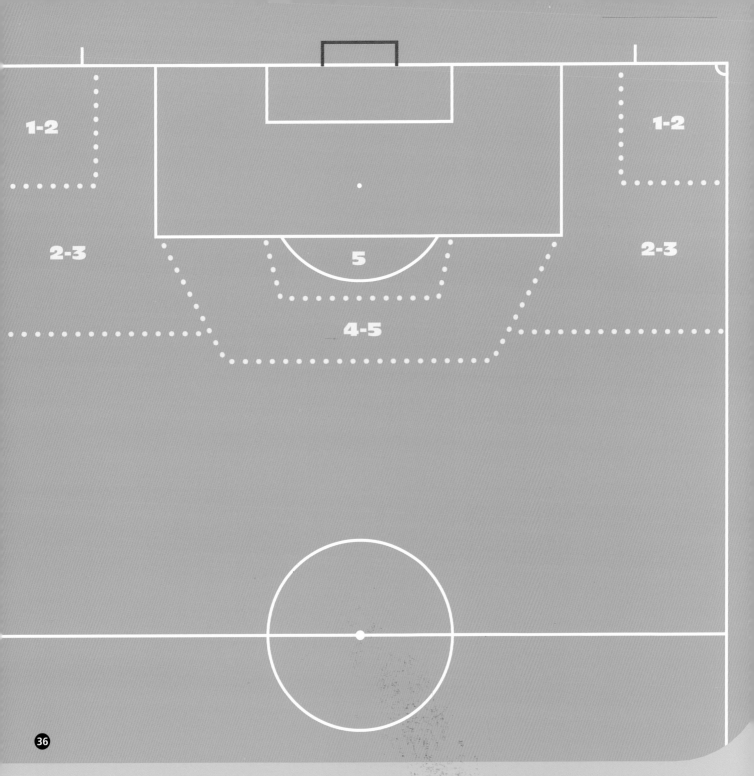

1-2

1-2

2-3

5

2-3

4-5

The Size of the Wall

The number of players used in the wall takes into account the ability and tendencies of the opposition's free kick specialist(s). As a general guideline, the above diagram provides the most common number of players used based on the position on the field where the free kick is awarded.

PART 6

The following pages present model training sessions for a technical and tactical training practice. In each case a theme is selected by the coach and then applied to all phases of the practice. Following this section are 104 games we recommend, annotated with specific training benefits and applications.

TECHNICAL TRAINING SESSION: Dribbling for Individual Possession

The format of each of the activities in this practice replicates a situation that really occurs in the game. Players must repeatedly execute a skill in a certain manner in order to be effective and successful in the activity. The activities are fun due to the realistic challenge and competitive environment provided by the conditions of each activity. High-intensity work is interspersed with brief rest periods so players are performing under soccer-like physical demands. The practice progresses from simple to complex activities as work is isolated in small numbers around the ball.

The cool-down period is also a necessary component of the technical training session in order to prevent injury and mentally wind down the players; refer to the cool-down activity following the Tactical Training Session section.

Warm-Up: Introduction of Technical Coaching Points and Preparation of the Body for Rigorous Activity

In general, the warm-up should consist of a mid- to moderate-intensity activity that introduces a soccer technique and allows players to get a lot of repetitions while preparing the body and focusing the mind for more vigorous activity. The ball is the key element here although the playing space may also be important, perhaps defined by a grid and the size adjusted in order to provide more or less pressure without opposition. Toward the end of the activity players can be encouraged to move at game pace to increase the demand on their performance and further prepare them for the next phase of practice. Static stretching of the large muscle groups should be done at the end or interspersed throughout the warm-up.

In this warm-up, the highlighted skill is dribbling—specifically, turning away from trouble to maintain individual possession. Each player has a ball and the activity challenges players to move in and out of traffic with the ball under control, to turn or change direction with the ball to avoid collisions, and to recognize and move into open space. The coach observes the behavior of the players in this environment and makes coaching points to the group or to individuals as they work. The skill is isolated in a very simple form but players are moving, controlling the ball, and recognizing situations that are realistic to the game.

Match-Related Activity 1 and 2:
Skill Practiced in Game-Like Exercises

This phase should consist of one or two medium- to high-intensity activities in which players can use the information from the warm-up to improve performance in small-sided games. The practice progresses from a very simple stage toward more complex activity. The introduction of opposition is a key element at this stage, as are goals or objectives, the field of play, rules, and realistic decision-making opportunities. Small-sided games provide repetitions of similar soccer situations from which players learn while playing. It is easier for the coach to observe the players around the ball and provide appropriate coaching points to improve performance. In this sample practice, Match-Related Activity 1 is a 1-v-1 game that isolates players in situations where they have to turn away from defenders to keep the ball and find open gates to dribble through to score goals. The coach and players can focus on the individual skill and decisions related to the dribbling topic in this game. In Match-Related Activity 2, the introduction of a teammate further complicates the decisions but still requires similar execution of dribbling technique. The beauty of both games is that players get many repetitions of realistic soccer situations and they both require intense periods of work followed by brief rests so players are performing under the same physical demands of a soccer game; the environment can be intensified by keeping score and determining a winner.

Match-Condition Activity:
The Conditioned Game and "Scrimmage"

In this most complex phase of the practice, the final game-like element, direction, is added and players are allowed to play in larger numbers. Direction dictates that the game is played to two goals and each team attacks one goal and defends the other. There may be some restrictions in order to highlight the practice topic, but eventually the game must be free of conditions to allow the players to perform the practiced skill in a game enviroment. The coach must observe and evaluate whether the objective of the practice has been transferred to the game.

The conditioned activity, the Zone Game, forces players into situations that they have practiced earlier activities but allows them to play in larger number and under more complicated circumstances. The shape of the field (rectangular) and the method of scoring (dribble under control into an end zone) create dribbling and turning opportunities similar to those practiced but now in a specific area of the field. To complete the practice, add goals on each end and play. When all restrictions are lifted, players should be able to recognize the situation, execute good skill, and make sound decisions under pressure.

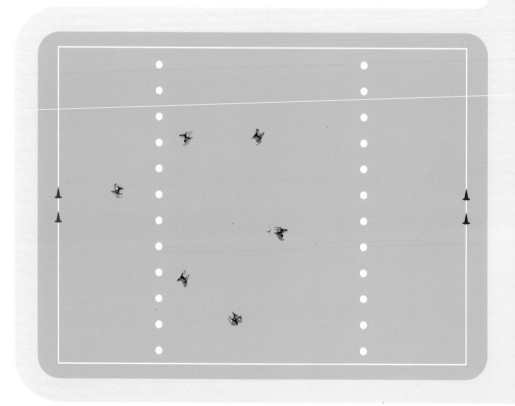

Match-Related Activity 1: One-v-One

Organization

Circle of Fire

- Four to six goals arranged in a 15–yard square or circle

- Group of 12 players is divided into two teams, each player has an opponent.

- One pair enters the game. The players compete to score by dribbling the ball through the goal.

- Keep track of time so game doesn't last longer than one minute (monitor fitness); the next pair then enters the game.

Key Coaching Points

- Turning away from opponent; Change of direction and pace

- Increase intensity by keeping score and playing to determine a winner

Match-Related Activity 2: Two-v-Two

Organization

Cone Game

- Players in pairs play against another pair in a triangle of approximately 5 to 7 yards, marked by 3 cones. Group of 12 players is divided into teams. One pair from each team enters the game and tries to score by dribbling and knocking down the cones.

- 1 point to score, 1 or 2 points to win game; when the game is won, 2 or more pairs enter the game.

- Keep track of time so each game doesn't last longer than 2 minutes (monitor fitness).

Key Coaching Points

- Turning away from opponent; change direction and pace

- Support of teammate; combining with teammate

- Increase intensity by keeping score and determining a winning team

Match-Condition Activity: 3-v-3 or 4-v-4

Organization

Zone Game

- Two zones at each end of a 25/30-x-35/40–yard area, teams score by dribbling ball into zone. Add goals at end to finish.

Key Coaching Points

- Technical application and corrections; tactical application

The focus of a tactical training session is the decision-making process. The format of each of the activities in this practice replicates a situation that really occurs in the game. Players must recognize situations and make sound decisions in order to be effective and successful in the activity. Ability to execute technique may also affect a player's success in tactical situations. Transition is involved in the activities so players must always be alert, whether they are attacking or defending. This creates motivation either to keep or win the ball and provides a flow to the activity. The practice progresses from simple to complex activities and work is isolated in small numbers around the ball. This allows players to make simple yet realistic decisions under increased pressure and game-like demands. We have chosen "penetration" as the theme of this sample practice, for which even the warm-up should be an instructive part of the session.

Warm-Up: Introduction of Tactical Coaching Points and Preparation of Body for Rigorous Activity

In general, the warm-up should consist of a mid- to moderate-intensity activity that introduces basic decisions related to the tactical objective of the practice. The activity should allow players to get many repetitions while preparing the body and focusing the mind for more vigorous or complex activity. The ball is the key element, although the playing space may also be adjusted in order to provide more or less pressure without opposition. Toward the end of the activity, players can be encouraged to move at game pace to increase the demand on their performance and further prepare them for the next phase of practice. Static stretching of the large muscle groups should be done at the end or interspersed throughout the warm-up.

Individual Activity: Decision-Making Practiced in Game-Like Exercises

This phase of the practice further defines and isolates the decisions required of the individual player both on and off the ball. It is played in a restricted, rectangular-shaped space in order to provide direction and illustrate that decisions are based on where the player is located in relation to the sideline and different areas of the field. The format of the grid should create simple but realistic decisions and provide repetition of situations that challenge players and provide opportunities to improve performance. Small-sided games allow the coach to observe the player's behavior around the ball and provide feedback to improve performance.

In this 1-v-1 game, the attacking player works on creating space to receive the ball, creating a passing angle, being patient and not giving the ball away, and deciding whether it is more appropriate to penetrate the defender by dribbling or passing. A poor decision or poor technique will result in a loss of possession and immediate transition to defense. This increases the pressure on the attacking player by motivating the defending player.

Small Group Activity:
Decision-Making Practiced in Game-Like Exercises

In this phase of the practice the activity becomes more complex by the addition of one full-size goal, a goalkeeper, and more field players. The goal focuses players on an urgent objective and reminds them of the third of the field in which they are operating. Players should attack/defend in one direction and have a counter to provide transition and motivation to both sides. The players now have an opportunity to apply the information gained from earlier activities in a more challenging environment. The tactical cues that were isolated previously give them the foundation to make sound decisions as the game is built up around them.

The activity in this phase of the practice is a 2-v-2 game with a goal, a goalkeeper, and target players at the other end. The coach can observe and either correct or reinforce the recognition of penetrating opportunities and the decisions made to execute those opportunities in this activity.

Large Group Activity:
The Conditioned Game and "Scrimmage"

This is the most complex phase of the practice, a second goal and more players are added and an even-sided game is played. The game allows players to perform the tactical decisions from previous activities in a game environment with larger numbers. The coach observes and evaluates if the tactical objective of the practice has been transferred to the game. The coach may initially place some restrictions to maintain the theme of the practice but all restrictions should eventually be lifted in order to determine the improvement of play.

In this practice, we have suggested a 6-v-6 game with goals and goalkeepers and no restrictions. The coach should continue to observe the behavior of the players and evaluate whether there has been a transfer of knowledge over the progression of the practice.

Cool-Down: Injury Prevention and Warm-Down

Low-intensity activity that physically and mentally winds down the players. Light jogging and static stretching are the main ingredient of the cool-down. Coaches may or may not choose to include a ball.

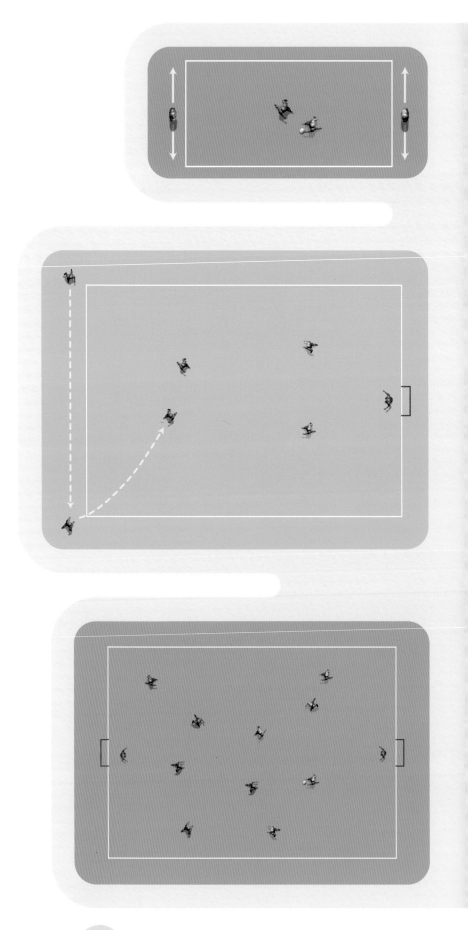

Individual Activity: One-v-One

Organization
- Two players compete inside a 10-x-20–yard grid; two players are targets behind endline.
- Targets may move only along the line to create passing angles.
- Target plays ball to one middle player whose objective is to play the ball to the other target to score a "goal" and retain possession.
- Opposing middle player defends and tries to win the ball.
- Compete to score goals and determine winner.

Key Coaching Points
- Create space to receive the ball; create passing angles
- Controlling the ball; playing the ball with accuracy and appropriate pace
- Not giving the ball away unnecessarily

Small Group Activity:

Organization
- A 2-v-2 game played in a 25-x-35–yard area with a regulation-size goal and goalkeeper on one end and targets on corners facing the goal
- One pair attacks the goal, the other pair defends it until a loss of possession, then the roles reverse.
- Play starts with target on one corner playing to the other target and then into the attacking pair. Repeat process anytime the ball is played to a target.
- Attacking team scores 2 points for a goal, the defending team scores 1 point each time they play the ball to a target.

Key Coaching Points
- Recognition of penetration opportunities: dribbling, passing, timing of runs, or finishing
- Support, including visual communication and cues
- Pace and accuracy of passes

Large Group Activity:

Organization
- A 6-v-6 game (outfield players plus goalkeepers) in a 45-x-30–yard area with two regulation-size goals, match-realistic conditions, including corners, goalkicks, throw-ins

Key Coaching Points
- Tactical application and corrections; technical breakdowns

(1) The Game: Shark Attack

Rules: Ten players each dribble a ball within a 20-x-30–yard grid while two "sharks," in identifiable bibs, jog around the outside of the area with no balls. The sharks yell "shark attack" and enter the area in an attempt to dispossess the players and kick the balls out of the area. A player whose ball exits from the area stays in the game without his ball (he can receive passes from and can pass to the remaining players with balls). The game ends when the last ball leaves the area or one minute has elapsed. Assign new sharks and play again. *Benefits: Dribbling, passing, receiving, and tackling. Phase: Individual. Ages: 6+ (most appropriate for ages 6–12)*

(2) The Game: Monsters Loose

Rules: Two "monsters" in scrimmage vests jog around the outside of a 20-x-35–yard playing area. Each of six pairs of players inside the zone has a ball and must keep it moving by dribbling and passing. The monsters shout "monsters loose" and enter the area to kick away their victims' balls. The monsters may not double-team any pair of players. Play for one minute, change monsters, and play again. You might also add another competitive component by keeping score: the team whose ball leaves the area the least times wins. *Benefits: Passing, receiving, dribbling, tackling, and decision-making. Phase: Individual. Ages: 6+ (most appropriate for ages 6–8)*

(3) The Game: Highway Robbery

Rules: In all four corners of a 30-x-30–yard grid are 10-x-10–yard zones. Within each corner are three or four players, with the same number of balls as there are players placed in the grid. When the game begins, any or all of a team's members may serve as "hunters" by running to the other areas and "stealing" a ball from any of the other zones by dribbling it back to their own zone (and then immediately going after more balls). No more than one "prison guard" at a time may stay at home to protect a grid. The group with the most balls after one minute is the winner. Avoid having the same players serve as guards in consecutive games. *Benefits: Dribbling. Phase: Individual. Ages: 6+ (most appropriate for ages 6–8)*

(4) The Game: Simon Says

Rules: The players follow the coach's directions. Played without eliminating any of the participants. Examples of "Simon Says" commands: 1. Touch the ball quickly from side-to-side between your feet. 2. Take turns tapping the ball with the bottoms of your right and left foot without moving the ball. 3. Jump over the ball. 4. Hop around the ball. 5. Skip around the ball. 6. Toss the ball up, hit it with your head, and catch it. 7. Use the bottom of one foot to move the ball in a circle. 8. Kick the ball in the air and catch it. 9. Kick the ball over your head, turn, and catch it. *Benefits:* Ball control and motor skills. *Phase:* Individual. *Ages:* 6+ (most appropriate for ages 6–8)

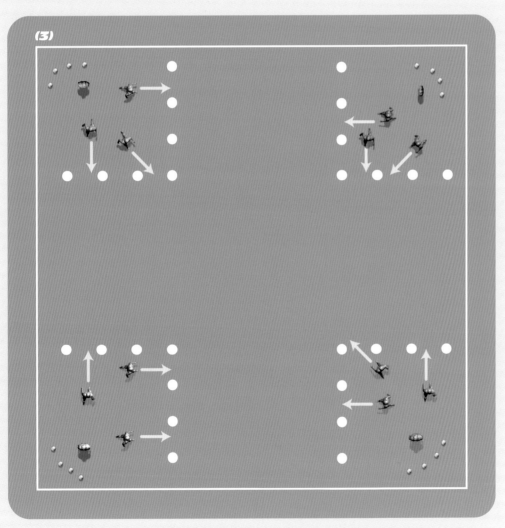

*All measurements for games are given as length x width

(5) The Game: Tidy Up Your Room

Rules: Two teams of six players, each player with a ball, are in a 20-x-40–yard grid that is divided by a midfield line of saucers. Each team has to stay in its own half of the grid. The objective is to keep one's "room" neat by kicking balls into your "brother's" or "sister's" room. The coach should keep all balls in play by returning stray balls to the players. When two minutes elapse, the team with fewer balls in its room wins. *Benefits:* Passing, receiving, and shooting. *Adjustments:* Can award bonus points for a ball that crosses over the opponents' end line (but inside of the sidelines). The game may be played with more or fewer players; increase or reduce the size of the grid to accommodate the number of participants. *Phase:* Large group. *Ages:* 6+

(6) The Game: Raceway

Rules: Twelve players, each dribbling a ball inside a 15-x-20–yard "racetrack," try not to "crash" into the "rail" that is marked by saucers. When "cars" (players) collide or hit the rail they move outside of the track for repairs by doing fast footwork (alternating feet to tap the ball rapidly with the inside of each foot), ball taps (alternating feet to tap the top of the ball with the front of the sole of each foot), or another technical task (turning with the ball with the left foot, turning with the right foot) before reentering the "race." All cars obey the "race director's" (coach's) instructions, such as: "Shift gears"—Change direction. "Red flag"—Stop the ball. "Blue flag"—Stop the ball with a knee. "Yellow flag"—Dribble slower. "Green flag"—Accelerate to top speed. "Change cars"—Change direction dribbling with the opposite foot than was used with the most recent touch. As you play, gradually introduce one new instruction at a time. *Benefits:* Dribbling. *Phase:* Individual. *Ages:* 6+ (most appropriate for ages 6–8)

(7) The Game: Red Light/Green Light

Rules: All players stand on the goal line with a ball while facing the midfield line about fifty yards away. When the coach yells "green light" the players dribble forward at full speed while maintaining control of the ball. On the coach's command ("Red light!") each player stops the ball with the bottom of a foot. Any player failing to do so returns to the starting line. The first player to stop the ball on the midfield line is the winner. *Benefits:* Dribbling. *Variations:* More skills can be included, for example: on the shout of "Red light," players turn with the ball using the inside of one foot; turn back with the ball using the outside of the other foot; then stop the ball using a knee. *Phase:* Individual. *Ages:* 6+ (most appropriate for ages 6–8)

(8) The Game: Passing Wars

Rules: Two teams of five players face each other while lined up on opposite end lines across a 20-x-20–yard area. Every player starts with a ball and can only move along the end line—not forward or backward. All the players start kicking at once. The objective is to kick balls across the field and past the line of opponents facing them. The team with the least number of balls behind it after 60 seconds is the winner.

Benefits: Passing and receiving. *Adjustments:* Game may be played with four-v-four teams, up to eight-v-eight. Alter the length (distance between teams) to accommodate the kicking strength of the participants. *Phase:* Large group. *Ages:* 6+ (most appropriate for ages 6–8)

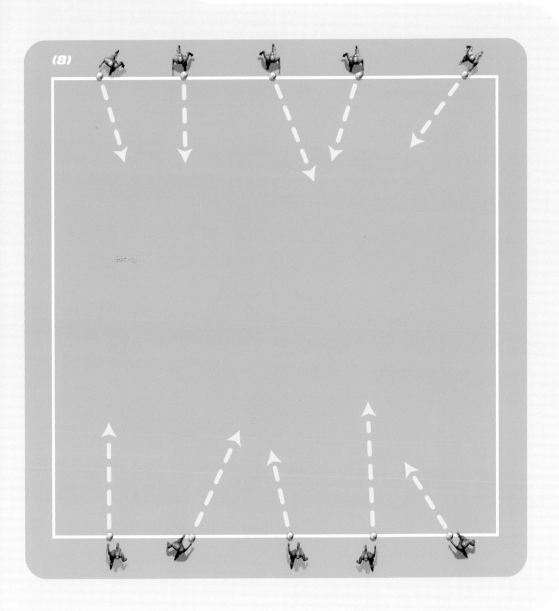

(9) The Game: Knockout

Rules: Eight or more players, each with a ball, dribble inside the center circle and keep their ball moving at all times while trying to kick the other players' balls out of the circle. When a participant's ball leaves the circle, he must retrieve the ball and complete a relatively simple challenge (such as fast footwork, ball taps, or a set number of juggles) before reentering the game. The winner can be the last player to have his ball kicked out, the player whose ball leaves the circle the least times in a set time frame (60–90 seconds), or the player who kicks the most opponents' balls out in a set time frame.

Benefits: Dribbling and tackling. **Note:** *This game has traditionally been played on an elimination basis, with players eliminating others by kicking their ball out of the circle. When five players remain, the boundary becomes one-half of the circle and is narrowed by half again when three players are left. The last player remaining with a ball wins. The game is also played with an individual who had been put out reentering the action when the opponent who knocked him out is, in turn, knocked out. However, these versions cause a lot of inactivity for many of the players and virtually assure that those who need the most practice get the least. It is recommended that this game should be played on an elimination basis only with older players and then only if the coach takes care that each round does not last too long.* **Phase:** *Individual.*
Ages: *6+ (most appropriate for ages 6–8)*

(10) The Game: Statue Tag

Rules: Twelve players, each with a ball, try to avoid two "defenders" in a 20-x-35–yard rectangle. Players with balls are transformed into "statues" when tagged by the hand of a defender or if their ball leaves the area or is kicked out by a defender. A statue retrieves the ball, returns to the area if necessary, and holds the ball overhead with legs spread far apart. Statues may be revived by one of the remaining attackers kicking a ball through the statue's legs. The game ends after two minutes or when every attacker has been turned into a statue. Change defenders and play again.

Benefits: Dribbling. **Phase:** *Individual.* **Ages:** *8+*

(11) The Game: Stampede

Rules: One "defender," without a ball, is inside of a 20-x-15–yard grid. Eight "attackers," each with a ball, stand at one of the longer end lines, facing into the grid. Upon the coach's signal each will attempt to dribble through the grid and stop the ball on the opposite end line. Players who are dispossessed by the defender, or whose ball leaves the area, become defenders (without balls) for subsequent rushes, with the winner being the last attacking player with a ball. *Benefits:* Dribbling and tackling. *Variations:* Can mandate that the defender must retreat five to ten yards from the line of attackers until play starts. To work on dribbling at speed, have the defenders start five to ten yards (depending upon the age and ability of the players) behind the line of attackers and attempt to tag the attackers (if tagged, the dribbler joins the defender for the subsequent rush). The game can also alternate between having defenders behind when going in one direction and in front when returning the other way. *Phase:* Individual. *Ages:* 6+ (most appropriate for ages 6–12)

(11)

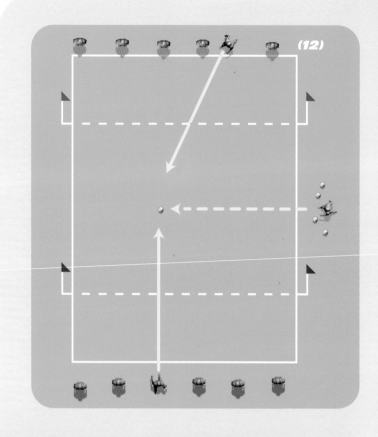

(12)

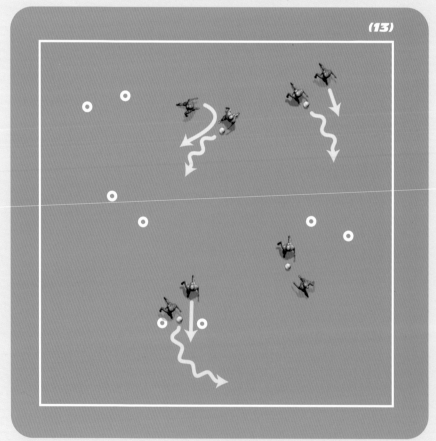

(13)

(12) The Game: One-v-One Zone Soccer

Rules: Two teams send out one player each to a 15-x-10–yard area with 2-yard-deep zones at either end. A server rolls a ball into the area. The two players compete for the ball: whoever is in possession attempts to score by stopping the ball with the bottom of a foot in the opponents' zone. Possession of the ball should change hands, with one player attacking, then defending, and then attacking again, depending on how evenly matched the players are and how much time is allowed. A new ball is immediately served should the ball leave the area. The pair of players is changed following a goal or when 45 to 60 seconds elapse. The first team to score a set number of goals wins. *Benefits: Dribbling and defending.* **Variations:** *Widen the grid and/or increase the zones' depth if needed to help the attackers. Can also be played as two-v-two or three-v-three, but still with only one ball. The game can end after every player has taken three turns.* **Phase:** *Small group.* **Ages:** *6+*

(13) The Game: Multiple-Goal Dribbling, Part One

Rules: Four six-foot-wide goals made up of flags or cones are positioned inside a 20-x-20–yard grid set up as the coach chooses. Eight players are divided into pairs, each pair with a ball. One player begins as the attacker, the other as the defender. Four simultaneous games of one-v-one therefore occur with players attempting to score as many times as possible by dribbling through any of the goals, in either direction, while maintaining possession as play continues. If the defender wins the ball, he returns it to the attacker. A player may not score consecutively at the same goal. Change the players' roles (switch attackers and defenders) after 60 seconds and start again. After each player has had a turn on both offense and defense, the player who has scored the most goals is the winner. Switch partners and play again. **Benefits:** *Dribbling and defending.* **Note:** *Have an ample supply of spare balls in the corners to help keep the game moving.* **Variation:** *To foster a more match-realistic environment, have the attacker and defender switch roles after a turnover.* **Note:** *This is a high-intensity activity. Allow players adequate recovery time between rounds.* **Phase:** *Individual.* **Ages:** *8+ (most appropriate for ages 8–12)*

(14) The Game: Multiple-Goal Dribbling, Part Two

Rules: Five six-foot-wide goals, made up of flags, saucers, or cones, are spaced evenly on the center circle. Simultaneous games of one-v-one occur for 60 seconds. Each game has 4–5 pairs and begins with one player per pair in possession of a ball inside the circle. This player tries to score while the other defends. If the defender wins the ball, he returns it to the attacker. A goal is awarded when a player stops the ball with one foot between a set of cones (the goal). Play then continues immediately. *Benefits:* Dribbling and defending. *Variation:* To foster a more match-realistic environment, have the attacker and defender switch roles after a turnover. *Phase:* Individual. *Ages:* 8+ (most appropriate for ages 8–12)

(15) The Game: Multiple-Goal Dribbling, Part Three

Rules: Five six-foot-wide goals, made up of flags, saucers, or cones, are spaced evenly on the center circle. Simultaneous games of one-v-one occur for 60 seconds each. The games begin with one player per pair in possession of a ball outside the circle, the other defending. The attacker attempts to enter the circle at any point but may only score by exiting, with the ball, through one of the goals. If the defender wins the ball he returns it to the attacker. *Benefits:* Dribbling and defending. *Variation:* To foster a more match-realistic environment, have the attacker and defender switch roles after a turnover. *Phase:* Individual. *Ages:* 8+ (most appropriate for ages 8–12)

(16) The Game: Nutmegs

Rules: A one-v-one game in a 20-x-15–yard-long area (although two players are active, more can feel directly involved). The "goal" on each of the shorter ends is made up of an inactive player who stands with feet spread wide apart while holding a spare ball. A chaser is positioned behind each "goal." The active players can score by shooting or passing the ball through the legs of the opponent's goal. Following a score or a shot that goes over the end line, the player who is the goal drops the new ball for his teammate. After 45 to 60 seconds (for older players 60 seconds is better) the chasers become the goals, the goals become active, and the active players become the chasers. Because of the high intensity of this game, allow adequate recovery time between rounds. **Benefits:** *Dribbling and defending.* **Variations:** *May be played two-v-two in the middle and/or with neutral players who move up and down the sidelines and immediately return a loose ball to the scrimmaging players.* **Phase:** *Individual.* **Ages:** *6+*

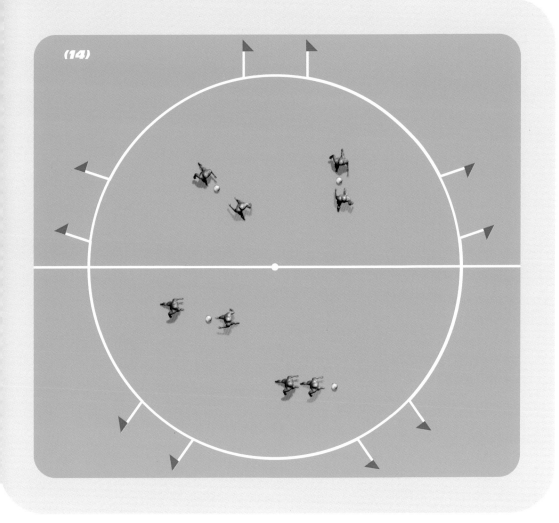

(14)

(17) The Game: Soccer/Bowling

Rules: Teams of two players facing each other from across the center circle pass a ball back and forth and attempt to score "strikes" by kicking the ball so it knocks over objects (such as pylon cones) randomly placed inside the circle. The kick should be hard and accurate enough to reach the teammate across the circle. All shots must be kicked from outside of the circle's boundaries. When all objects have been toppled, the team with the most strikes wins. *Benefits:* Passing. *Adjustments:* Use a much smaller circle (marked with saucers) for young players. *Variations:* Can award two strikes for a ball that hits a cone on the fly, for knocking over a cone by using the weaker foot, and/or for a first-touch pass. Older players may direct the ball with the instep or chip the ball across the circle for a teammate to head at the targets. *Note:* Use for fun but not as a steady diet, as it offers minimal problem solving. *Phase:* Individual. *Ages:* 6+

(18) The Game: Receive and Pass

Rules: Set up two grids, each 10 yards square, with two six-foot-wide goals behind each of them. Four players alternate as server, active player, and chasers (but no goalkeeper). The server passes to the active player, who is five yards behind the grids. With his first touch the receiver touches the ball into either grid, runs to catch up to it, looks up at his target, and attempts to shoot the ball, with his subsequent touch, through one of the goals, preferably before the ball leaves the grid. Rotate the players after 10 serves. When everyone has taken a turn, the player with the most goals wins. *Benefits:* Receiving and passing. *Variations:* In subsequent rounds place specific demands, such as: 1. Receive with the outside of a foot and pass with the inside of that same foot. 2. Use the inside of one foot to cut the ball across the body and pass with the inside of the other foot. To emphasize vision, have the chasers decide which one will raise his hand as the ball is received. The active player must then pass the ball through the goal that the chaser is behind. *Phase:* Individual. *Ages:* 9+

(19) The Game: Soccer/Golf

Rules: Map out a field with several small grids (as many as you like), following any route you wish, using four corner flags, cones, or saucers to form a rectangle to indicate each "hole." Each player has a ball and kicks, doesn't dribble, around the course. A "putt" is in the hole when the ball stops inside the rectangle. The winner is the player who takes the least "strokes" (kicks) to complete the course. Adjust the degree of difficulty to accommodate the age and ability level of the players. *Benefits:* Long and short passing. *Note:* Recommended for small groups of players. Use only on occasion as a fun diversion but not as a steady diet. *Phase:* Individual.

Ages: 6+ (most appropriate for ages 6–8)

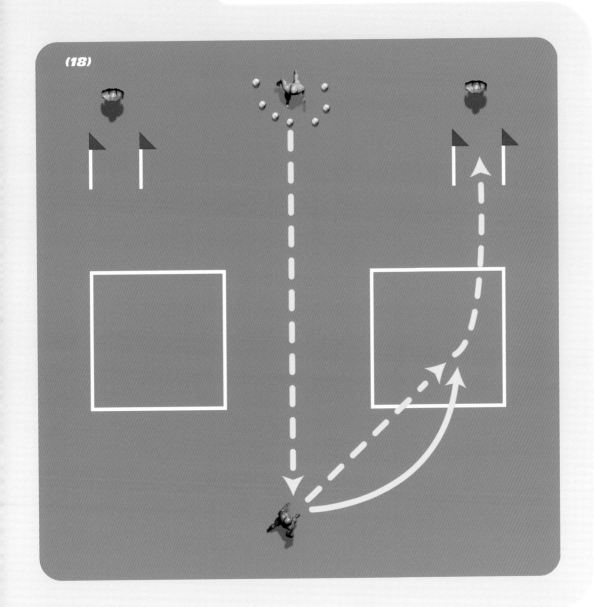

(18)

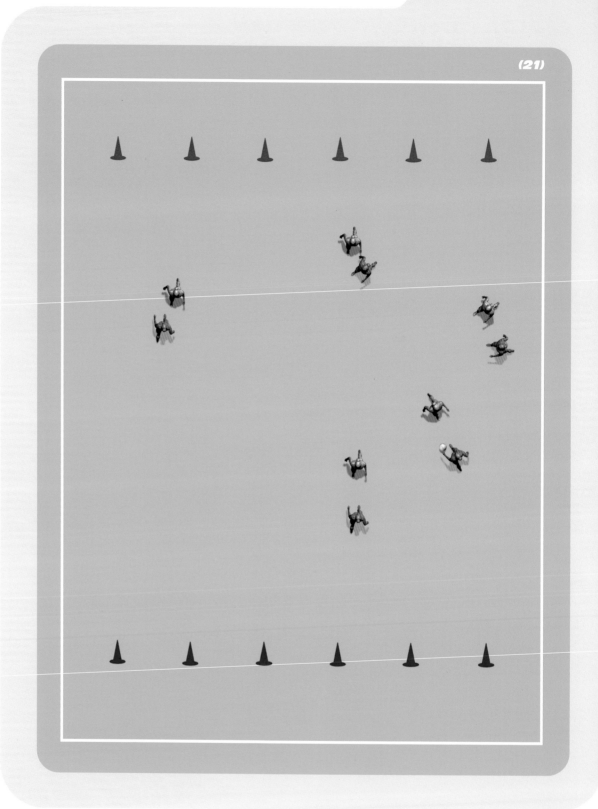

(20) The Game: Target Hunt

Rules: Various stationary targets are inside a 20-x-30–yard area in addition to a moving "goal" of two players who run around while holding each end of a six-foot rope at waist height. Eight players in the grid, each with a ball, attempt to kick the ball (no higher than knee height) through the moving goal (worth three points) and to hit the set targets (one point each) during 60-second periods. This is organized mayhem, but it inspires a lot of movement and shooting. *Benefits: Dribbling and passing.* *Variations: Double point value for targets hit with passes struck by a player's weaker foot. Can also be played with two-player teams, each team sharing one ball (and with double-point value for scoring on the first or second touch following a pass).* *Phase: Individual/small group (when teams).* *Ages: 8+ (most appropriate for ages 8–12)*

(21) The Game: Cone Barbarians

Rules: A five-v-five game played with one ball in a 40-x-30–yard area. Evenly intersperse six cones, five yards inside of each end line (as shown). The objective is to shoot (not dribble!) the ball to topple the opposition's cones. Whenever a cone is knocked over the scoring team takes that cone and places it within the line of cones that it is defending. When the ball leaves the area restart play with a kick-in. The team that has more cones in its defensive line after five minutes is the winner. *Benefits: Passing and receiving.* *Adjustments: Can play four-v-four up to eight-v-eight, adjusting the area, as appropriate, but always with one more cone per team than there are players per squad (seven-v-seven has eight cones per team). Neutral players can be added on the sidelines to return the ball quickly to the players. The game may be played with more cones.* *Phase: Large group.* *Ages: 10+ (most appropriate for ages 10–12)*

(22) The Game: Serve and Finish

Rules: A one-v-one confrontation in a penalty area between the front player of a (short) line of finishers versus the defender at the front of another (short) line of players. The two lines stand on either side of the penalty area. The front defender in line passes to the first attacker in line and follows the pass to close down the attacker as soon as possible. The attacker has six seconds to score into a regulation-size goal that is protected by a goalkeeper. All rebounds are live. If the defender kicks the ball out of the penalty area, he scores. (For older players, the defender should try to clear the ball in a controlled manner.) The players then switch lines. After 10 minutes the player with the most goals wins. *Variations: For highly skilled players/teams the initial pass may be chipped. Benefits: Receiving, finishing, defending, and goalkeeping. Phase: Small group. Ages: 9+ (most appropriate for ages 6–12)*

(23) The Game: Two-v-Two Finishing

Rules: Inside a penalty area with a regulation-size goal are two teams of two players. The coach/server is within the penalty-area arc (or the "D"). Chasers are behind the goal. The ball is served into the area by the coach and is live until saved by the 'keeper, enters the goal, or leaves the area. Whichever team has possession tries to score; the other team attempts to win possession so it can score. *Benefits: Passing, dribbling, finishing, receiving, defending, and goalkeeping. Variations: Allow resting players to serve from varying spots. For younger players, reduce the size of the playing area. Phase: Small group. Ages: 9+*

(24) The Game: Three-v-Two Finishing

Rules: A team of defenders stands in two lines just behind the goalpost of a regulation-size goal. A team of attackers stand in three lines a few yards beyond the top of the penalty area. A goalkeeper is needed, plus the coach/server who, with an ample supply of balls, serves (or, for older players, chips) a pass into the area. The front players in all five lines run into the box. The attackers attempt to score while the defenders try to clear the ball; older defenders should pass to each other to escape the area. Play continues until a goal is scored, the ball leaves the area, or the goalkeeper gains possession. Five more players then compete. After four minutes, the teams switch places. *Benefits: Receiving, passing, dribbling, finishing, defending, and goalkeeping. Phase: Small group. Ages: 9+*

(22)

(24)

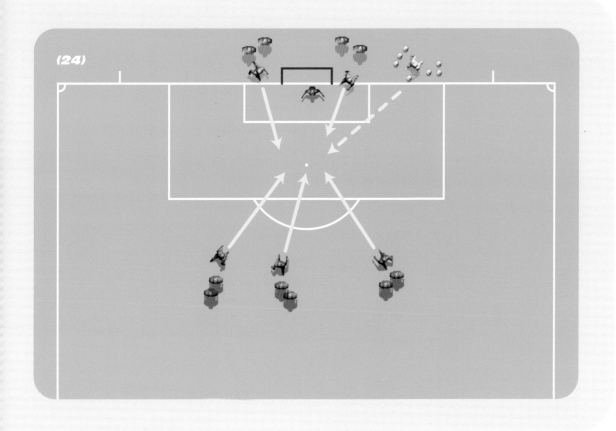

(25) The Game: One-v-One-v-One

Rules: An excellent game to work on dribbling towards space, as well as finishing breakaways and upgrading fitness. This game involves three teams of three competing on a 36-x-44–yard area with regulation-size goals with goalkeepers on each of the longer sides. The coach/server, who has an ample supply of balls, is stationed near the middle of a sideline. Each team sends out one player at a time. Any of the three players winning possession at any time, tries to score at either end. The other two players try to defend and win possession so they can score. (Thus, the attacking player is always outnumbered by two defenders.) Play begins with the coach/server kicking the ball into play. A new ball will immediately be served after a goal or when the ball goes out of play or is caught by one of the goalkeepers. After 45–60 seconds (depending upon the age of the players) the players are changed (except for the goalkeepers). Play a set number of rounds or to a set number of goals. The team scoring the most goals wins as does the goalkeeper who concedes fewer goals. **Benefits:** *Dribbling, finishing (especially breakaways), tackling, and goalkeeping.* **Adjustments:** *You may opt to manipulate the line up so players of comparable ability work against each other.* **Note:** *This is a very demanding exercise; allow adequate recovery time between rounds.*
Phase: *Small group.* **Ages:** *8+*

(26) The Game: Breakaways Wild

Rules: Played in a penalty area, two teams take turns on offense against a goalie. The teams alternate sending one player to the top of the "D" to receive a throw from the goalkeeper. Starting with the first touch, the player has five seconds to beat the goalkeeper and to score. The game ends after every attacker has had five attempts.
Benefits: *Receiving, finishing, and goalkeeping.* **Adjustments:** *The goalkeeper may serve the ball in the air but it cannot be thrown beyond the attacker.*
Considerations: *The goalkeeper only advances forward when the ball cannot be contacted by the attacker. The goalie's knees are bent with the palms exposed to the ball. He looks to pounce on any long touch that escapes from the attacker's control.*
Phase: *Small group.* **Ages:** *8+*

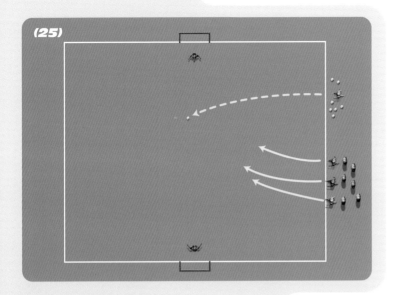

(25)

(27) The Game: Rapid Fire

Rules: Two teams of six players, each player with a ball, dribble inside a 55-x-70–yard area. On each end line is a regulation-size goal with a goalkeeper. When a field player makes eye contact with the centrally positioned coach/server standing in the middle of the field, or the player's name is called by him, the ball is passed to the coach/server who then lays it off in any direction. The player catches up to the ball and then shoots in a match-realistic manner (but may not run around the ball to strike it with the stronger foot). Every few seconds a player should be shooting. The other players should be working on their dribbling skills. The team with more goals after five minutes wins, as does the goalkeeper who yields the least goals. *Benefits: Dribbling, passing, finishing, and goalkeeping. Phase: Small group. Ages: 8+*

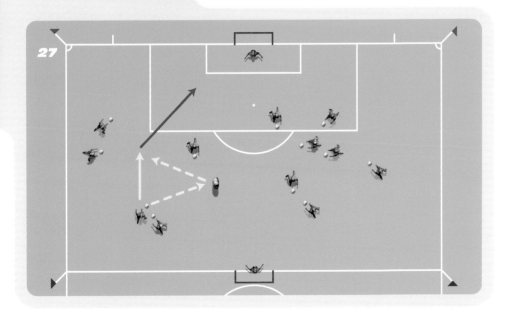

27

(28) The Game: Head It/Catch It

Rules: A circle of participants surround the coach/server. The coach/server moves around inside the circle and softly tosses the ball underhand at an individual's head. As the ball is airborne the coach/server calls out "head it" or "catch it," and the player must successfully do the opposite of what has been stated. A mistake sees the player given a "point." The player with the least number of points at the end is the winner. *Benefits:* Introduction to heading. *Adjustments:* Increase the ratio of coach/servers to participants or have two players serving to each other, with a point awarded every time an opponent errs. *Phase:* Individual. *Ages:* 8+

(29) The Game: Multiple-Goal Heading

Rules: Four regulation-size goals are placed in a square facing into a 40-x-40–yard area. For each goal, there is an attacker, a goalkeeper, a server to one side, and a chaser behind. A ball is tossed or kicked by the server to the attacking player, who attempts to score on a header. After five serves the players change roles. *Benefits:* Heading and goalkeeping. *Variations:* Vary the position of the servers and the type of serves between those driven and those chipped. Use two-handed underhanded tosses to serve gently to younger players. *Phase:* Small group. *Ages:* 10+

(30) The Game: Cooperative Head Juggling

Rules: Two players must head the ball back and forth to each other with every contact and compete against other pairs to see who can complete the most headed exchanges without the ball touching the ground. *Benefits:* Heading. *Variations:* Each participant may juggle a set number of times before heading the ball to his teammate. Very talented players might compete while seated or on their knees. Alternatively, the objective could be to advance the ball across or up the field without the ball touching the ground. *Phase:* Small group. *Ages:* 10+

(31) The Game: Throw/Head/Catch

Rules: Two teams of seven players without goalkeepers play in a 40-x-44–yard area with regulation-size goals. The objective is to head the ball into the opponents' goal. Play starts with a two-handed, underhand throw by a member of the attacking team. The receiver attempts to head the ball to any teammate who, in turn, must catch the ball before it hits the ground. He then can take up to two steps and within five seconds must throw it to the next player, who must head it to another player, who catches it, throws it to a player, and so on. All shots must come on a header. The team not in possession challenges for the ball, but defenders are not allowed into their own six-yard box unless marking an attacker. They are prohibited from blocking any throws; they may only contest headers and/or intercept the ball immediately after it has been headed. A turnover occurs on an interception or when the ball touches the ground (with the restart awarded from that spot to the team that did not last touch the ball). **Benefits:** Heading. **Adjustments:** May be played with more or fewer players. **Phase:** Large group. **Ages:** 10+

(32) The Game: Heading for Glory

Rules: Five two-player teams play with a regulation-size goal and a neutral 'keeper. Alternating turns, the teams compete to see who can score more goals on headers during a set time frame or for a predesignated number of attempts. One team member stands behind the goal with a ball at his feet, while his partner is stationed on the "D." The goalie is in the goal and must have at least one foot touching the goal line at the start of every play. To begin play, the server chips the ball over the crossbar as his teammate rushes into the penalty area. The runner attempts to score with a first-time header from outside the six-yard box. The play is dead when a serve fails to clear the crossbar, touches the ground, does not get beyond the six-yard box, or is contacted more than once or with any body part except for the shooter's head. **Benefits:** Heading. **Adjustments:** Alternate 'keepers and have them compete to see who can yield fewer goals. For younger or less skilled players, allow the server to punt the ball over the crossbar. A similar game can be played in which shooters finish with either a header or a volley. **Note:** To incorporate match-realistic diagonal goalward runs, allow the shooters to stand anywhere to start as long as each is outside the penalty area. Avoid inactivity by playing with no more than six teams. **Phase:** Small group. **Ages:** 15+

(33) The Game: Soccer/Baseball

Rules:: A field is marked with four bases 60 feet apart with saucers used beyond first and third bases to mark the foul lines. A goal is positioned behind "home plate." The ball is gently "pitched" with the inside of the foot. The hitter must kick the ball so it lands in fair territory (if on the ground the ball must pass first or third base in fair territory or land beyond them in fair territory). A foul ball is an out. The hitter must round the bases and touch home plate before the fielding team can kick or head the ball on the fly into the unguarded goal. There are no singles, doubles, or triples; the hitter either gets a run or is out. The fielders are limited to three collective touches and no player may use more than two consecutive touches on the ball. The team scoring more runs in three innings is the winner. *Benefits: Receiving, passing, and finishing. Good for teaching very young players to pass and move, but merely an enjoyable diversion to be used rarely for older teams. Adjustments: With advanced teams stipulate that all goals must be headed. Note: Only use as an occasional fun-filled diversion but not as a steady diet. Phase: Large group. Ages: 7+*

(34) The Game: World Cup

Rules: In a penalty area a regulation-size goal is guarded by a goalkeeper while a server, with an ample supply of balls, hits crosses into the area. All participants, as many as the coach wishes, except for the 'keeper, try to score. Credit for a goal is awarded to the last attacker to touch the ball before it entered the goal. The first player to score three times is the winner. The original version was an elimination game in which a scorer was declared "safe" and would go to the sideline. When only two contestants remained, the one who failed to score was eliminated, and the "safe" players would return for another round. When only two players remained the "Final" was held with the first player to score twice becoming the World Cup champion. The great amount of inactivity using the elimination version is not desirable, even if the eliminated players are working on their crossing skills as servers. *Benefits: Dribbling, receiving, finishing, tackling, and goalkeeping. Adjustments: You may allow that all goals scored on the first touch count double. It can also be played in an 18-x-44–yard area with two regulation-size goals (each with a 'keeper) with the attackers permitted to score on either goal. Note: Play only on occasion as an enjoyable diversion, but not recommended as a steady diet. Phase: Individual. Ages: 9+*

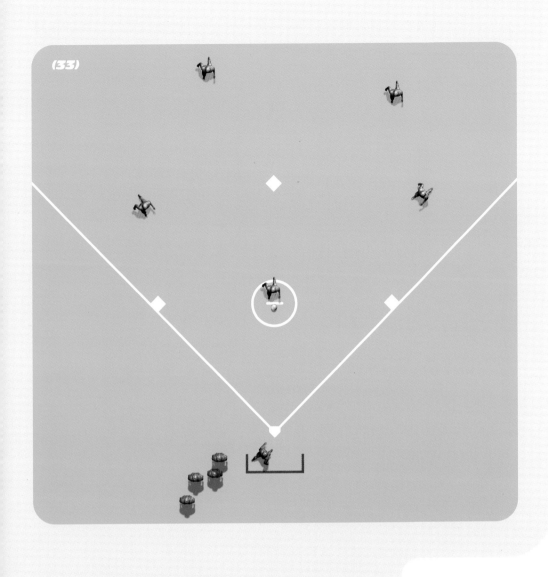

(33)

(35) The Game: Team Tag

Rules: Twelve players with two balls in a 40-x-25–yard area pass to each other and move. Two players are made defenders. When in possession of the ball, an attacker can be tagged on the body by either defender. A player is eliminated when tagged, and the game ends when no attackers remain. New defenders are appointed and a new game begins. The set of defenders who play the shortest game is the winner.

Benefits: Dribbling, passing, and receiving. **Note:** *As with any elimination game, do not allow long periods of inactivity with eliminated players. Toward that end, the game can be played for a set time frame (two minutes) with the teams' defenders competing to see how few attackers remain when time expires. A useful warm-up activity.*

Phase: Small group. **Ages:** *9+*

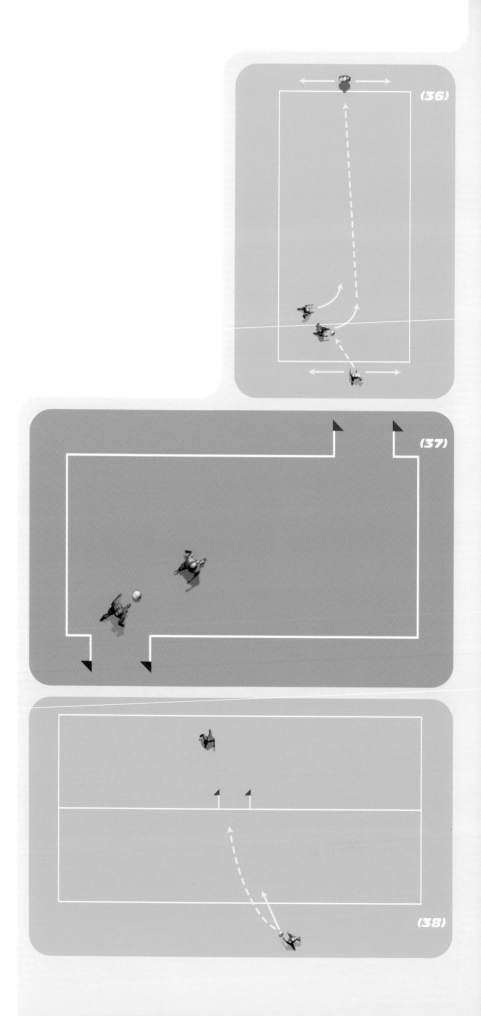

(36)

(37)

(38)

(36) The Game: One-v-One Turning

Rules: Two competing, active players are in a 20-x-10–yard area, with a neutral player on each end line. One of the neutrals passes to the nearest active player, who is facing him. The active player "scores" by turning with the ball and then passing across the field to the opposite neutral. (He is permitted to pass back to the first neutral and move to get a return pass, but there is no point value.) A player who scores gets the ball back and tries to score again in the opposite direction. The other active player tries to win possession and score a goal. After one minute the neutrals switch places with the active players, and a new game begins. **Benefits:** *Shielding, turning with the ball, passing, and tackling.* **Phase:** *Small group.* **Ages:** *9+*

(37) The Game: One-v-One to Channel the Attacker

Rules: A one-v-one game in a 10-x-20–yard area, with two four-foot-wide goals, each placed in opposite corners of the end lines. Each player is assigned one goal to attack and one to defend. The player in possession attacks the other's goal. Games can be won by whoever scores three goals, or play can simply last for a maximum of 60 seconds (45 seconds for younger players). **Benefits:** *Funneling, tackling, and dribbling.*
Adjustments: *May also be played as a team game (two-v-two up to five-v-five) to work on group defending. Appropriately increase the field and goal size to accommodate the larger number of participants. Increase the length of the game by one minute per player added. For example, three-v-three is played for three-minute intervals.*
Phase: *Small group.* **Ages:** *8+*

(38) The Game: Hot Shots

Rules: A one-v-one game in a 50-x-25–yard area with a 10-foot-wide "goal" (two cones, saucers, or corner flags) in the middle. Each player must remain in his half. The ball is served from behind the end line with the receiver having to kick it through the goal while using no more than two touches. A point is won when the opponent fails to return the ball through the goal or the ball crosses the end- or sidelines in his half (after going through the goal first). All shots must remain below knee height. Alternate servers after every point. The first player to earn 21 points wins. **Benefits:** *Receiving, passing, and shooting.* **Variations:** *Decrease or increase the goal size.*
Phase: *Individual.* **Ages:** *9+ (most appropriate for ages 9–12)*

(39) The Game: Dual Hunters

Rules: Up to seven two-player teams run while holding hands inside a 50-x-40–yard area. Two hunters use one ball, kicking it (with either the inside or outside of the foot—for safety, it is prohibited to use the instep) to try to hit any of the two-player team members below knee height. When either member of a team has been struck, the pair gets a ball and becomes hunters. The last surviving team wins. If the hunters are not very successful, decrease the playing area. A good warm-up exercise. *Benefits:* Dribbling, passing, receiving, and shooting. **Note:** *To promote safety, be sure that only hand-stitched balls are used and that none is over-inflated.*

Phase: Small group. **Ages:** *8+*

(40) The Game: Competitive Group Juggling

Rules: A circle of six players take turns juggling a ball. As a player finishes his turn he calls out a name of another player and the number of times that player must juggle the ball and then lofts a pass to the player whose name was called. The receiver must then touch the ball the demanded number of times without using his hands or allowing the ball to hit the ground. Play continues until an individual fails and is given a "strike." Three strikes and a player is eliminated. The last remaining player is the winner. *Benefits: Ball control, passing, and receiving.* **Variations:** *For more skilled players, add some restrictions such as: 1. Only juggle using the right (or the left) foot. 2. All balls must be passed with a designated body part (instep, inside of foot, thigh, chest, head, or shoulder). 3. Players may not use the same body part for consecutive touches.* **Note:** *Have eliminated players join an "out-bracket" and play the game among themselves.* **Phase:** *Small group.* **Ages:** *12+*

(41) The Game: Rapid Fire; Three-v-Three Plus Two

Rules: In a 30-x-50–yard grid with a regulation-size goal at each end, are teams of two field players plus a goalkeeper. Each team also has a fourth player, who runs up and down one flank and who may not be challenged but must stay on the flank. The action starts or restarts after a goal, as the goalkeeper distributes to his flank player. He has two or three touches to pass or strike a cross. The field players then compete for the ball and whichever team has possession tries to score. When the goalkeeper makes a catch (or after a goal) or a defender wins the ball, that player distributes to his flank player to start a counter. The game is played in two-minute intervals, after which point all the players rotate positions. *Benefits:* Crossing, heading, volleying, finishing, and goalkeeping. *Adjustments:* You can make one of the defending central players inactive (to create a two-v-one edge for the offense) and/or add a third attacking player. To work on cutbacks, the flank player may be granted more touches and allowed to dribble into the playing area. *Considerations:* Goalkeepers provide early information to teammates. Clearances should be high and wide; goalward runs by attackers well-timed and diagonal. Headed shots usually should be struck downwards. *Phase:* Small group. *Ages:* 12+

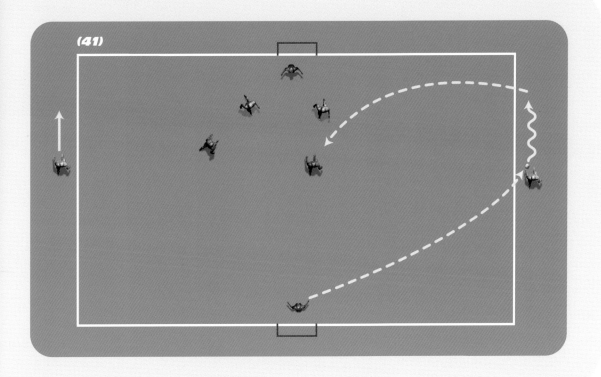

(41)

42) The Game: Two-v-Two, Heading

Rules: Two teams of two players compete in a 14-x-10–yard grid divided by saucers into two halves. Players are restricted to their own half of the grid. At each end are goals. Play starts as the deeper player on one team tosses the ball up and heads it to his teammate. The receiver may either try to shoot a goal with a header or head the ball to a teammate, who has to score with a header, and so on. The defending team stands in their goal and both players serve as goalkeepers. A player who makes a save restarts by serving to his partner. Play for a set time or until one team scores three goals. **Benefits:** *Heading and goalkeeping.* **Adjustments:** *Make the field longer for senior players and shorter for younger participants. May be played for a set time frame (five minutes recommended).* **Phase:** *Small group.* **Ages:** *12+*

(43) The Game: Soccer/Tennis

Rules: Played in a 20-x-10–yard grid with a six-foot-high net, this two-v-two game is like doubles tennis, except that the ball may not be touched with hands or arms while it is in play. While standing on the end line the "server" starts a point by drop-kicking the ball over the net. There are no "faults" and a "serve" that goes out is a lost point. The receiving team must return the ball over the net into their opponents' grid in three or less touches. The ball is permitted to touch the ground once before being returned. A point is won when the other team fails to return the ball successfully. The first team to earn 11 points wins. **Benefits:** *Receiving, heading, passing, and volleying.* **Adjustments:** *May be played in the singles boxes of a tennis court. It can also be played one-v-one or three-v-three. And, as with volleyball, it can be played so that a team may only win a point on their own serve with the serving team switching after the non-servers win a rally. An option for more advanced participants is to prohibit players from taking two consecutive touches.* **Phase:** *Small group.* **Ages:** *12+*

(44) The Game: Chip-To-Grid

Rules: A two-v-two game with each pair of players restricted to its own 15-x-15–yard grid, with 25 yards between the grids. The ball is served by one pair with a lofted kick into the opponents' zone. It must be returned on the first or second touch in a game-like manner (better players are prohibited from running around the ball to kick it with a preferred foot and/or to take excessive time to strike it). Alternate serves. Points are awarded when a team misses their opponents' grid or fails to return the ball in two touches. The first team to 11 points wins. **Benefits:** *Receiving air balls, first-touch, and* long passing. **Adjustments:** Grid size and distance between areas varies from a 12-yard square and 40 yards for advanced players to a 20-yard square with 15 yards for less skillful players. With advanced players nobody is permitted to touch the ball twice in succession while with less skillful participants that rule is waived and a third touch is permitted. **Phase:** Small group. **Ages:** 14+

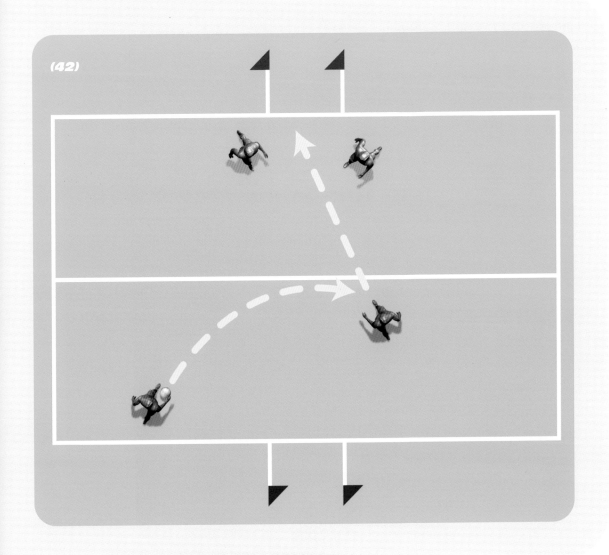

(45) The Game: Quick Draw

Rules: A team technical exercise in which the objective is to beat the clock. Station two to three players at each corner of a 25-x-25–yard grid with 10 balls behind corner #1. The front player in the first corner plays a long ball to the front player in the opposite corner (diagram 1). After each pass, the passer sprints to the back of the line of the corner to his immediate right. The receiver first-times a pass to a checking player from the corner perpendicular to him. As that player receives the ball, the player opposite runs toward the next corner (diagram 2). The ball is then passed into his path and he dribbles it to the back of the line of the corner to his right (diagram 3). The exercise ends when all 10 balls have been delivered. **Benefits:** Passing, receiving, and dribbling. **Adjustments:** Play the game in the opposite direction or restrict players to using only the left foot. **Considerations:** Players are encouraged to attack incoming balls and to strive for technical proficiency at speed. **Phase:** Large group. **Ages:** 12+

(46) The Game: Power Heading

Rules: In a 60-x-20–yard area two seven-player teams try to drive the other team behind their own goal line. Two coaches serve as the "net" by standing opposite each other on a respective sideline. The net moves up and down the field to the spot at which a team failed to return the ball, or a five-yard penalty is taken when a ball lands out of bounds (or half the distance to the end line when within 10 yards of the goal line). To clear the net the ball must cross the imaginary line between the two coaches at or above shoulder height. Any ball that does not clear the net results in the net moving five yards in the direction of the team that lost the rally. Teams have a maximum of three touches to head the ball over the net but no player may touch the ball twice consecutively and the ball may not hit the ground. A point is scored when the ball lands over the other team's goal line or crosses the goal line without being returned (a ball crossing the end line is in play as long as it remains airborne). **Benefits:** Receiving, passing, and power heading for distance. **Adjustments:** Can mandate that while playing the ball over the net the player must have both feet off the ground. **Considerations:** Encourage players to head with power by striking the ball while airborne, snapping forward of the upper body but keeping the neck muscles rigid. **Phase:** Large group. **Ages:** 14+

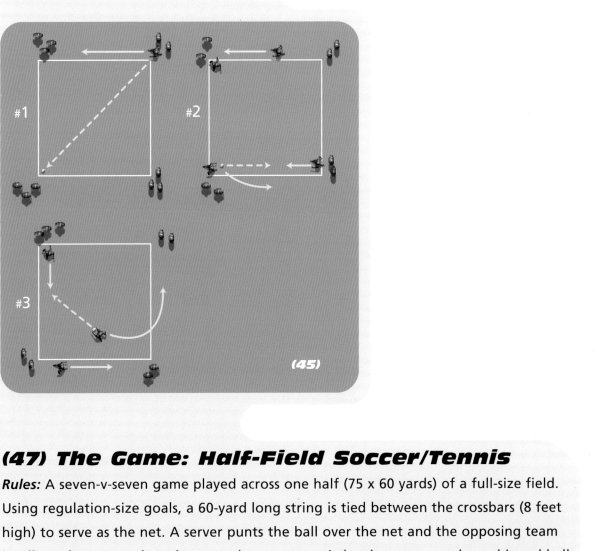

(45)

(47) The Game: Half-Field Soccer/Tennis

Rules: A seven-v-seven game played across one half (75 x 60 yards) of a full-size field. Using regulation-size goals, a 60-yard long string is tied between the crossbars (8 feet high) to serve as the net. A server punts the ball over the net and the opposing team is allowed no more than three touches to return it (or the serve may be a chipped ball or an instep drive). The ball may not hit the ground and no player may touch the ball consecutively. A point is won when a team fails to return the ball into its opponents' zone or the ball touches the ground before it is returned. There are no "faults;" a bad serve is a lost point. Teams alternate serving. The first team to 21 points wins.

Benefits: Receiving, passing, heading, and volleying. **Adjustments:** *May be played with more or fewer players. The game can also be played with any one of the following stipulations: 1. The ball may only be headed back over the net. 2. The ball may only be volleyed back over the net. 3. Any goalkeeper(s) participating are permitted to box (fist) the ball.* **Phase:** *Large group.* **Ages:** *14+*

(48) The Game: Goalie Wars

Rules: Two goalkeepers, with a healthy supply of extra balls in each goal, compete on a 20-x-44–yard field with full-size goals. They strive to shoot, throw, or drop-kick the ball into the other 'keeper's goal. Play starts with one player striking a dead ball from just in front of his own goal line. That goalkeeper stays on offense if he scores or his shot is parried. To win possession, the opposing goalkeeper must make a catch or let a ball run that is off target. After making a catch, a goalkeeper is permitted four steps before shooting. The first goalkeeper to score 21 goals is the winner.

Benefits: Diving on the line, distribution, foot skills, and fitness.

Phase: Individual. **Ages:** 11+

(49) The Game: Boxing Volleyball

Rules: A six-v-six game of volleyball in a 36-x-44–yard area with a 10-foot-high net. Every ball must be boxed (fisted) and spiking is prohibited. A team must return the ball with three or less touches and no player may touch the ball consecutively. Points are only awarded on a team's serve. *Benefits: Dealing with crosses, boxing. Adjustments: It can be played with as few as 2-v-2 while decreasing the area's size. It may also be played with a mixture of field players (who are prohibited from using their hands/arms) and goalkeepers (who must box the ball). Phase: Large group. Ages: 12+*

(50) The Game: Crossing Baseball

Rules: An excellent game for helping goalkeepers develop the ability to command their box. Playing in a penalty area, the team "at bat" has a server in a wide position and two central attackers. The defending team sends out one of its three goalkeepers while the other two act as chasers. The server's cross must be within 12 yards of the goal line and must be shot on the first or second touch (any rebound must be shot the first time). The defending goalkeeper is credited with an "out" for a clean save, for fisting the ball out of the penalty area on the fly, for a shot that misses the target, or for a bad serve. A shot parried for a corner kick is a "foul ball." Both teams rotate after each of the goalkeepers on the team at bat has recorded three outs.

Benefits: Handling crosses, shots on the line, and foot skills. Adjustments: Have serves sent in from both sides. Even though there are no defenders, to promote organizational skills and good habits, award a penalty kick against a goalkeeper who fails to shout "'keeper" (asking imaginary defenders to clear the way) or "away" (asking imaginary defenders to clear the ball from danger). Considerations: Position the goalkeeper's

body at an "open" angle with the starting position slightly to the front half of the goal for an inswinging cross and deeper for an outswinger. Balls should be caught, if possible. Only when a collision is anticipated is boxing encouraged. Whenever possible crosses should be cut out above the head height of the opponents. When attempting to catch the ball, the goalie's elbow should be slightly bent, if possible.
*Phase: Small group. **Ages:** 10+*

(51) The Game: 'Keeper Tag

Rules: Eight to twelve 'keepers play inside a regulation-size penalty area. Three are "taggers," who compete while holding brightly colored scrimmage vests. The remainder are active players, three of whom have balls in their hands. Each of the taggers attempts to tag any opponent not in possession of a ball. Thus, each active player in possession should throw his ball to a teammate who is in danger of being tagged. A goalie who is tagged without a ball or who leaves the area to escape being tagged changes places with the player who tagged him. **Benefits:** *Goalkeeping.* **Adjustments:** *Require more skilled goalies to pass the ball by volleying it out of their hands or with a drop kick. To work on saving low shots, stipulate that all passes be bowled to the receiver.* **Note:** *Allow for adequate rest, as this is a very active game. For saftey's sake, move the goal so that it is not in the players' way.* **Phase:** *Individual.* **Ages:** *9+*

(52) The Game: The Numbers Game

Rules: Seven players stand between the goalposts of their own goal on a 30-x-50–yard field. (Goals are in the middle of the end lines.) Each team's players are assigned a number. The coach/server stands near the middle of a sideline with a number of balls. The coach calls out one or more numbers from each team and kicks a ball into play. Those whose numbers are called race onto the field and combine with their teammates to try to score. All others remain on the goal line and try to prevent the opponents from scoring goals (but are prohibited from using their hands). The players on the line may be used for a back pass but are restricted to one touch to return it, are not permitted to shoot, and may not venture more than a few yards away from their goal. *Benefits:* Passing, receiving, combination play, mobility, finishing, and defending. *Adjustments:* May be played five-v-five up to eight-v-eight. Generally, use three-v-three or two-v-two confrontations in the field. A shout of "boxcars" by the coach means that all players may enter onto the field. **Note:** For younger players, play six-v-six with two groups of three players that alternate being on the field and being on the goal line. For safety's sake, use only hand-stitched balls that are not over-inflated. *Phase:* Small group. **Ages:** 6+

(53) The Game: Backpasses Wild

Rules: This game introduces rudimentary tactics by teaching youngsters that not every attacking movement must be first toward goal. Try this two-v-two game (one outfield player plus a goalkeeper for each team) on a 15-x-20–yard field with two 12-foot-wide goals, one in the middle of each of the 20-yard end lines. The outfield rivals try to score. If a player passes back to his goalkeeper (who may not use the hands when receiving the pass, only when stopping a shot on the goal line) the passer (outfield player) and the receiver (goalkeeper) must change roles. To help the outfield players defend or start a new attack, encourage them to pass to their goalkeeper when they are under pressure and/or facing their own goal. **Benefits:** Dribbling, passing, receiving, finishing, goalkeeping, and tactical awareness. **Adjustments:** If no backpass occurs in 45 seconds, switch positions. Progress from this game to Game 54. **Considerations:** On a backpass, the receiver's (goalkeeper's) first touch should usually be played to the opposite side of the field from where the pass came, in order to reduce defensive pressure. **Phase:** Small group. **Ages:** 7+

(54) The Game: Backpasses Wild, Part Two

Rules: This is a four-v-four game (two outfield players plus two goalkeepers for each team) on a 20-x-40–yard field with four 12-foot-wide goals (two on each endline). The outfield players try to score. When an outfield player passes back to one of the goal-keepers (who may not use hands when receiving passes) the passer and the receiver/ goalkeeper change roles. *Benefits: Dribbling, passing, receiving, finishing, goalkeep-ing, and tactical awareness. Considerations: Play to space and off-the-ball movement. Backpasses should generally be aimed at the goalkeeper's far foot, whose first touch should put the ball into an area away from any pressurizing opponent. Note: Ensure rotation of players so everyone has a chance to play as the sweeper/'keeper. Phase: Small group. Ages: 8+*

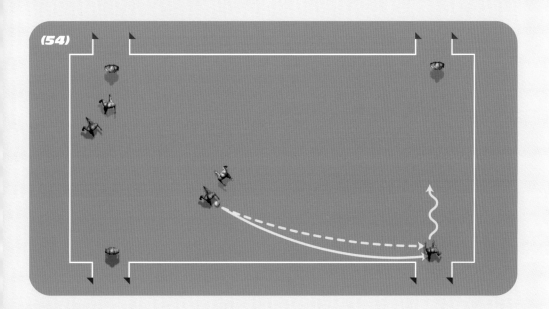

(55) The Game: Line Soccer

Rules: This four-v-four game encourages incorporating a dynamic first touch to set up chances to penetrate defenses by dribbling. The game is played in a 25-x-35–yard grid. There are no goals and no goalies. The objective is for the players on a team to pass to each other until one finds an opportunity to dribble the ball, with control, over the opponents' end line. *Benefits: Dribbling, passing, receiving, combination play, and defending. Adjustments: May be played with more or fewer participants, altering the size of the grid accordingly. Considerations: Taking initiative whenever appropriate. Phase: Small group. Ages: 8+*

(56)

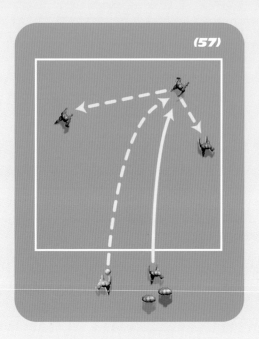

(57)

(56) The Game: Five-Cone Knockoff

Rules: Playing away from defensive pressure with a good first touch is sure to be improved by playing this four-v-four game. Set up a 35-x-35–yard area with five cones. Points are earned by kicking the game ball so that it knocks over any of the cones, with the action continuing and the scoring team keeping possession as the cone is picked up and put back on its spot by the coach. A ball leaving the area is kicked in by the team that did not last touch the ball before it left the area. The first team to score five points is the winner. *Benefits:* Passing, receiving, turning with the ball, mobility, vision, and defending. *Adjustments:* Alter the playing area as needed. Older players can play up to six-v-six. For less advanced and/or younger teams, it can be played with uneven numbers (i.e., six-v-three) for 60-second intervals. If defenders win the ball, the play is restarted with a kick-in for the attackers. *Phase:* Small-group. *Ages:* 8+

(57) The Game: Small-Group Keepaway

Rules: The objective of this game is to learn to maintain possession of the ball for an extended period of time. Set up a 12-x-12–yard area. Three attackers stand inside the grid and three members of the defending team stand in a line behind a saucer next to the coach. Play starts with the coach rolling a ball into the playing area and starting his watch. The first defender in line sprints into the grid in an attempt to clear the ball from the area, while the attackers try to play keepaway. If the defender wins possession or clears the ball out of the area, a new ball is served, and the defender runs to tag the hand of his teammate in the front of the line, who then takes his place. The action is repeated. After the ball has been cleared by the final defender, the watch is stopped. The teams swap places. Whichever attacking team held possession longer wins the round. **Benefits:** *Passing, receiving, and playing under pressure in a confined area.* **Adjustments:** *The game can be played with two teams of six players. Divide the attacking team in half. The first three players play an entire round (challenged consecutively by six different defenders) and then the next three attackers do the same. Compare their total time to that of the opposition. For players age 12 and older, play four-v-two in a 15-x15–yard area. Be prepared to adjust the space to suit the age and ability level of the participants.* **Considerations:** *Passing to the farther foot, a good first touch out of pressure, and attackers off the ball moving to provide immediate support.* **Phase:** *Small group.* **Ages:** *8+*

(58) The Game: Five-v-Two

Rules: In a 12-x-12–yard grid five attackers form a circle and play keepaway from two defenders in the middle. A player whose pass is intercepted, or who loses possession in a tackle, exchanges places with the defender who won the ball. If an errant pass exits from the grid, the passer trades places with the defender who has been in the middle longer. **Benefits:** *Passing (pace and accuracy), support, and receiving.* **Adjustments:** *May also be played so that the attackers get one point for a predesignated number of consecutive passes as determined by the coach, based on the age and ability of the players, and two points for successfully completing a penetrating pass that splits the defenders. The defenders earn a point every time they touch the ball or when a ball leaves the area. The first team with ten points wins. Switch defenders and play again. Advanced players can be limited to one- or two-touch play.* **Considerations:** *Attackers support each other in open-body position with emphasis on pre-reception vision. Good first touch away from defensive pressure is a main objective. The nearer defender pressures the ball and makes the play predictable while the covering defender prevents a penetrating pass.* **Phase:** *Small group.* **Ages:** *9+*

(59) The Game: Team Breakaways

Rules: To improve your team's finishing efficiency and goalkeeping sharpness, outline a central 15-x70-yard grid across the width of a 70-x-70–yard area. Play a four-v-four game in this area. In the middle of each end line is a regulation-size goal guarded by a 'keeper. Only after a team has completed a predesignated, minimum number of passes (usually three or four) may a player send a diagonal pass beyond the grid for a team-mate to run onto the ball. The attacker who "escapes" the grid attempts to score—as defenders are not allowed to chase him, he faces a one-on-one with the goalkeeper. The first team to score ten goals wins. *Benefits: Passing, receiving, dribbling, finishing, and goalkeeping. Adjustments: May also be played for a specific amount of time. To add pressure to the attacker, allow the member of the defending team who is the far-thest from the attacker to give chase. The coach can alter the number of players in the grid and/or play with one or two neutral players. Phase: Small group. Ages: 10+*

(60) The Game: Two-v-Two Plus Two; Penetration

Rules: A more challenging game that hones combination play for penetration purposes, this two-v-two game is played on a 15-x-15–yard grid with two neutrals, one stationed at each end line. The objective is to receive a pass from one neutral, who stays outside the grid (but may move anywhere along the end line), and to play it to the neutral on the opposite side. The neutral players can take no more than two touches and may play to each other, but points are only awarded when the inside players "connect" the outside, neutral players. The action continues after a point is earned; the scoring team gets the ball from the neutral and attempts to penetrate in the opposite direction. After one minute the losing team trades spots with the neutrals. *Benefits: Passing, receiving, mobility, defending, and combination play. Adjustments: To reinforce posi-tive attacking play, double the point value for a successful first-touch pass to the tar-get player. Phase: Small group. Ages: 11+*

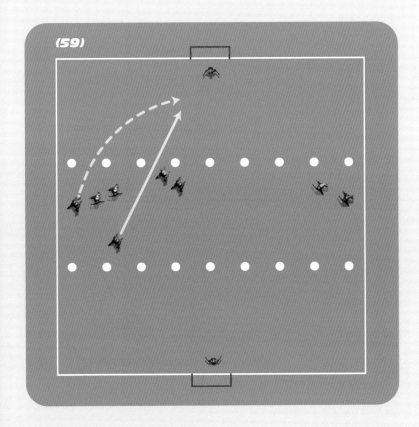

(59)

(61) The Game: Find the Target

Rules: Combining to achieve penetration is the point of this game. It is a two-v-two confrontation in a 15-x-15–yard area with four extra players, one assigned to each sideline—neutral players—and one to each end line—target players. The neutral and target players may not enter the grid, but can move up and down their lines. There are no goals or goalies. Each team starts with assigned ends to attack and defend. During a one minute to ninety-second period the objective is for one of the players in the field to pass the ball over the opponents' end line to the target player behind the end line. The active players may combine passes with either of the two neutral players and/or with the rear target player. The neutrals must return the ball to the passing team on the first or second touch or within two to three seconds. After "scoring" with a pass to the forward target player, the target player passes back to the "scoring" team, which immediately attacks in the opposite direction. *Benefits: Passing, receiving, and combination play.* **Adjustments:** *Advanced players can play with limited touches. Adjust the grid size to accommodate the age and ability of the players.* **Considerations:** *Off-the-ball movement with the neutral and target players seeking supporting positions. Attack at speed.* **Phase:** *Small group.* **Ages:** *11+*

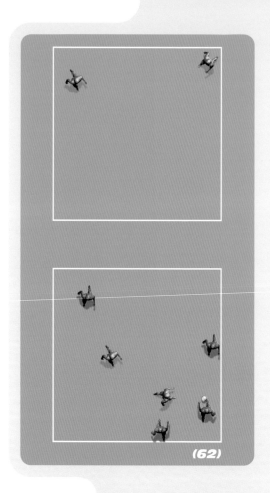

(62)

(62) The Game: Double-Grid Possession

Rules: In this possession game, players off the ball learn to support the player on the ball better. Set up two adjacent 15-x-15–yard grids. In one grid four reds play keep-away from two blues with two inactive blues in the other grid. When the blue defenders win the ball they play it to a teammate in the other grid and then sprint to join their teammates as attackers. Meanwhile, two reds race to the opposite grid to act as defenders. Any ball leaving the playing area results in a kick-in. A point is awarded for a predesignated number of consecutive straight passes or for a first-touch pass that splits the defenders. The team with more points after five minutes wins. *Benefits:* Passing, receiving, mobility, support, and defending. *Adjustments:* Alter the grids' sizes per age and abilities of the players. *Considerations:* Play quickly with accurate passes. One defender pressures the player on the ball and makes the pass predictable while the covering defender prevents a penetrating pass. *Phase:* Small group. *Ages:* 11+

(63) The Game: Grid Combination Play

Rules: This is a two-v-two game played in a 20-x-20–yard grid with a neutral player along each of the four sidelines. Neutrals are limited to no more than two touches or two to three seconds with the ball and must not pass to another neutral, only to the team that passed to them. A team earns a point for completing a predesignated number of successive passes based upon the age and ability of the players. The other team challenges for the ball. If it wins possession, it tries to complete passes, and so on. After a one-minute period, the active players and the neutrals trade places. The team with more points after three rounds wins. *Benefits:* Passing, receiving, mobility, combination play, and tactical awareness. *Adjustments:* May play three-v-three in a 30-x-30-yard area. You may also award points for other forms of combination play, such as takeovers, wall passes, and overlaps. To make the game easier, increase the size of the playing area. For more advanced players, neutrals may be limited to one touch.

Considerations: Neutrals available in support. Verbal communication and pre-reception vision. *Phase:* Small group. *Ages:* 13+

(63)

(64) The Game: Four-v-Four Plus Two

Rules: In a long but narrow area (40 x 20 yards) two teams of four players are aided by two neutral players on the long sidelines. One team attempts to maintain possession for as long as possible, while the other team challenges for the ball. A neutral is restricted to one or two touches or two or three seconds to pass the ball and must try to pass back to a member of the team from which he received the ball. The team that completes the most consecutive passes (including to or from the neutrals) in a four-minute period wins. **Benefits:** Passing, receiving, support, mobility, defending, the weighing of risks vs. rewards, and the performance of techniques while under pressure. **Adjustments:** To promote mobility and combination play, allow only the passes completed between interior (active) players to be counted, with three consecutive passes required for scoring a point. The game may also be played with direction for penetration as players try to work the ball to a teammate who can attempt to run with the ball under control over one of the short end lines. As soon as that is accomplished, the game immediately continues, but the team attacks in the opposite direction. **Considerations:** Players support at angles to maximize options before receiving the ball. Quality of first touch. Defensive organization. **Phase:** Small-group. **Ages:** 13+

(65) The Game: Inside-Outside

Rules: To work on principles of support and to improve the ability of players to complete penetrating passes, try this game. Players are divided into two teams and then assigned and restricted to one of four zones, so as to set up a game of two-v-one confrontations within a 26-x-26–yard area around the center circle. One point is awarded for completing a pass through the opponents' half of the center circle to a teammate on the opposite side (either from the outside of the circle to the inside or vice versa). Players whose team is in possession should try to be open for a pass; defenders challenge for the ball when it's in their zone as well as mark opponents. Play continues after a point is scored. Any ball leaving the area is restarted with a throw-in taken by the team that did not kick it out. The first team to earn 21 points wins. **Benefits:** Passing, receiving, support, mobility, and defending. **Adjustments:** With 14 players, make one outside zone three-v-two (both outside zones are three-v-two if there are 16 players). To emphasize quick play award two points for a first-touch penetrating pass. **Considerations:** Intelligent support. Vision followed by a sharp first touch. Quick ball movement. Weighing risk-taking vs. safety. Numbers-down defender makes play predictable. **Phase:** Large group. **Ages:** 11+ (best for ages 11–14)

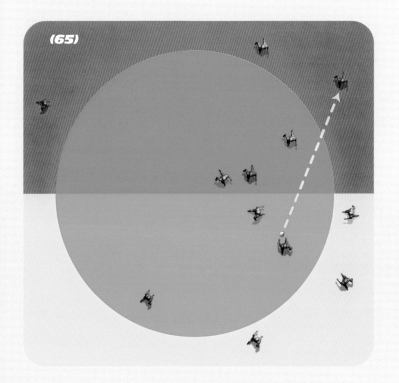

(65)

(66) The Game: Volley/Tennis

Rules: On a wide but narrow, 70-x-25–yard playing area, two seven-player teams try to get the ball over the opponents' end line (25-yard-wide line) so that it cannot be returned. Two coaches serve as a "net" by standing opposite each other on the side lines. Each team must stay on its side of the net. All balls played "over the net" must be above the coach's shoulder height. Teams have three touches to volley the ball into their opponents' zone and may not let it touch the ground. The net moves up and down the field after every rally—rather like the line of scrimmage in American football—to the spot at which a team failed to return the ball or five yards forward or back when a ball lands out of bounds, thereby moving the teams up and down the field. The game is won when the ball lands on the ground past the other team's goal line or crosses the goal line without being returned (a ball crossing the end line is in play as long as it is in the air). All rallies start by the coach serving to the team that won the previous rally. *Benefits: Receiving, passing, heading, and volleying using the insides of the feet and the insteps.* **Considerations:** *Quality of the pass to the player who will volley. Volleying technique.* **Phase:** *Large group.* **Ages:** *14+*

(67) The Game: Cross & Finish

Rules: A six-v-six crossing and heading game in a 50-x-44–yard area, with two goals, one in the middle of each short end line. Both 'keepers face four opponents (one server and three strikers) and are aided by two defenders. Attackers must stay in the opponents' half and defenders must stay in their half. The objective is for the defenders to get the ball to the server, who is the only player who can dribble forward and cross into the attacking zone. One striker makes a looping, far-post run while another striker runs diagonally toward the near post and a third attacker holds near the penalty spot. The players challenge for the ball. Any rebound is live and may be struck with any legal body part. As soon as a defender clears to a server or a goal, or a save occurs, the goal-keeper distributes the ball to his team's server, in which case the action moves in the opposite direction. The first team to score three goals wins. **Benefits:** Crossing, heading, finishing, timing of runs, and goalkeeping. **Adjustments:** Can be played with four neutral players (two per sideline). **Phase:** Large group. **Ages:** 14+

(67)

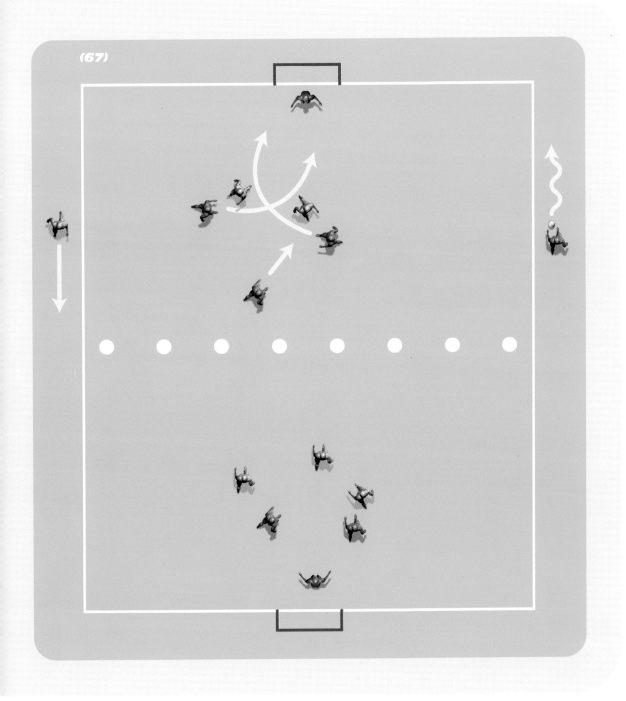

(68) The Game: Conditioned Game/ Forward Passes Banned

Rules: A regular soccer match with one rule change; players may not pass or cross forward. Violations of this type are punished by awarding an indirect free kick to the opponents from the spot where the ball was played. Play four-v-four in a 35-x-25–yard grid or up to seven-v-seven in a 50-x-40–yard grid, with adjustments for field size allowed per the age and ability of the players. *Benefits:* Quickness of thought/action, first touch, dribbling for penetration. *Phase:* Small-group. *Ages:* 8+

(69) The Game: One-Goal Soccer

Rules: A five-v-five game in a 45-x-60–yard grid with one regulation size goal (preferably consisting of corner flags or use two saucers or cones) in the middle of the field and guarded by a neutral goalkeeper. A goal may be scored by shooting the ball through the goal, but each team must attack the goal from a different, predetermined direction. When the goalkeeper catches the ball he throws it to any part of the field and the action continues. The first team to score ten goals wins. *Benefits:* Passing, receiving, dribbling, heading, finishing, mobility, combination play, defending, and goalkeeping. *Adjustments:* Play three-v-three for younger players and up to eight-v-eight for older players, while adjusting the grid and goal size accordingly. May add a neutral player or two on the sideline to help create more finishing opportunities. May also be played for a set time frame (ten minutes suggested); the team scoring more goals is the winner. *Considerations:* Quickly play away from defensive pressure. Extra attackers provide width and depth. Shoot at the first opportunity. *Phase:* Large-group. *Ages:* 8+

(70) The Game: Zone Soccer

Rules: A four-v-four game that is played in a 30-x-20–yard grid with three-yard-deep zones behind both of the end lines. A goal is scored by stopping the ball anywhere in the opponents' zone with the bottom of a foot. The team scoring more goals after five minutes wins. *Benefits:* Passing, receiving, dribbling, vision, mobility, combination play, tactics (changing the point of attack), and defending. *Adjustments:* It can involve three teams. Two teams compete with the resting teams' members surrounding the field and acting as neutral players who are limited to one or two touches or two to three seconds and are not allowed to pass to another neutral. Older players can play up to seven-v-seven, while adjusting the grid size. The depth of the end zones should be tailored to the age and ability of the players (less depth for older and better players).

The game can also be played so that after a goal the scoring team keeps possession of the ball and immediately attacks in the opposite direction. **Considerations:** *Efficient attacking play with minimum number of touches and intelligent movement off the ball. Defensive pressure and making the play predictable.* **Phase:** *Small-group.* **Ages:** *8+*

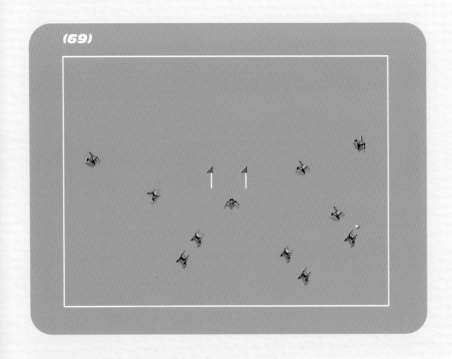

(69)

(70)

(71) The Game: Four-Goal Soccer

Rules: A four-v-four game with one ball and no goalkeepers in a 25-x-35–yard area in which each team attacks either of two four-foot-wide goals just inside each corner of the opponents' goal line. **Benefits:** Passing, receiving, dribbling, decision-making, combination play, and defending. **Adjustments:** Widen the goals slightly if defenders are trying to defend their goals by acting as de facto goalkeepers. May be played five- or six-a-side for older or more advanced players, while adjusting the size of goals and grid as needed. **Considerations:** Playing away from defensive pressure by changing the point of attack. Efficiency of touches and off-the-ball movement. Accurate passes (mostly to feet). **Phase:** Small-group. **Ages:** 9+

(72) The Game: Four-Goal Soccer, Sideline Version

Rules: This game is excellent for recognizing space and playing away from defensive pressure. It is played in a 50-x-50–yard area with four 12-foot-wide goals that are marked by cones, saucers, or corner flags. Each five-player team attacks the goal on the opposite end line and the sideline goal to its left, while defending the other two. There are no goalkeepers. To score, the ball must be passed through either goal (front to back or vice versa) to a teammate on the other side. Play continues after a goal is scored. The first team to score ten goals wins. **Benefits:** Passing, receiving, dribbling, vision, decision-making, combination play, mobility, and defending. **Adjustments:** Demand quick play from senior players (3 seconds to pass). You may add neutral players for less-advanced teams or for young players. Award a point for any ball played through an 8-foot-wide goal, even if there is no teammate to receive it. Narrow width of the goals for advanced players. **Considerations:** Some of the attackers must provide width and depth. **Note:** If possible, use one color of saucer for the goals that one team is attacking and another color of saucer, or corner flags, for the goals the other team is attacking. **Phase:** Large-group. **Ages:** 9+

(71)

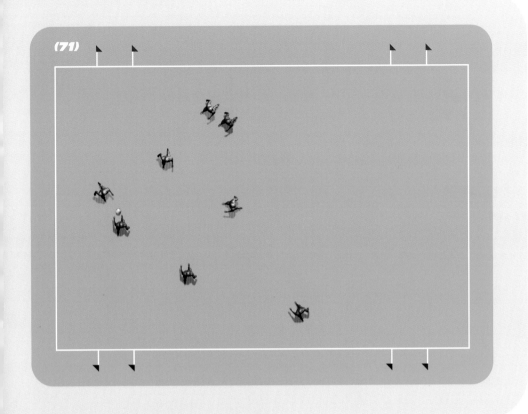

(72)

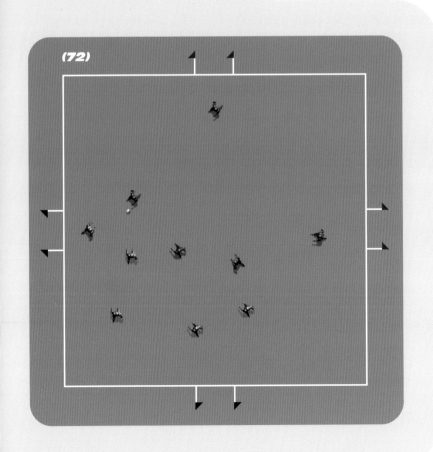

(73) The Game: Six-v-Six Minus Two

Rules: This six-v-six game on a 40-x-50–yard field with a regulation-size goal in the middle of each of the longer endlines teaches players to find the open attacker. There are no permanent goalkeepers. Instead, when a team loses possession its two deepest members must drop back into their own six-yard box and become temporary goalkeepers. Thus, the offense always enjoys a two-player numerical advantage. *Benefits:* Passing, receiving, combination play, finishing, mobility, tactical challenges (possession vs. risk-taking), and goalkeeping. *Adjustments:* May also be played five-v-five or up to eight-v-eight with the appropriate field-dimension changes. *Considerations:* Efficiency of touches (pass and move). Taking initiative to shoot at the first good opportunity. *Phase:* Large-group. *Ages:* 10+

(74) The Game: Four-v-Four Plus Four; Possession

Rules: To work toward minimizing turnovers while on offense, two four-player teams play with one ball in a 25-x-30–yard area and earn points by completing a predesignated number of consecutive passes. The team not in possession challenges for the ball. Four neutrals—one on each boundary line—may be used, but they cannot play to each other and are limited to no more than one or two touches and/or two to three seconds with the ball before attempting to return a pass to the team that last passed it to them. *Benefits:* Passing, receiving, vision, mobility, and combination play. *Adjustments:* Can be played up to seven-v-seven, while altering the size of the grid appropriately. You may add one or two neutrals inside the zone (if so, widen the area). Rather than awarding points for consecutive passes, reward combination play (such as a wall pass, takeover, or double pass). To work on finishing, include regulation-size goals with goalkeepers. A team may shoot on either goal but only after having completed a specified number of passes. *Phase:* Large-group. *Ages:* 10+

(75) The Game: Five-v-Five Plus Four; Finishing

Rules: Superb for working on finishing, this game takes place in a compact, 36-x-44–yard area with two five-player teams (four plus a goalkeeper) playing regular soccer and attempting to score on regulation-size goals, one each in the middle of the wider end lines. Two neutral players are assigned to each of the goal lines, one to either side of each goal. They are limited to two touches to return the ball to the team that passed it to them, and they may not pass to another neutral. Many match-realistic scoring opportunities should be presented in a short period of time. Throw-ins are used if the ball crosses the sidelines. The team scoring more goals in five minutes wins. The losing team then switches places with the neutral players. *Benefits: Passing, receiving, dribbling, crossing, finishing, vision, mobility, combination play, and goalkeeping.*

Adjustments: You may award two points for all goals scored on the first touch. Goalkeepers may be restricted to distributing a ball with a rollout. Position extra neutral players on the sidelines. *Considerations: Accuracy over power when finishing.*

Phase: Large group. Ages: 10+

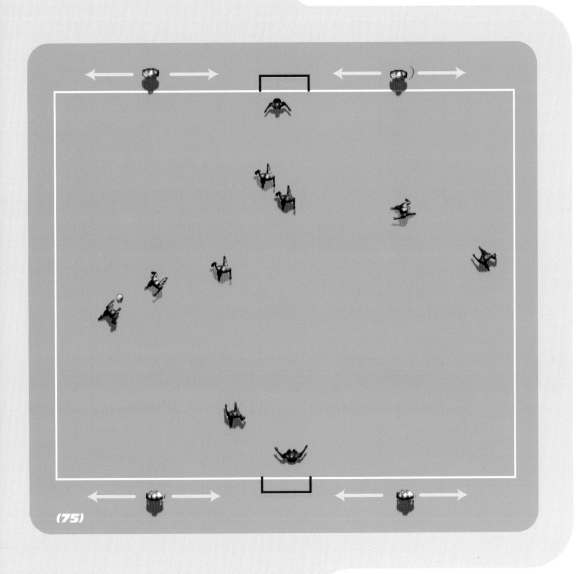

(75)

(76) The Game: Numbers Up and Numbers Down

Rules: A regular six-v-six soccer game (five field players plus a goalkeeper) in a 60-x-45–yard area with a regulation-size goal in the middle of each of the two shorter end lines. The outfield players on each team are assigned a number from one to five. After every change of possession the coach calls out one or two numbers. The corresponding player (or players) on the defending team stands still and cannot participate until his team wins the ball back or concedes a goal. The team scoring more goals in ten minutes is the winner. *Benefits:* Passing, receiving, dribbling, heading, finishing, and goalkeeping, as well as the tactical demands of attacking with the advantage of an extra player. *Adjustments:* Can be played up to eight-v-eight while adjusting the area to accommodate the age and ability of the players. Can also be played by dividing the squad into three teams so that the members of each team receive an occasional rest. *Considerations:* Quick, efficient, and intelligent attacking. *Phase:* Large group. *Ages:* 10+

(77) The Game: Forced Marking

Rules: A regular six-v-six soccer game (five field players plus a goalkeeper) in a 60-x-45–yard area with regulation-size goals in the middle of the end lines. Four of the field players are paired with a specific opponent and may only mark and tackle that player. Each team has a deep defender, or sweeper, who must stay in his own half of the field and may challenge anyone, but no opponent may tackle him. The deep defender is limited to playing up to two touches at a time. Play for 15 minutes, alternating the sweeper every three minutes. The team that scores more goals wins.
Benefits: Full range of defensive skills as well as passing, receiving, dribbling, finishing, mobility, support, and goalkeeping. Ample one-v-one confrontations. *Adjustments:* Can be played up to eight-v-eight while appropriately altering the dimensions of the playing area. *Considerations:* Immediate recovery to get goal-side of opponents upon loss of possession. Defensive judgment (not challenging recklessly). *Phase:* Large group. *Ages:* 10+

(78) The Game: Five-v-Five/Short and Wide

Rules: To highlight possession playing while being patient on attack, play a regular five-v-five (four outfield players plus a goalkeeper) game in a 36-x-60–yard area (short but wide) with two regulation-size goals, one in the middle of each of the longer end lines. The ability of attackers to pass and move and to dribble for penetration is underscored, as is individual and collective defending. **Benefits:** *Passing, receiving, vision, mobility, combination play, dribbling, heading, finishing, defending, and goalkeeping with many tactical demands.* **Phase:** *Large group.* **Ages:** *10+*

(79) The Game: Total Football

Rules: A regular six-v-six (five outfield players plus a goalkeeper) game designed to teach team compactness and based on the premise that when a team has the ball all members are on offense and when without it they must defend. To reinforce the principle of players moving as a team, saucers mark the midfield line on a 60-x-44–yard field with regulation-size goals at each end, guarded by goalkeepers. All five outfield players on the attacking team must be in the opponents' half of the field before their team may attempt a shot. A goal is disallowed if any attacking outfield player is in his own half of the field when the shot was struck. In addition, all goals count double if any player on the defending team is not in his own half of the field when the ball enters into his team's goal. **Benefits:** *Finishing, passing, receiving, dribbling, support, team shape/compactness, mobility, combination play, defending, and goalkeeping.* **Adjustments:** *For younger players, may be played as four-v-four and, for older players, up to eight-v-eight, while changing the field dimensions accordingly.* **Considerations:** *Ability of striker to "hold" the ball until support arrives after receiving a long ball. Also key: speed of support, possession in attack, defenders reading runs and pressing collectively, and transition play.* **Phase:** *Large group.* **Ages:** *10+*

(80) The Game: The Three-Colors Game

Rules: A game used to improve possession play and team transition. Two four-player teams combine to form an eight-player team that plays keepaway in a 50-x-50–yard area against a third team of four players that tries to win the ball. A "goal" is scored after ten straight passes are completed. A second goal is awarded for the 15th straight pass (and again at 20, and so on). When a turnover occurs the entire four-player team whose member was responsible for losing the ball switches roles with the squad that won the ball. After ten minutes the side with the best net (goals for minus goals against) wins. **Benefits:** *Passing, receiving, vision, mobility, combination play, speed of transitional play, and fitness.* **Adjustments:** *May be played with teams of three to*

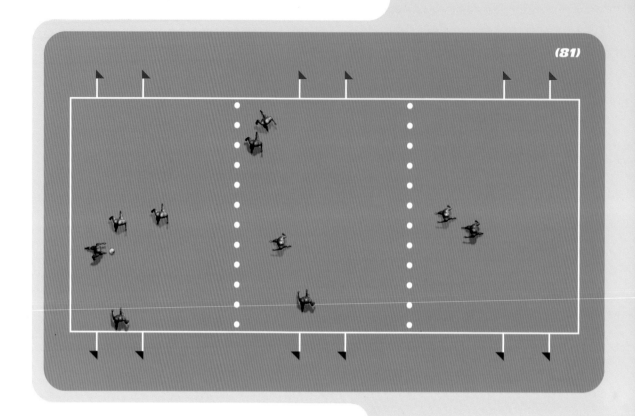

(81)

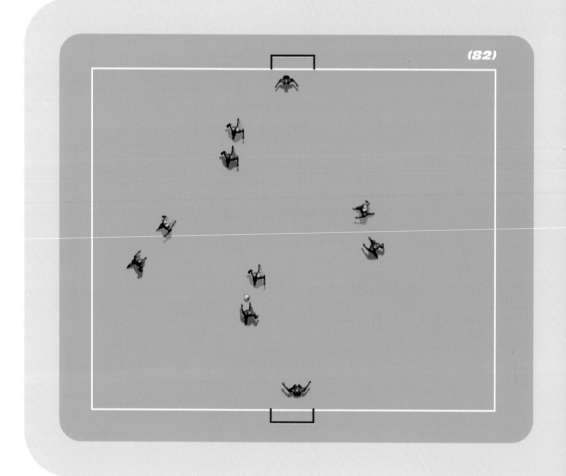

(82)

seven members. For advanced teams you may restrict touches or time on the ball while for younger players the number of passes needed to score may be lowered. Alter the grid size to accommodate the age, ability, and numbers of players. **Considerations:** Changing the point of attack. Movement off the ball and after passing. Some attackers must provide width and depth. Intelligent and determined defending. Quickness of thought and action in transition. **Phase:** Large group. **Ages:** 11+

(81) The Game: Six-Goal Soccer

Rules: A game that encourages playing away from defensive pressure and changing the point of attack. Using one ball, two five-player teams attack three six-foot-wide goals spaced along the opponent's end line while defending the three on their own goal line in a 20-x-45–yard area. There are no goalkeepers. The first team to score ten goals wins. **Benefits:** Passing, receiving, support, vision, mobility, combination play, and defending. **Adjustments:** May mandate that a goal be awarded only if the attacking team has at least one player in each vertical third of the field and/or that all goals must be scored on the first touch. May wish to put in a three-second rule or limit touches to encourage quick combination play. The game may be played up to eight-v-eight, while increasing the size of the area and the goals. **Considerations:** Focus is on defensive balance, pressure, and team shape; keep defenders no more than one vertical zone away from the ball. Width and depth in attack, combination play, quickness of thought and action during transition are highlighted. **Phase:** Large group. **Ages:** 10+

(82) The Game: Five-v-Five

Rules: Regular five-v-five (four outfield players plus a goalkeeper) soccer in a 36-x-44–yard area, with regulation-size goals in the middle of each end line.
Benefits: Passing, receiving, vision, mobility, dribbling, heading, finishing, defending, and goalkeeping with many tactical demands. **Phase:** Large-group. **Ages:** 10+

(83) The Game: Five-v-Five/No Keeper

Rules: To encourage players to shoot quickly and more often, play five-v-five (five out-field players and no goalkeepers) in a 36-x-44–yard area, with regulation-size goals in the middle of each of the longer end lines. The attackers should seize half-chances by shooting at every opportunity while defenders close down with urgency. *Benefits: Passing, receiving, vision, mobility, dribbling, heading, finishing, defending, and many tactical demands. Phase: Large-group. Ages: 10+*

(84) The Game: Long-Range Finishing

Rules: To work on scoring from a distance, play this five-v-five-plus-two game (four out-field players and a 'keeper per team plus two neutral players) in a 54-x-44–yard area using saucers to mark three 18-yard-deep zones. In the central zone each team has two players plus two neutral players. All initial shots must be taken from the central or rear zone with the lone advanced member of the offensive team "poaching" for deflections and rebounds without wandering offside. The ball may be passed into the front third to the front player who then lays a pass back to the players in the middle zone who can shoot. *Benefits: Long-distance finishing and goalkeeping. Adjustments: Shorten the field for younger players (example: for 11 year olds, the zones should be no more than 14 yards deep apiece). Considerations: Players encouraged to shoot at the first opportunity.*
Phase: Large group. Ages: 11+

(85) The Game: Volleys Unlimited

Rules: A seven-v-seven game played in a 50-x-70–yard area, with a regulation-sized goal in the middle of each of the longer end lines guarded by a 'keeper. The ball can only be passed by a player volleying (punting) out of his hands to a teammate, who must catch the ball before it hits the ground to avoid a turnover. There is no dribbling or running with the ball. No defender may attempt to block a volley but may challenge the intended receiver to win the ball. All shots on goal must be volleys. *Benefits: Volleying, mobility, and goalkeeping. Adjustments: Can be played as five-v-five up to nine-v-nine while making appropriate adjustments to the dimensions of the playing area. Considerations: Proper technique for volleys. Phase: Large group. Ages: 12+*

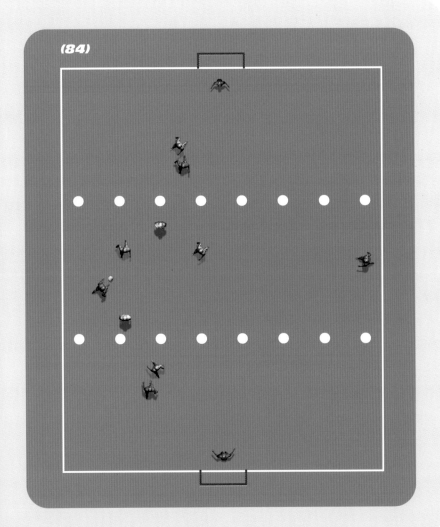

(84)

(86) The Game: Five Plus Four-v-Five Plus Four; Finishing

Rules: To sharpen your team's ability to make the most of scoring chances, play five-v-five (four field players plus a goalkeeper) with regulation-size goals (in the middle of the longer end lines) in a 36-x-44–yard area. Both teams have four extra teammates surrounding the offensive half of the field, on the sidelines and the end lines, with whom they may combine. The outside players are limited to no more than two touches, are encouraged to put in crosses, and may not shoot or pass to each other. Meanwhile, the team without possession has its outside players inactive until it gains possession. Every five minutes the inside/outside players swap roles. The team scoring more goals in 20 minutes wins. *Benefits: Finishing, passing, receiving, dribbling, heading, and goalkeeping with the constant creation of match-realistic scoring opportunities.*

Adjustments: If squad size is inadequate, play with three teams of four (plus 'keepers) with all resting players used as neutrals. May emphasize first-touch and/or long-distance shooting by awarding two goals for scoring on any such shot. An alternative is to allow a flank outside player to cut into the field after receiving a pass. That player temporarily becomes "live," has unlimited touches, and may be challenged. As soon as he plays the ball he returns to the flank. *Considerations:* Balls served from near the goal line should generally be cut back to attackers, who delay their runs into the box and who move, whenever possible, diagonally to goal. Near-post crosses are forcefully struck. Selection of the appropriate finishing technique. *Phase:* Large-group. *Ages:* 12+

(87) The Game: Conditioned Game; Three-Touch (for younger or less-advanced teams)

Rules: Introducing combination play rather than relying upon dribbling as a primary offensive tool is aided by a regular six-v-six (five outfield players plus a goalkeeper) game in a 50-x-44–yard area but with one rule change: every player is restricted to no more than three consecutive touches of the ball. Any violation is punished by awarding a free kick to the opposition. *Benefits:* Vision, immediate support, team mobility, combination play, passing, receiving, finishing, defending, goalkeeping, and fitness. *Adjustments:* If your teams struggles with this game they are either not quite ready for its demands or they might benefit from using one or two neutral players. Also you can adjust the field size as needed. *Considerations:* Accurate passing. Communication. Intelligent off-the-ball movement by the attackers. *Phase:* Large-group. *Ages:* 12+

(88) The Game: Conditioned Game; One-Touch/Multiple-Touch

Rules: Learning to combine to penetrate is underscored by this six-v-six (five plus a 'keeper) match in a 50-x-60–yard area. It is a regular, small-side game but with one rule change: whenever a player uses multiple touches the teammate that he passes to is limited to one touch. A violation is punished by awarding a direct or an indirect free kick (coach's choice) to the opponents from the spot of the extra touch. *Benefits:* Free kick organization for attackers and defenders; vision, speed of play, mobility, combination play, verbal communication, passing, receiving, dribbling, finishing, defending, and goalkeeping. Demands a rhythm of play in which quick and efficient action is

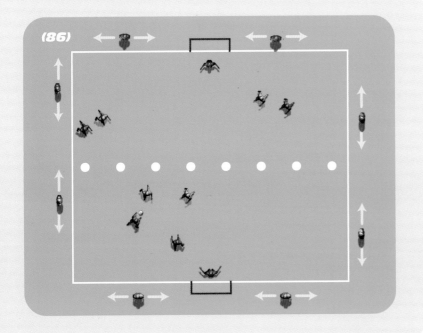

needed to exploit a defense that has been temporarily unbalanced. **Adjustments:** May add a neutral player or two if a team struggles to string together passes. **Considerations:** Dribbling to attack a space in order to create an opening that can subsequently be exploited. Potential receivers must have vision. **Phase:** Large-group. **Ages:** 12+

(89) The Game: Five-v-Five Long and Narrow

Rules: This game emphasizes penetrating passing. Play five-v-five (four outfield players plus a goalkeeper) in a 50-x-16–yard area (long but narrow), with two regulation-size goals, one in the middle of each end line. This game demands longer passing and attackers who are in advance of the ball immediately showing for a pass when there is a "window" between defenders. As the ball is quickly passed forward, the withdrawn attackers move rapidly into supporting positions with one trying to get in front of the ball when appropriate. **Benefits:** Passing, receiving, vision, mobility, dribbling, heading, finishing, defending, and goalkeeping with many tactical demands. **Phase:** Large-group. **Ages:** 12+

(90) The Game: Hit the Goalkeeper

Rules: Getting your players both to "see" and play a long, accurate pass is a vital aspect of their development. Play six-v-six on a 55-x-44–yard area. Each team has one additional player limited to playing in a ten-yard-radius semicircle behind the opposition's defense. No other players are permitted in that area. A goal is scored by chipping a pass to that player for him to catch on the fly. *Benefits: Defensive organization, with the first defender closing down the first attacker to deny penetration and/or the opportunity for a long pass. The game also should create lots of long passing, crossing, receiving, and dribbling as the attackers try to gain width and depth. The game may also be used to improve goalkeepers' skills to receive balls. Adjustments: May be played over a larger area up to eight-v-eight. If more repetitions of striking long passes are desired, add neutral players. For advanced players, place an outfield player into each of the semicircles, with a score only being awarded when that player receives and juggles the ball five times without it hitting the ground.*

Phase: Large-group. Ages: 12+

(91) The Game: The Gates Game

Rules: An excellent game for teaching players to pass and move by working to support each other. Two teams of six-players with one ball play in a 50-x-50–yard area with eight six-foot-wide gates. A team scores when a player passes the ball through a gate to a teammate on the other side. The team not in possession attempts to win the ball and then to score itself. Play continues following a goal, but a team may not score consecutively through the same gate. The first team to score 15 times is the winner. *Benefits: Passing, receiving, mobility, support, vision, combination play, defending, and fitness. Adjustments: Unless working with a very advanced team, there should be two to three more gates than there are players per team. Adjust the size of the area and the gates appropriately. For advanced players you can stipulate that all goals must be scored on the first touch or award two points for doing so. May opt to limit touches or time on the ball. For younger and/or less-advanced teams a neutral player or two can be added. Considerations: Quickness of thought and action during transition. Efficiency of play and accuracy and pace of passing. The ability of some of the attackers off the ball to provide width and depth. Phase: Large-group. Ages: 12+*

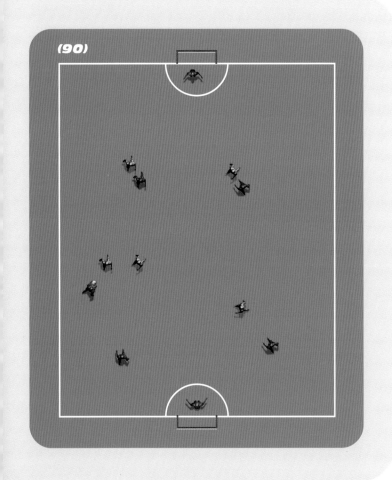

(90)

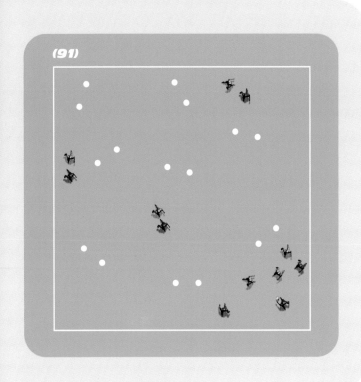

(91)

(92) The Game: Vertical Soccer

Rules: To create opportunities to penetrate the defense, a team often attacks diagonally. Play seven-v-seven (six plus a 'keeper) in a 75-x-70–yard area using regulation-size goals. The field has 10- to 12-yard-wide vertical corridors extending from end line to end line. Unless shooting, attackers must dribble or pass into a different corridor than the one in which they received or won the ball. A violation results in a "foul," with an indirect free kick awarded to the defending team. *Benefits: Finishing, passing, receiving, dribbling, heading, mobility, combination play, defense, tactical demands, and fitness.* **Considerations:** *Attackers in advanced positions bend runs at angles to receive passes while sideways-on, play effective diagonal penetrating passes, and dribble to space to create angles that promote chances to pass or shoot.* **Adjustments:** *May be played with as few as seven-v-seven, with a smaller field and narrower zones.* **Phase:** *Large-group.* **Ages:** *12+*

(93) The Game: Five-v-Five Flank Zones

Rules: To hone crossing and finishing, play five-v-five (four outfield players plus a goalkeeper), with regulation-size goals in the middle of each end line, in a 50-x-74–yard area, including 15-yard-wide flank zones on each side. One neutral, flank player (who may not be challenged and is either limited to two touches or two to three seconds with the ball) is positioned in each of the wide alleys. A premium is placed on attackers timing runs into the box so as to get free from a marker and to be open to receive a cross from the flank player. There are ample heading and volleying opportunities, while the goalkeepers must command their penalty areas. *Benefits: Passing, receiving, vision, mobility, dribbling, heading, volleying, finishing, defending, and goalkeeping with many tactical demands.* **Phase:** *Large-group.* **Ages:** *13+*

(94) The Game: Conditioned Game; Five-Touch Minimum

Rules: To work on vital principles of defense, this six-v-six game is played in a 50-x-44–yard area with one rule change: all outfield players may not pass or shoot until they have made at least five consecutive touches of the ball. A violation results in the opposition being awarded an indirect free kick. This condition allows defenders to learn to position themselves to restrict the options of the attacking players. However, any ball won in the front half of the field lifts that restriction for that possession for

(92)

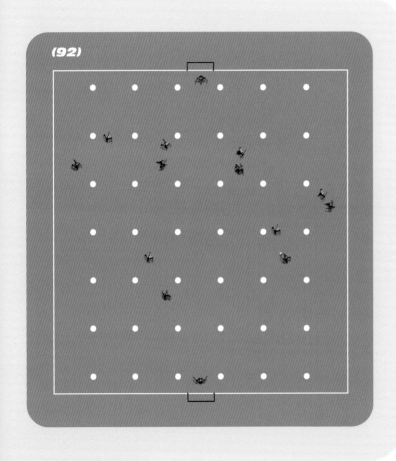

(93)

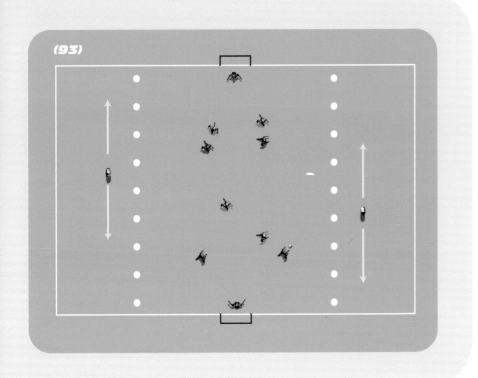

the team that created the turnover. **Benefits:** *Emphasizing collective and high-pressure defending tactics coupled with the ability to launch a quick counterattack after forcing a turnover.* **Adjustments:** *All goalkeeper distributions must be to a player in the rear half of the field. Can play five-touch/one-touch so that the defending team that fails to immediately force a turnover is more vulnerable to being "punished."* **Considerations:** *The first defender should attempt to close quickly while making the first attacker predictable as the nearest covering defender "reads" the situation and moves quickly to tackle.* **Phase:** *Large-group.* **Ages:** *13+*

(95) The Game: Three-Colors Game With Two Goals

Rules: A game that is intended to minimize dribbling by giving the team in possession many passing options. On a half-field with regulation-size goals in the middle of each end line play six-v-six (five players plus a goalkeeper). A third team of five outfield players serves as neutrals within the playing area. They must pass back immediately to the team that passed to them and they cannot pass to each other. They can be tackled. Play five-minute periods with teams taking turns serving as neutrals. **Benefits:** *Improved speed of play and off-the-ball mobility.* **Adjustments:** *To emphasize mobility and players interchanging positions off the ball, stipulate that no player can pass to anyone who is wearing the same colored bib (thus when reds have the ball and are playing against whites with neutrals in blue a red may only pass to a blue and a blue may only pass to a red). Can be played up to eight-a-side, adjusting the field length.* **Considerations:** *Participants are strongly encouraged to "make the ball do the work" by passing and moving as quickly as their tactical awareness and technical ability will allow.* **Phase:** *Large-group.* **Ages:** *13+*

(96) The Game: Three-Colors Game With Three Goals

Rules: Three five-player teams (four field players plus a goalkeeper) compete in a 55-x-75-yard area with three goals. When a turnover occurs, the team whose member was responsible for losing the ball goes on defense, and the other two teams attack that defending teams' goal. The offside law is waived. The team that scores keeps possession, with the action restarted with a goal kick by the goalkeeper who is a teammate of the player who scored. *Benefits:* Passing, receiving, dribbling, heading, finishing, vision, mobility, combination play, and goalkeeping. *Adjustments:* To prevent defenders from retreating to "pack" the area near their own goal the attackers are awarded a penalty kick for stringing a predesignated number of consecutive passes. Especially for older squads, the game may be played with teams of five or six (plus a goalkeeper). *Considerations:* Quick and efficient play. Speed of thought and action in transition. Taking initiative by shooting when appropriate. *Phase:* Large-group. *Ages:* 13+

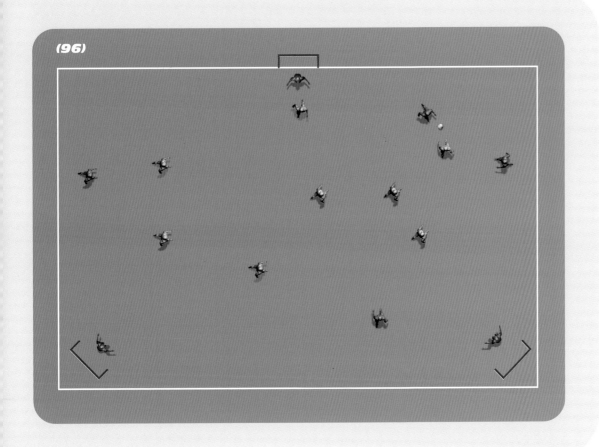

(96)

(97) The Game: Half-Field Restriction

Rules: A six-v-six (five plus a 'keeper) game in a 60-x-44– up to 60-x-75–yard area with a midfield line marked with saucers. Three defenders on each team are restricted to their own half of the field while two forwards must remain in the attacking half (thus, the ball must be passed over the midfield line for a team to attack). Goalkeeper distributions may only be to a teammate in their own half of the field, and the defenders marking the strikers must stay goal-side of the attackers when the ball is in the other half of the field. *Benefits:* Passing, receiving, dribbling, finishing, defending, and goalkeeping with great tactical demands. Incorporates functional play for all participants. *Considerations:* Strikers show when a "window" exists between defenders but clear the space if no pass is forthcoming. *Adjustments:* To help the offense, mandate that one of the defenders becomes inactive when the other team has the ball. *Phase:* Large-group. *Ages:* 14+

(98) The Game: Half-Field Restriction; One Joins In

Rules: A game with one variation on the rules for Half-Field Restriction (Game #97). After the ball is played across the midfield line, one of the members of the attacking team in the rear half of the field is permitted to cross the line and join in on the attack to create a three-v-three situation. *Benefits:* Passing, receiving, dribbling, finishing, defending, and goalkeeping with great tactical demands. Incorporates functional play for all participants. *Considerations:* Strikers show when a "window" exists between defenders but clear the space if no pass is forthcoming. *Adjustments:* To help the offense, mandate that one of the defenders becomes inactive when the other team has the ball. *Phase:* Large-group. *Ages:* 14+

(97)

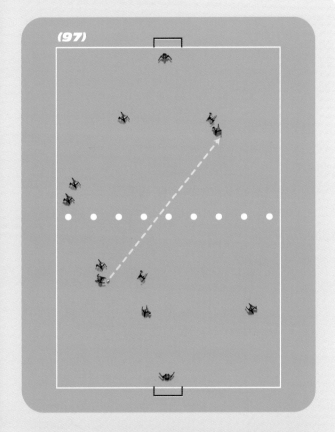

(98)

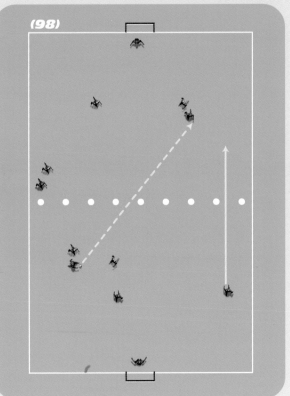

(99) The Game: Half-Field Restriction; Neutral Zone

Rules: To hone long-distance shooting, play six-v-six (five plus a 'keeper) in a 50-x-44– up to 50-x-75–yard area with a 10-yard-deep midfield zone marked with saucers. Three players on each team are restricted to their own half of the field (with no one in the neutral zone) while their two teammates remain in the attacking half (thus, the ball must be passed over the midfield zone). After the ball is played ahead, the rear attackers may move from the back half of the field into the neutral zone (but no opponent may do so). The players are available for support and also for the ball to be laid back for a long shot (20+ yards for senior players but shorten the field for others) until their team scores or loses possession, then they must retreat. Goalkeeper distributions may only be to a teammate in their own half of the field, and the defenders marking the strikers must stay goal-side when the ball is in the other half of the field. *Benefits:* Passing, receiving, dribbling, finishing, defending, and goalkeeping with great tactical demands. Incorporates functional play for all participants. *Considerations:* Strikers show when a "window" exists between defenders but clear the space if no pass is forthcoming. *Adjustments:* To help the offense, mandate that one of the three defenders becomes inactive when the other team has the ball. *Phase:* Large-group. *Ages:* 14+

(100) The Game: Conditioned Game; Two-Touch

Rules: Six-v-six game in a 50-x-44–yard area, but with one rule change: every player is restricted to no more than two consecutive touches of the ball. Any violation is punished by awarding a free kick to the opposition. *Benefits:* Vision, immediate support, team mobility, combination play, passing, receiving, finishing, defending, goalkeeping, tactical demands, and fitness. *Adjustments:* If your team struggles with this game they are either not quite ready for its demands or might benefit from using one or two neutral players. Alter the area of play based on the age and ability of the participants. All conditioned games may be played with greater numbers while adjusting the field size as needed. *Considerations:* Accurate passing. Communication. Intelligent off the ball movement by the attackers. *Phase:* Large-group. *Ages:* 14+

(101) The Game: Two-Ball Soccer

Rules: A six-v-six up to nine-v-nine game (including a 'keeper) played with two balls in a 40-x-60–yard area with regulation-size goals in the middle of each end line. Play begins with one 'keeper putting both balls into play. An adequate supply of balls in both goals assures that whenever a ball leaves the area play restarts quickly by kick-ins, throw-ins, or goalie roll-outs. The team scoring more times in 10–15 minutes is the winner. **Benefits:** *Passing, receiving, dribbling, vision, mobility, defending, finishing, goalkeeping. Extremely physically and tactically demanding.* **Adjustments:** *The game may be played so a team may only score when it is in possession of both balls. Can also be played with as many as 11-a-side. Unlike with most games, the more advanced the players, the fewer the number of participants.* **Note:** *The team that defends with greater purpose and collective understanding will almost always win. Without stopping the action, verbally encourage players to recognize when and how to defend.* **Considerations:** *Players must read situations (numbers up versus numbers down on offense and defense) and respond accordingly. Off-the-ball movement and intelligent support. Verbal communication and fitness are emphasized. Defenders seek man-up situations to win the ball with a marking defender forcing an attacker toward the covering defender. The game demands vision, as all players should be aware of the play occurring around both balls.* **Phase:** *Large-group.* **Ages:** *14+*

(102) The Game: Conditioned Game; One-Touch (for very advanced teams)

Rules: Learning to attack with great technical and tactical speed is demanded when playing six-v-six game (five plus a 'keeper) in a 50-x-44–yard area with one rule change: every player is restricted to one touch of the ball. Any violation is punished by awarding a free kick to the opposition. Thus, an attacker may only pass or shoot. **Benefits:** *Vision, immediate support, team mobility, passing, combination play, receiving, finishing, defending, and goalkeeping.* **Adjustments:** *If your team struggles with this game they are either not quite ready for its demands or might benefit from using one or two neutral players. Alter the area of play based on the age and ability of the participants. All conditioned games may be played with greater numbers while adjusting the field size as needed.* **Considerations:** *Accurate passing. Communication. Intelligent off the ball movement by the attackers.* **Phase:** *Large-group.* **Ages:** *15+*

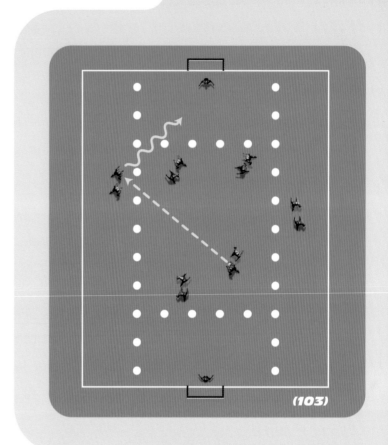

(103)

(103) The Game: Numbers-Up; Delay

Rules: Five-v-five (four outfield players plus a 'keeper) in a 54-x-44–yard area with a goal at each end and two lines of saucers going across the field, each 18 yards from the goal line. An attacker can only be offside when beyond that line. Each team also has a wide (neutral) player outside of the zone on either sideline. After receiving a pass the wide player dribbles or passes into the 18-yard zone and joins in on the attack to give the offense a numerical advantage. If possession is lost the extra player immediately leaves the area. The team scoring more goals in ten minutes wins. *Benefits: Teaches defensive concepts of covering for each other while collectively applying pressure. Also involves passing, receiving, mobility, combination play, dribbling, finishing, defending, and goalkeeping. Adjustments: Can have neutral players in the central area so as to be playing five-v-five plus two. Considerations: Quick and prudent attacking play while numbers up with efficient finishing. Zonal defensive principles with constant pressure on the ball, especially when out-numbered. Goalies act as sweeper/'keeper and are responsible for balls played behind the last defender. Phase: Large-group. Ages: 14+*

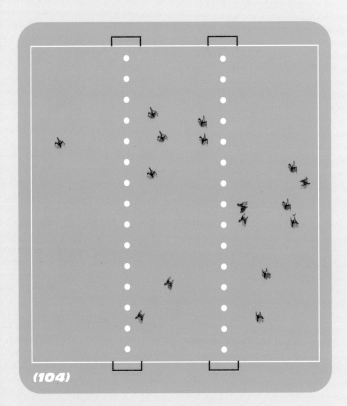

(104)

(104) The Game: Defensive-Zone Game

Rules: Pressuring to win the ball and principles of defensive compactness are empha-sized by an eight-a-side game (with or without goalkeepers) on a 70-x-75–yard field with saucers marking three vertical zones. Each team attacks the two 15-foot-wide goals on the opposite goal line. Defenders must try to prevent all goals, but if a goal is to be scored on them they must make sure they are all in the same, or the adjacent, third of the field as the goal into which the goal was scored. If any defender is in the far zone as the ball enters the goal that goal counts double for the attacking team. *Benefits: Individual, group, and team defending plus defensive shape. On offense: changing the point of attack, going forward to penetrate when numbers up, and establishing a rhythm of play. **Adjustments:** Attackers' touches may be limited. Change the number of players and the dimensions as needed. **Considerations:** Attackers pro-viding width and depth must read the game and react when penetration possibility exists. Defenders must close down foes while forcing the first attacker to move in one direction so as to make the offense predictable. **Phase:** Large-group. **Ages:** 14+*

PHOTOGRAPHY CREDITS

The photographs are copyright © of
the photographers and institutions,
as noted below.

Allsport:
pages 17, 50, 93-95,
109,143,177, 222-23, 252-53

Any Chance Productions:
pages 19, 21, 27, 31, 33, 38, 49, 54, 57, 60,
83, 97,118-19, 124, 127-28, 149, 153, 155,
156, 164, 184-85, 192-93, 200, 203, 204,208,
246-47, 258-59, 292-93

Dan Herbst:
page 38

Charles Miers:
Eastchester Youth Soccer Association:
pages 98, 232-33

Mark Leech:
pages 23, 25, 27,
60, 66, 73, 102, 123, 132, 135, 137-39,
145-46, 158-59, 161, 164, 169-71, 175,
178-80, 182-83, 186, 212, 214-16, 219-20,
238-39, 278-79

Jim Reinman:
page 87

**J. Brett Whitesell/
International Sports Images:**
pages 28, 45-47, 50, 54, 93, 102, 122, 130
134, 140, 147, 150, 169, 172, 196,
199, 262-3, 274-5

**Pam/International
Sports Images:**
page 189

Paul Dooley:
page 142